DATE DUE

NO 1 0 '94			
DE 2 3 '95			
DE 3 '96			
MR 1 8 '97			
SE 1 7 '98			
JE 1 1 01			

DEMCO 38-296

D1603958

THE MASKS OF DIONYSOS

SUNY Series in Ancient Greek Philosophy
Anthony Preus, Editor

THE MASKS OF DIONYSOS

A Commentary on Plato's
Symposium

Daniel E. Anderson

State University of New York Press

Published by
State University of New York Press, Albany

For information, address the State University of New York Press,
State University Plaza, Albany, NY 12246

Production by Christine M. Lynch
Marketing By Theresa A. Swierzowski

Library of Congress Cataloging-in-Publication Data

Anderson, Daniel E., 1928–
    The masks of Dionysos : a commentary on Plato's Symposium / Daniel
E. Anderson.
        p.   cm. — (SUNY series in ancient Greek philosophy)
    ISBN 0-7914-1315-2 (alk. paper). — ISBN 0-7914-1316-0 (pbk. :
alk. paper)
    1. Plato. Symposium.   2. Plato. Meno.   3. Love.   4. Knowledge,
Theory of.   5. Metaphysics.   I. Title.   II. Series.
B385.A96   1993
184—dc20   91-48020
                                                                    CIP

To the Memory of Helen Hooven Santmyer

Contents

Preface

The characters in the *Symposium* are clear about the fact that their intention is to compose speeches in praise of Eros. Some of those present are paired as lovers, and the theme of love—both as a god and as a relationship—is woven through the fabric of the entire dialogue. Recent works on the dialogue have tended either to treat love as secondary to other themes, or as showing the incompatibility of love with the philosophical life exemplified by Sokrates. The present interpretation rejects both positions, treating the theme of love as central to any effort to interpret the dialogue; arguing that Sokrates' rejection of Alkibiades does not constitute a rejection of love, and that other themes in the dialogue, including metaphysical themes, can be understood only through an understanding of Plato's treatment of love. The conclusions derived from such an approach are somewhat startling, leading to the claim that in this dialogue Plato was not defending the doctrine of forms. Instead, immutables, including immutable forms, are seen only as a possibility, with Plato steering a narrow course between a metaphysics grounded in process and one that allows for the possibility of such immutables.

The traditonal interpretation of Plato's metaphysics portrays the forms, the ground of possibility of understanding, as wholly apart from the world. The doctrine of forms, therefore, is seen as integrally bound up with the claim that learning is actually a process of recalling knowledge that has been acquired prior to birth—the doctrine of recollection. The latter doctrine is not found explicitly in the *Symposium*, but *Meno*, which is taken by many to be one of Plato's clearest expressions of the doctrine of recollection, gives the same definition of knowledge as does the *Symposium*. This definition appears to be incompatible with both the doctrine of forms and the doctrine of recollection. An analysis of *Meno* has therefore been added as an appendix.

My greatest departure from the usual interpretations of characters other than Sokrates is probably in my understanding of Aristophanes' place in the dialogue. I see Eryximakhos' speech and his as linked by Empedokles, whose views are distorted by the one and satirically "corrected" by the other. I do not see Plato as portraying Aristophanes in an unfavorable light. Rather do I see Aristophanes not only as correcting Eryximakhos' distortions of Empedokles, but also as laying important groundwork for major themes Sokrates is to bring out in his speech.

I have (of course!) used the *Symposium* in my classes since I first began teaching some thirty years ago. The interpretation here has been developed in conjunction with those classes. It does not rest on an understanding of highly technical material. Neither does it rest on an understanding of Greek, although where the material seems to require it I have included the occasional Greek word or phrase. All of my teaching has been on the undergraduate level, and although this essay has been written for a professional audience the material has proven not to be beyond the scope of competent undergraduates—including the better students in my introductory courses.

Although my deepest debt is to those students who over the years have forced me to hone my interpretations of Plato to whatever fine edge they may have, I find at this distance that with two exceptions I cannot attach their names to specific contributions. The exceptions are Christine Stephenson, who, tragically, died last year, and Alberto Mendez, who at this writing is a first-year student in my introductory philosophy course. I also owe a debt of gratitude to my colleagues at Ohio Wesleyan University, Bernard Murchland and Loyd Easton, both in the Philosophy Department, and to Donald Lateiner in Humanities and Classics, who have read and criticized the entire manuscript at various stages of its development.

My debt to Anthony Preus, editor of this series on Ancient Philosophy is beyond calculation. I showed him a monograph with the main lines of my argument. He showed me how to turn it into a book. And the book in its present form could not have come into being without his help, his sharp and rigorous criticism, his occasional harpoons, and his unwavering encouragement. For all of these I owe him my thanks.

I have also benefited greatly from the comments of my anonymous readers. Occasionally it has been possible to pinpoint their contributions, and I have noted these. Most of their contributions, however, are woven into the fabric of the text in a way that makes attribution impossible.

Unfortunately, R. E. Allen's text and careful, extended commentary (*The Dialogues of Plato*, vol. II, *The Symposium*, Yale University Press, 1991) did not come to hand until too late for consideration in the present study.

Needless to say I take full responsibility for all of the faults that remain.

I have used modern transliterations of the Greek (Sokrates, Phaidros, Eryximakhos, etc.). The translations are (except as noted) from Lamb's translation for the Loeb Classical Library edition. Since he used the Latinized spellings (Socrates, Phaedrus, Eryximachus, etc.) I have felt obliged to retain those spellings when quoting from his translation.

Finally, I owe debts of gratitude to Hilda Wick, who, when asked to produce an index, did that—then went on to give me a critical analysis of the entire manuscript, and to Linda Dixon, for secretarial assistance and for help in the proofreading.

Ohio Wesleyan University
1991.

Introduction: A Note on Method

Readers familiar with Stanley Rosen's sprightly *Plato's Symposium*[1] will recognize the depth of my debt to his analysis—particularly of the characterizations of Phaidros and Pausanias—as well as the depth of my disagreement with many of his conclusions and some of his method. Even in those cases where I am in agreement with Rosen (and there are many) I frequently arrive at those positions by a different route. As a result, a note on method seems in order.

A problem any student of Plato encounters very quickly is how to deal with the enormous complexities of his writing. He approaches his material through myth, religion, drama, literary symbolism and humor on the one hand, and through careful observation, science (as he knew it) and meticulous philosophical analysis on the other. Nothing seems to be ruled out. At times he seems to range from one method to another, often without warning or explanation. At other times his writing seems to thicken and to layer several of these methods into a single passage. The interpreters of Plato thus find themselves driven to use not just philosophical methods, but the methods of mythography, of religious analysis, of literary criticism, of humor, and at times even of science (or at least ancient science) as well. Many passages have to be unpacked several times in different ways, and tied in with various other passages on a number of different levels. Moreover, all of these complexities are further compounded by the fact that (at least in some cases) Plato seems to be playing games with his readers.

Thus, at times there will be very close, very careful scrutiny of what appear to be quite casual statements on the part of one character or another. Some passages that are often interpreted as supporting generally accepted theses, and which if read casually are open to such interpretation will, when subjected to tweezers and microscope, seem not to support the conventional interpretations after all. One can in such circumstances legitimately raise a question as to whether Plato intended that his works be read that closely. The scriptuararian's minute analysis of biblical texts is justified by the belief that that text was inspired or even indirectly written by an omniscient being. But Plato, after all, was human. Should we

1

not allow him an occasional lapse in his use of language, even a mistake or two?

The problem, of course, is that Plato, the human being who walked the streets of Athens and (perhaps) Syracuse, wrestled (perhaps) in the Olympics, and wrote philosophical dialogues, is dead. We cannot ask him whether this or that wording was intentional or just a slip of the stylus.[2] In an important sense Plato is today not so much a human being as a construction. Moreover, the materials out of which we construct him are by no means limited to the dialogues, or the dialogues in conjunction with other ancient sources we have. Those materials also include two and a half millennia of scholarly interpretations which in their turn are grounded in the values and perspectives of two and a half millennia of changing cultures. Nevertheless, although our way of constructing Plato is different in extent, it is not different in kind from our experiences of other people.

In our experiences of other living people any errors we might make in our construction of the other person are in principle at least, easily and quickly corrigible; however, some aspects even of these relationships rest on indirect evidence of the other's feelings, beliefs, intentions or expectations—love relations being in our culture a particularly clear example. In such cases we often find that the values one person attaches to the relationship so infuse that person's view of the other person that clarity in the relationship becomes virtually impossible—or can be corrected only in ways so painful that people often prefer preservation of the illusion to the clarification. In cases where the other is dead, the same hazards exist, but are more difficult to correct because the evidence is necessarily indirect.

Facts on this view take on a dialectical character. They arise in large measure out of values, but once established they are in turn to a great extent creative of the values of a later time, values through which these facts themselves will be seen and transformed. Nowhere is this more obvious than with Plato, where we have an overwhelming array of facts which, through Alexandrian Greece, Rome, Byzantium, Islam and the medieval and later European civilizations, have profoundly affected the values through which those facts are seen. This is the underlying truth of Whitehead's famous pronouncement that the whole of Western philosophy is but a footnote to Plato.

The hazard, of course, is that in seeing Plato through the lens of one's own culture and one's own values, one shall merely project that culture and those values on what is there, and that may be the underlying truth in J. K. Feibleman's remark that Plato has become "a philosopher's Rorschach."

The hazard arising out of the interpenetration of facts and values in the interpretation of Plato manifests itself in at least two ways. The first, and the one from which there is perhaps no protection, is the ubiquitous layer of Neoplatonism, a millennium thick, that lies between us and the work as seen by Plato's contemporaries. The second, more obvious problem is that in the pages that follow I may simply project upon Plato my own values and views, including an epistemology—or if that is avoided, project upon him a set of values and views, including an epistemology, which I see as more relevant to the needs of our own times than those of the more common interpretations of Plato. The reader should in particular be cautious of the claim that Plato may have held knowledge—and therefore presumably facts—to be dialectical.

Rosen makes the claim (*Plato's Symposium*, p. xlvii) that "the unspoken dimension of the dialogues is in fact a dimension of the dialogues and, for methodological purposes, the most important one." Ferrari makes a somewhat similar claim in his commentary on *Phaidros*:[3] "the limitations of [Plato's] arguments are as thematically important to the concerns of the dialogue as what can positively be claimed for them." Statements of this sort are sprinkled through the corpus of recent Plato scholarship, and although the temptation exists simply to disregard claims that what Plato did not write is as important as (or more important than) what he did write, the fact remains that what is omitted often is too clearly implied to be overlooked.

Equally clearly, such an approach to works as complex as Plato's middle dialogues opens a Pandora's Box of hazards that must be carefully weighed by any interpreter of Plato.

The most obvious is that when such a limitation is encountered a number of different possibilities for interpretation open up. The first possibility is that the character (say Sokrates) has intentionally structured the argument that way—as, for example, in *Meno* when Sokrates pushes the slave to try to give a number when the answer required is an irrational. If this is the case the commentator's task is to show reasons why the character would do so. (See Appendix for the way I have tried to unpack this in *Meno*.) The second possibility is that Plato has had the character structure the argument in that way in order to show something either about the personality of the character or about how the argument is flawed. (Thrasymakhos' outburst in Book I of the *Republic* comes to mind as an example of the former, while the exploration of logical fallacies in *Euthydemos* is a fairly obvious example of the latter.)

When the character is Sokrates this possibility must be approached with particular caution since he so often seems to be Plato's mouthpiece. In *Meno*, for example, Plato seems to portray Sokrates as deliberately giving circular definitions of "color" and "shape." The evidence for this as portrayal is worked out in some detail below (see Appendix). On the other hand, if such evidence is not forthcoming we are left with virtually unanswerable questions. Did Plato wish to portray Sokrates as having such a limitation? Or did Plato himself have such a limitation?

This is the point at which the risk is greatest of injecting the commentator's views and attributing them to Plato. We tend at this point to work "backwards" from our own views to what Plato says—or fails to say. If we can do this at several points we can create the illusion of convergence, the illusion that what Plato did not say at one point fits with what he did not say at other points, and that the fit is intentional. We can then claim that the omissions or limitations are intended by Plato when in fact they are little more than projections of our own illusions.

Although the quotes I have given above are from Rosen and Ferrari, the criticism is by no means limited to their work. *All* of Plato's modern commentators—myself included—are guilty. What makes these hazards so seductive, of course, is the fact that Plato clearly does do something of the sort from time to time. The reader is therefore confronted with the burden of deciding in any given instance whether this is one of those cases or something else. In short, sinful though such an approach may be, it is unavoidable, and anyone who hopes to take Plato seriously must run the risk.

Although a sampling of Plato scholarship over the millennia will show that these hazards lurk always in the shadows, some fairly obvious precautions can be taken, the most important of which is to stick to the text as closely as possible. Plato might have made mistakes. The probabilities are that he did. But that is a generality, and in any given instance there is a rather greater likelihood that the interpreters have made the mistake. As a general rule, therefore, I shall withhold the claim that Plato made a mistake until and unless I have convinced myself that no other interpretation is possible.

That is a protection from too facile an excuse for ignoring a text. But since any passage is likely with a little imagination to be subject to some interpretation or other, something is also needed as a protection against flights of fancy that have only a tenuous connection with the text. For an interpretation not to be in conflict with other passages in the text is necessary, but it is not enough. The second requirement, therefore, is that the interpretation, while grounded in the text, must fit in a coordinated, patterned way with the interpretations of other passages. We cannot ask Plato what his intentions might have been, but where such patterns exist we can reasonably argue that they are intentional. This implies, of course, that "intention" now has lost its reference to a person, and has become an aspect of our construction of Plato. It means just such mutually supportive patterns of interpretation.

On the other hand, such patterns found here and there across a number of dialogues constitute perhaps the most seductive hazard of all in Plato scholarship—a hazard to which all are susceptible, and which in the end may be unavoidable. Nevertheless, such comparisons must be regarded with suspicion for a number of reasons. Plato's philosophical writing life is believed to have begun shortly after Sokrates' death, when Plato was twenty-nine or thirty, and to have continued with only minor interruptions until he died at an age of more than eighty. According to Cicero[4] he was still writing at the time of his death. His writings therefore span half a century. We can reasonably expect that so great a thinker as Plato would have altered his views from time to time over half a century. Those alterations might have formed a smooth development of his thought, or they might not. The question of how his thought might have developed is further aggravated by the fact that we have only a few clues as to which dialogues were written when; still less do we have evidence of the actual order. An obvious danger, then, is that different dialogues, or sections of dialogues, will be interpreted as mutually supportive, and as representing a single view, when those dialogues or passages may have been separated by two or three decades or more,[5] and may have had significantly different purposes or even content if we could but see them in context with the development of Plato's thought.

A danger here, of course, is circularity: we start with a general idea of how Plato's thought might have developed, order the dialogues accordingly, then point out that the dialogues taken in this order support the claim that Plato's thought developed in this way.

As pointed out above, these problems are further complicated by the fact that Plato's work is given in dramatic form. Drama in Plato's time had reached a very high level of sophistication. Those who read his works are constantly confronted with the question of to what extent the dialogues should be read as drama, and to what extent as philosophical treatises. What is acted out is often to be viewed as being at least as important as what is said, sometimes perhaps as more important. Whether a character is giving Plato's or some other's view is not always clear, even when the character is Sokrates. And the risks incurred when one puts what Sokrates says in one dialogue together with what he says in another, especially one that might be from another period of Plato's life, compound accordingly.

Since such comparisons seem nevertheless to be inevitable, some ground rules seem in order here as well. The ones I try to abide by are, first, to limit my analysis as much as possible to a single dialogue.[6] Where another dialogue must be brought in, whatever is brought from it is to the greatest extent possible put in context with the dialogue from which it comes in order to avoid likely distortions ranging from fallacies of accent to outright misinterpretations. Where the entire dialogue cannot be treated, I try at least to treat extensive enough sections of the dialogue to give reasonable protections from such distortions. Any other references to other dialogues must be viewed as trivial. At any rate nothing of significance can be built upon them. Finally, anything in my interpretation that I see as significant is so only if the case for it can be built out of the dialogue at hand, even though that case may also receive support in other dialogues. (For more on method, see chapter 5, sections 3 and 4.)

How successful I have been is for the reader to decide.

Chapter 1

Plato's *Symposium*, particularly in conjunction with *Phaido*, is often viewed as giving one of the clearest explanations in all of Plato's work of the doctrine of forms. The *Symposium* is also generally recognized as one of the greatest literary masterpieces Plato produced. The purpose of the present essay is to suggest that, viewed from one perspective at least, the literary aspects of the *Symposium* suggest an interpretation of the philosophical side of the dialogue that is incompatible with the usual claims for the doctrine of forms. The literary side in particular will be discussed in the present chapter, and in chapters 2, 3 and 6. The philosophical side will be discussed in chapters 4 and 5.

1 Dionysos[1]

The most obvious fact about the *Symposium* is that its dramatic setting is a party in celebration of Agathon's prize in the festival of tragedy. This was a Dionysian festival, and there should be no surprise in the discovery that Plato uses Dionysian symbolism throughout the dialogue, or that he plays on the traditional conflict between Dionysos and Apollo. Two of those at the party, Agathon and Aristophanes, are playwrights, obvious creatures of the god of drama. Another, Eryximakhos, is a physician, and therefore a creature of Apollo, god of medicine.

Dionysos was god of wine, of madness, of prophecy as well as of drama, and Plato plays on all these themes on a number of different levels. But Dionysos seems also to have been much more than these. An Orphic creation myth tells of the birth of a god from the cosmic egg. This god was Phanes who (Orphic fr. 60; Aristophanes' *Birds*, 693ff.) was called Eros—but who (Diodorus Siculus, I. ii. 3) was also called Dionysos.[2] Whether this traditional identification of Eros with Dionysos is accurate or not, Plato seems to have intended some such identification. As Nussbaum[3] points out, ''[Dionysos] is the god who dies. He undergoes, each year, a ritual death and rebirth, a cutting back and a resurgence. . . . Among the gods he alone is not self-sufficient, he alone can be acted on by the world. . . . And yet, miraculously, despite his fragility, he restores himself and burgeons." Yet it is Eros who is described by Diotima as "neither immortal nor mortal,[4] in the selfsame day he is flourishing and alive at the hour when he is abounding in resource; at another he is dying, and then reviving again. . . yet the resources that he gets will ever be ebbing away." (203e).

On this level Dionysos was seen as the life force of the cosmos. He was run down by the Titans and devoured in the form of a bull (in the Orphic version, as a child). The Titans were then destroyed by Zeus, who incinerated them with his thunderbolts and scattered their ashes to the winds, thereby spreading the life force over the world (Olympiodorus on Plato's *Phaido*, 61c; Orphicorum fr. 220, p. 238 of Kern). Thus all living things may be regarded as manifestations of Dionysos.[5]

This was symbolized in the theater where one actor was expected to play many parts, and the audience knew which part only by the mask the actor wore. Symbolically then, Dionysos was god of masks. But as god of masks his essence is *to be masked*; there can be no Dionysos unmasked. Each living thing is a mask of Dionysos. As all living things, he is no one thing in particular. He has no individuality, no character peculiarly his own, so taking all the masks off Dionysos, like taking all the peelings off an onion, would leave nothing behind.

On these terms, each person is a mask of Dionysos. But if Dionysos' character is to be masked, self-knowledge must be viewed as a process of peeling one's mask away in order to discover not one's "true self," but the mask beneath, which in turn is to be peeled away. Since the act of removing a mask becomes an aspect, perhaps even a significant aspect, of the person who removed it, that act becomes an aspect of the mask that it reveals. In this way the removal of a mask is at least partly creative of the mask beneath. And the process of removing the mask is in actuality a process of growth in self-knowledge. This process can be brought to a halt only on the false supposition that what one has discovered is not a mask, but the "true self," an absolute self that underlies all the masks and will never change. That there can be no such immutable self is made clear in Diotima's speech.[6]

Only humans have the intellectual power to recognize such masks. Most humans have some skill in recognizing them in others, but they deeply resist recognizing those that they themselves wear. They must be persuaded that they are wearing them, and that process of persuasion is the dialectic. On these terms the elenchus, that part of the dialectic that leads to the recognition of one's ignorance, is the discovery that what one thought one knew was in fact a mask. One may like Anytos, simply refuse to listen and thereby avoid the discovery altogether; or like Meno, having once discovered the mask, skate around it refusing to admit that it is there; or like Meno's slave, try to correct the ignorance one has discovered, removing the mask to find the belief—the mask—that lies beneath. To be fully human is to engage in this dialectical process—to seek always to discover the masks one is wearing and remove them. In this sense the dialectical process is one of self-discovery and of self-creation as well. Only thus can humans grow, and as will be argued below (ch. 4, sec. 7), love, Eros, is a process of growth. As pointed out in the Appendix, the dialectic requires both the knowledge of one's ignorance and the desire to learn. Anytos lacks both; Meno lacks the desire to learn; and the slave, lacking neither, is more fully human than either of the others.[7]

Humility was not regarded by the Greeks as a virtue. Pride, so long as it was restrained by moderation, and limited to what one could properly take pride in, was a virtue. Only when it went beyond what was proper did it become hubris. Thus, hubris, believed by the Greeks to be the source of all sin, is arrogance, or "overweening pride," the belief that one is something that one is not. In other words, hubris is rooted in the failure of self-knowledge.[8] Thus, in the present framework the most common form of hubris would be the belief that there is such an immutable self, that there is some one level of discovery that is real, that is not a mask, some "knowledge" which, though open to question, remains unquestioned. Such a belief is necessarily beyond proof, since the most one could legitimately say is that *if* what I have now discovered is a mask I have not yet succeeded in stripping it away to see what lies beneath. One could not justifiably claim that the failure to remove it is evidence that it cannot be removed—still less that it is by nature such that it cannot be removed. The claim that there is a "true" or "immutable" self must therefore remain no more than a presupposition, and the claim that any self that happens to have been discovered *is* the "true" self must be a presupposition as well.

But to base one's claim for self-knowledge on the presupposition that one has it is so clearly circular as to approach the ultimate in self-deception, the failure of self-knowledge—the hubris from which springs all sin. True self-knowledge on these terms is a pursuit, not a discovery, and it is grounded in the realization that one cannot know even that there is a self to be known. All one can discover—either in oneself or in another—is a mask. Although exactly what the mask happens to be may be important, there is an underlying suggestion that for humans, to be is to grow, and any mask may therefore be fleeting.[9]

Although a theme of masks is not mentioned explicitly in the *Symposium*, such a theme does seem to loom ever in the background. For the ancient reader, any mention of drama would call to mind the masks through which the audience identified the persona the actor was adopting at a given moment. In addition to this rather obvious fact, the dialogue itself is presented in the form of a drama. Plato tells the story in the persona of Apollodoros, who tells it through Aristodemos. Each character is himself a mask for Aristodemos, and each is presented as masked.[10] The most important philosophical aspect of the dialogue is then presented through the character of Sokrates, who in turn puts it on the lips of Diotima—who apparently never existed.[11]

The first direct mention of Dionysos occurs after Sokrates' late arrival at the party. There is irony in the fact that Agathon, after trying repeatedly to send a servant to badger Sokrates into coming on to the party instead of standing in a neighboring portico (175a-b, 175c), demands that Sokrates share his couch "so that by contact with you I may have some benefit from that piece of wisdom that occurred to you there on the porch."[12] Then with added unwitting irony he continues, "Clearly you have made the discovery and got hold of it; for you would not have come away before" (175d-e). In the banter that follows, Sokrates suggests that knowledge cannot be acquired merely by hearing something said, as water flows through wool from one container to another—a theme that is to become increasingly important as the dialogue proceeds.

In reply Agathon says, "you [are hubristic ('Ὑβριστὴς εἶ ἔφη)], Socrates!... A little later on you and I shall go to law on this matter of our wisdom, and Dionysus shall be our judge" (175e).

From Agathon's point of view the reference to Dionysos is understandable. He has just received a favorable judgment from Dionysos in the awarding of the prize for tragedy, and is jokingly suggesting the god would award him another favorable judgment. The fact that Plato, the author, is not treating this merely as a passing remark becomes evident in the conversation that follows. Dionysos was god of wine, and a person who was drunk was regarded as literally possessed by the god, who spoke through the person's lips.[13] The Dionysian dictum reflecting this belief, "in wine, truth" ($o\hat{\iota}\nu o\varsigma$ $\kappa\alpha\grave{\iota}$ $\dot{\alpha}\lambda\acute{\eta}\theta\epsilon\iota\alpha$),[14] is to be paraphrased later by Alkibiades (217e). In context with this belief, then, the guests move almost immediately to deprive Dionysos of his role as judge when they agree "not to make their present meeting a tipsy affair, but to drink just as it might serve their pleasure" (176e). On the other hand their reason for not allowing the god to possess them is that Agathon, Pausanias and Aristophanes, described as "the stoutest drinkers" (176c) are hung over from the previous night's drinking, and the rest are described as "known weaklings" (176c)—suggesting that Dionysos has already passed one judgment on them, and it has not been favorable.

In contrast to this, Eryximakhos tells us, "Socrates I do not count in the matter: he is fit either way, and will be content with whatever choice we make" (176c). This appears to be an indication that Sokrates is unaffected by drinking—as is repeated later by Alkibiades (214a) and then acted out at the end of the dialogue.[15] This, in terms of the symbolism, would imply either that Sokrates' behavior does not change because, drunk or sober, he is always possessed by Dionysos, or that drinking does not affect him because he is immune to such possession. The former would imply that he is a creature of Dionysos; the latter presumably, since Dionysos' traditional rival is Apollo, that he is a creature of Apollo, who protects him from Dionysian possession. Eryximakhos, however, as a physician, should also come under the protection of Apollo, and Apollo seems clearly to be unable to protect him. Eryximakhos in fact admits his inability to handle wine, branding himself as a "known weakling" (176c), then goes on to tell us that: "the practice of medicine, I find, has made this clear to me—that drunkenness is harmful to mankind; and neither would I myself agree, nor would I recommend it to another, especially when his head is still heavy from a bout of the day before" (176d). Thus, Plato seems to be suggesting that Sokrates is a creature of Dionysos.[16]

As if to emphasize the banishment of Dionysos from the party, Eryximakhos somewhat contemptuously dismisses the flute girl with the comment, "let her pipe to herself or, if she likes, to the womenfolk within, but let us seek our entertainment today in conversation" (176e). The flute, of course, was a Dionysian instrument, and the flute girl's presence at the party was in part a symbol of the presence of the god in the wine. Flute girls at such banquets also were often expected to have sex with the guests,[17] and Eryximakhos apparently does not want any erotic byplay—or at any rate any heterosexual erotic byplay[18]—to disturb the discussion of Eros he is about to propose.

Despite the attempt to banish Dionysos, the reader soon finds that the god is still present, and is taking a hand even in the ordering of the speeches. Aristophanes, as a dramatist, is in Dionysos' train. As a comic playwright satire is his stock in trade, and he could reasonably be expected to satirize whatever speech precedes his own. If he were to speak when his turn comes his victim would be Pausanias. At this point, however, he has a case of hiccoughs and is unable to take his turn. He had already admitted (176b) that he is hung over from the parties of the previous evening. This time they have agreed "to drink just as much as it might serve their pleasure" (176e). The combination of a hangover and a few sips of wine (or any other alcoholic beverage) resulting in hiccoughs is common enough not to need further comment. The result is that instead of satirizing Pausanias, he will speak after Eryximakhos, the attendant of Apollo. The details of his satire of Eryximakhos are discussed below.[19] Part of the satire, however, arises directly from Dionysos in the form of the wine in Aristophanes' belly. Eryximakhos had given Aristophanes a prescription for his hiccoughs: "But during my speech, if on holding your breath a good while the hiccough chooses to stop, well and good; otherwise, you must gargle with some water. If, however, it is a very stubborn one, take something that will tickle your nostrils, and sneeze: do this once or twice and though it be of the stubbornest, it will stop" (185e).

Later we learn that the prescription was successful, but "not until it was treated with a course of sneezing" (189a). This latter comment, together with Eryximakhos' directive that this be done "during my speech," and Aristophanes' reply, "Start away with your speech. . . and I will do as you advise," (186a) emphasizes for the reader that all the while Eryximakhos is discussing Love as the binding force of the cosmos, bringing peace, and introducing harmony (or "attunement") into all levels of existence, Aristophanes is holding his breath (sputtering, no doubt, and belching), hiccoughing, gargling and finally sneezing, generally disrupting the harmony (or "attunement") of the discussion—as might be expected of Dionysos.

Or of a comic poet.[20]

Later, as Sokrates is finishing his speech, Alkibiades enters—or more accurately, perhaps, Dionysos enters in the person of Alkibiades—and Dionysos' role as judge becomes more explicit.[21] Alkibiades is described as "very drunken" and as "bawling" (βοῶντος) like a bull (212d), a Dionysian beast, and a form Dionysos himself assumed when he was pursued by the Titans. He is supported by a flute girl, just as the god is frequently portrayed as being supported in his drunkenness by maenads carrying and playing their flutes. And like the god and those in his train, Alkibiades is crowned with ivy (as well as violets; cf. ch. 6, sec. 1).

Agathon's original challenge to Sokrates was to allow Dionysos to judge which of them was wiser (176a). Now Alkibiades' initial request is, "will you admit to your drinking a fellow very far gone in liquor, or shall we simply set a wreath on Agathon—which indeed is what we came for—and so away?" (212e). The god, then, if we carry out the implied symbol, has again come to crown the tragedian as he had the previous day in the theater. Although he addresses Agathon as "the cleverest and handsomest" (212e), he has not yet noticed Sokrates.

After he crowns Agathon, he somewhat petulantly puts his drunkenness together with "speaking the truth:" "Ah, you would laugh at me because I am drunk? Well, for my part, laugh as you may, I am sure I am speaking the truth" (212e). Then with more than a little impatience, he adds: "Come, tell me straight out, am I to enter on the stated terms or not? Will you take a cup with me or no?" (212e–213a).

The impatience and the petulance are quite in character for Alkibiades, but in context with the previous effort to keep Dionysos out of the party, they are equally in character for the god, who is petulant because they fail to recognize that he speaks through the lips of the drunken Alkibiades, and impatiently demands that they decide whether or not to admit him, not just to the party—he has covertly at least, been there all along—but into their bodies in the form of wine, allowing him to possess them. Once admitted, Alkibiades and his train join the party (213a).

This is the point at which Alkibiades notices Sokrates. He immediately takes back the crown he had awarded to Agathon, splits it, and awards part of it to the tragedian, part to the philosopher, saying: "He [Sokrates] shall not reproach me with having made a garland for you [Agathon] and then, though he conquers everyone in discourse—not once in a while, like you the other day, but always—bestowing none upon him" (213e).

This appears to be one of the judgments of Dionysos.[22]

It is not the last.

Although the guests, at Alkibiades' request, invited him and those with him to join the party, Alkibiades does not accept the role of party crasher, and those who invited him soon find, perhaps to their dismay, that instead of Alkibiades joining the party, the party in fact has joined the train of Alkibiades. This, of course, fits well with the character of the god, who in a number of the myths turns up uninvited, disguised as a human, then imposes his will upon the others.[23] Alkibiades takes more seriously than they may have wished their agreement to "take a cup" with him, and he takes over Phaidros'[24] office as symposiarch, or "master of the feast," all with the peremptory manner of the petulant god: "Now then, gentlemen, you look sober: I cannot allow this; you must drink, and fulfill our agreement. So I appoint as president [ἄρχοντα] of this bout, till you have had a reasonable drink—myself" (213e).

His idea of a "reasonable drink," we find, is to chug down a cooler full of wine—which he does. He then orders the others to do the same.

At this point Alkibiades unwittingly repeats what Eryximakhos had said at the beginning of the evening: "Against Socrates, sirs, my crafty plan is as nought. However large the bumper you order him, he will quaff it all off and never get tipsy with it" (214a).

Coming from Alkibiades this is both a prediction and a Dionysian judgment. Moreover, Alkibiades clearly shows Sokrates to be a creature of Dionysos, identifying him first with Silenos, then with Marsyas,[25] both of whom are satyrs, creatures of the god.

Yet another judgment is found in the fact that Alkibiades chooses not to praise Eros, but to praise Sokrates instead—even going so far as to say "I could praise none but you in your presence" (214d). Then, in the description he gives of Sokrates he goes on to say that Sokrates' speeches "are the only speeches which have any sense in them; and. . . [no others] are so divine, so rich in images of virtue, so largely—nay, so completely—intent on all things proper for the study of such as would attain both grace and worth." If this is the case, then no speeches written or produced by Agathon can measure up. The judgment of Dionysos again goes to Sokrates.

In the banter that follows Alkibiades' speech, Sokrates arranges the seating so that he will be in a position to praise Agathon (222e–223a). Since Sokrates has by this point been identified as the clay through which Dionysos speaks,[26] this would suggest that

Dionysos, through Sokrates, is about to praise Agathon. But Dionysos in another manifestation prevents this, "when suddenly a great crowd of revelers arrived at the door, which they found just opened for someone who was going out. They marched straight into the party and seated themselves: the whole place was in an uproar and, losing all order, they were forced to drink a vast amount of wine" (223b).

In the end, the judgment is given by Dionysos in the form of the wine itself when, at the end of the dialogue, we are told that Aristodemos, having passed out, "awoke towards dawn, as the cocks were crowing; and immediately he saw that the company were either sleeping or gone, except Agathon, Aristophanes and Socrates [i.e., Sokrates and the two playwrights, the three dearest to the god], who alone remained awake and were drinking out of a large vessel, from left to right; and Socrates was arguing with them" (223c).

The movement from left to right had been part of Eryximakhos' proposal for the second stage of the evening's entertainment, in which each was to "prescribe" for his neighbor on the right. The "prescription," then, is that each in turn drink from the "large vessel."

> As to most of the talk, Aristodemos had no recollection, for he had missed the beginning and was also rather drowsy; but the substance of it was, he said, that Socrates was driving them to the admission that the same man could have the knowledge required for writing comedy and tragedy—that the skilled tragedian could be a comedian as well [i.e., both are inspired by the same god, Dionysos]. While they were being driven to this, and were but feebly following it, they began to nod; first Aristophanes dropped into slumber, and then, as day began to dawn, Agathon also (223d).

Thus, both in argument and in wine, the judgment of Dionysos went to Sokrates.

The above account gives only the bare bones of the Dionysian symbolism that runs deep through the whole of the dialogue. The skeleton will be fleshed out in the pages that follow.

2 The Lovers

That Pausanias and Agathon are lovers is made explicit by Aristophanes who, as he ends his speech, says, "And let not

Eryximachus retort on my speech with a comic mock, and say I refer to Pausanias and Agathon; it may be they do belong to the fortunate few, and are both males by nature" (193b–c).

Although the evidence is less concrete, the same appears to be the case with Eryximakhos and Phaidros. They do appear together in *Protagoras*, but there is no mention there of their being lovers. The fact that they were both accused along with Alkibiades of the desecration of the herms may suggest something of the sort as well.

In the *Symposium* such a relationship is strongly hinted at in the initial exchange between them (176d–e) where Phaidros says, "why you know I *always* obey you, above all in medical matters" (emphasis mine). The use of "always" ($\epsilon\check{\iota}\omega\theta\alpha$—"in my customary manner") clearly suggests that their relationship is not just one of physician and patient. This suggestion is then strengthened when Eryximakhos says that Phaidros:

> is *constantly* [$\dot{\epsilon}\kappa\acute{\alpha}\sigma\tau\sigma\tau\epsilon$] complaining to me and saying,— is it not a curious thing, Eryximachus, that while other gods have hymns and psalms indited in their honour by the poets, the god of Love, so ancient and so great, has had no song of praise composed for him by a single one of all the poets that have ever been?. . .I recollect coming across a book by somebody, in which I found Salt superbly lauded for its usefulness, and many more such matters I could show you celebrated there. To think of all this bustle about such trifles, and not a single man ever essaying till this day to make a fitting hymn to Love! So great a god, and so neglected (177a–c, emphasis mine).

In addition to the improbability of such a claim, this is hardly the sort of remark one would make casually to a friend. That Phaidros would make such a complaint to Eryximakhos once is suggestive; that he would "constantly complain" to him in this way seems conclusive. Moreover, if we accuse Eryximakhos of embellishing Phaidros' complaint—or even of making it up—a statement such as he makes here would pass without comment only if the others present perceived them as lovers.

The fact that Agathon and Pausanias, Eryximakhos and Phaidros, are thus paired as lovers will cast a somewhat different light on their speeches.

3 The Symposiarch

Although Eryximakhos proposes the subject for the evening's discussion, the fact that he attributes it to Phaidros seems to be enough to give Phaidros the office of symposiarch,[27] the master of the feast. Although nothing is said directly of this, Phaidros is referred to as the "father of our debate" (177d), and is allowed to speak first, perhaps in order to clear the way for him to exercise his duties afterwards. At any rate, Phaidros merely presents his speech to the company at large ("So there is my description of [Eros]..." 180b), but a number of the other speakers present their speeches to Phaidros.

Pausanias begins by addressing a complaint to him: "I do not consider, Phaedrus, our plan of speaking a good one..." (180c). He ends by presenting his speech to Phaidros: "Such, Phaedrus, is the contribution I am able to offer you, on the spur of the moment, towards the discussion of [Eros]" (185c). Agathon, at the beginning of his speech addresses Phaidros directly, although this might be because he is criticizing a point made in Phaidros' speech: "Thus I conceive, Phaedrus, that [Eros] was originally of surpassing beauty and goodness, and is latterly the cause of similar excellences in others" (197c). As he closes, he formally presents his speech to Phaidros: " 'There, Phaedrus,' he said, 'is the speech I would offer at his shrine' " (197e). Even Sokrates goes through a similar formality at the end of his speech: "This, Phaedrus, and you others, is what Diotima told me" (212b); then a moment later: "So I ask you, Phaedrus, to be so good as to consider this account as a eulogy bestowed on [Eros], or else to call it by any name that pleases your fancy" (212c).

The three speakers who do not address their speeches to Phaidros are Eryximakhos, Aristophanes and Alkibiades. Eryximakhos and Aristophanes have each spoken in place of the other, and that probably explains the fact that each presents his speech to the other. Alkibiades takes over the office of symposiarch, and addressing his speech to Phaidros would be inappropriate. This fact may also explain Eryximakhos' and Phaidros' early departure after Alkibiades' speech: "Then, as Aristodemus related, Eryximachus, Phaedrus and some others took their leave and departed" (223b–c)—thereby possibly (through the exit of the follower of Apollo) letting in the group of drunken revelers who broke up what was left of the party.

Finally, we get a hint of the symposiarch's duties when we see Phaidros exercising his authority at three points in the dialogue. The first takes place after Aristophanes' speech when Phaidros interrupts the conversation between Sokrates and Agathon, preventing the development of a philosophical dialogue in order to allow the agreed order of the entertainment to continue, even though he admits that he would be happy to allow Sokrates to continue the dialogue: "For my part, I enjoy listening to Socrates' arguments; but I am responsible for our eulogy of Love, and must levy his speech from every one of you in turn. Let each of you, then, give the god his meed before you have your argument" (194d).[28]

The second takes place after Agathon's speech when Sokrates complains to Eryximakhos that he misunderstood what was expected of him, and offers to withdraw from the entertainment: "I find I was quite mistaken as to the method required; it was in ignorance that I agreed to take my turn in the round of praising. 'The tongue,' you see, undertook, 'the mind' did not; so good-bye to my bond. I am not to be called upon now as an eulogist in your sense; for such I cannot be" (195a).

He then offers to speak anyway, but in his own way—an offer he addresses to Phaidros: "Nevertheless I am ready, if you like, to speak the mere truth in my own way; not to rival your discourses, and so become your laughing-stock. Decide then, Phaedrus, whether you have any need of such a speech besides, and would like to hear the truth about Love in whatsoever style of terms and phrases may chance to occur by the way" (199b).

The third occurs immediately after this. When "Phaedrus and the others" ask him to speak, Sokrates again appeals to Phaidros, this time almost formally, for permission to have a short dialogue with Agathon as an introduction to his speech:

> "Then allow me further, Phaedrus, to put some little
> questions to Agathon, so as to secure his agreement before
> I begin my speech."
> "You have my leave," said Phaedrus; "so ask him."
> (199b–c).

Thus Phaidros seems beyond doubt to be the symposiarch. As such he has the duty—and the authority—to see that whatever entertainment has been agreed upon is carried out. He can "levy a speech" from each of those present, cut off conversation, and even decide whether a speech about to be offered is admissable or not. Later, of course, when Alkibiades "elects" himself symposiarch, we find that the office carries the power to order everyone to get drunk—even after the physician has told them it is harmful to their health.

Chapter 2

A number of themes are touched on, then developed in the speeches of Phaidros, Pausanias, Eryximakhos, Aristophanes and Agathon: the rewards of love, prostitution, self glorification, the relation of love to excellence ($\dot{\alpha}\varrho\epsilon\tau\acute{\eta}$), the relation of lovers to the state, the role of love in the world, and love as a way of transcending death. These themes are to be picked up later in Sokrates' speech. Some will be incorporated, some will be rejected, and most will be transformed in the process.[1] The purpose of this and the following chapter will be to analyze these speeches in order to show what these themes are and how they are developed.

One of the things that will become clear in the course of this analysis is that although others might describe the relations between Pausanias and Agathon, and between Phaidros and Eryximakhos, as love relations, Plato does not. An exploration of exactly why this is the case will show that the theme of love is central to the dialogue, and not just a convenient way of connecting several speeches leading up to a metaphysical dissertation by Sokrates, which is at best only tenuously related to the subject of love. With the exception of Aristophanes' speech, these earlier discourses constitute a rather thorough exploration of why and how love relations fail. Aristophanes, by contrast, will point the way mythologically that Sokrates will travel philosophically in exploring what love relations must be if they are to succeed. I shall argue in chapters 4 and 5 that Sokrates' discussion of his metaphysical views cannot be understood apart from his view of love.

1 Phaidros

In terms of the anthropological distinction between "guilt" and "shame" classical Greece was clearly a "shame" culture. As Dover[2] points out: "any act or condition is $\alpha\dot{\iota}\sigma\chi\varrho\acute{o}\nu$ which makes the agent *seem* inferior, for any reason, in the eyes of others, but especially if it is induced by cowardice,...meanness, sloth or lack of ambition. $\Phi\iota\lambda o\tau\iota\mu\acute{\iota}\alpha$ 'love of honour' is what makes us strive for achievements which will earn us the admiration of others....It is a common Greek belief that the desire to be honoured and the fear of incurring contempt are the essential motives of good action" (emphasis mine).

I have argued in my analysis of *Meno* (Appendix) that for Plato the ἀρετή, the excellence, of the human is the human capacity to reserve to the self the power of defining the self; and that to yield that power to others is the fundamental corruption out of which arise all other forms of corruption of the person.[3] Thus, if Dover is correct, Plato would have seen the emphasis on appearances in Greek culture as profoundly corruptive of the people in it. And if Plato held this view at the time of writing the *Symposium*, in which a central issue is the relation of the human individual to the cosmos, consideration of such a thesis would be unavoidable.

Phaidros' speech reflects this aspect of Greek society in a very clear, if also very shallow way. He is concerned not with what one does, but with what one gets caught at; not with guilt, but with shame. The power of Eros, we are told (178c–e) is:

> The shame [αἰσχροῖς] that we feel for shameful [αἰσχύνην] things, and [love of honor (φιλοτιμίαν)]; without which it is impossible for city or person to perform any high and noble deeds. Let me then say that a man in love, should he *be detected* in some shameful act or in a cowardly submission to shameful treatment at another's hands, would not feel half so much distress at anyone *observing* it, whether father or comrade or anyone in the world, as when his favourite [παιδικῶν] did; and in the selfsame way we see how the beloved [ἐρώμενον] especially [feels shame (α ἰσχύνεται) towards] his lovers[4] when he *is observed* to be about some shameful business. . . . For a man in love would surely choose to have all the rest of the host rather than his favourite [παιδικῶν] *see* him forsaking his station or flinging away his arms (emphasis mine).

The implication of this passage is that what one is is less important than what one seems to be. But Phaidros sees this as so central to a love relation that it is the source of love's power. If taken seriously, this implies that lovers will mask what they are with a pretense of being what each believes the other wants. Pathetically, each wants the other to love him for what he is, and each in his effort to attain this creates just the situation which renders such a deeper relationship impossible. If *A* puts on a mask in order to attract *B* then if *B* is attracted, what *B* is attracted to is not *A*, but the mask that *A* wears. And *A* has failed to fulfill his desire to be loved. On the other hand, if *B* is not attracted by *A*'s mask, the effort failed— even though, ironically, *B* might have been attracted if no mask had been donned. On the other hand, if *A* now removes the mask, or tries to wear a different mask, *A* will be seen by *B* not as what the new mask is, but rather as the sort of person who puts on masks—a more accurate perception of *A*, perhaps, than *A* would want *B* to have.

The case is similar, of course, if *B* attempts to appear as what *B* believes *A* wants. Moreover, neither dares put the mask aside for fear of losing the little that has been gained. As a result, all that remains is two masks dancing with each other while the human individuals behind the masks are unable to meet. Neither can allow the other beyond the surface, and deeper relationships grounded in exploration of each other as persons become impossible.

Yet without such a deeper relationship neither can discover what the other actually wants. For this reason the mask each wears cannot have its source in the other. Since each is unable to know the other, each is reduced to viewing what the other wants in terms of socially defined stereotypes. The mask each dons to attract the other is therefore the mask of conventional virtues. The society defines for them what constitutes courage, honor, nobility or good citizenship, and since each is acting a part, each has no alternative but to play the role and conform. In this way they *become* the mask; they render to the society the power to define their being. And we should not be surprised to find that for Phaidros Eros is a force for conformity "without which it is impossible for city or person to perform any high and noble deeds"(178d); or again (178e–179a): "So that if we could somewise contrive to have a city or an army composed of lovers and their favourites, they could not be better citizens of their country than by refraining from all that is base in a mutual rivalry for honour." That is, for prestige in the eyes of the others. Although Phaidros allows this reference to a city to slide while he goes on to speak of such an army, he may well have seen the homosexual conventions of the Greeks as having just such an effect—particularly since women had no social status either in citizenship or in love.

His discussion of that army, ironically, reduces courage to the fear of shame, thus debasing the virtue he is trying to praise. There is for him no such thing as courage, but the appearance of courage can be achieved precisely because some fears are greater than others. And this, we are told (180a) is the "sort of valour...respected [most] by the gods."

Since each of the lovers is unable to know the other, the basis of their attraction cannot get beyond what initially attracted them to each other. The only individuality either can have in the eyes of the other is physical appearance. The rest is conventional.

Predictably, then, Phaidros is unable to find any value in the relationship itself. Instead, he locates the value of love outside the relationship, and sees the relationship only as a means to other things. Eros is (178c) "the cause of all our highest blessings," one of which is "the [beautiful ($\varkappa\alpha\lambda\tilde{\omega}s$)] life" (178c), but these "blessings" seem all to lie outside the relationship itself. Alkestis, through her sacrifice, is rewarded by being allowed to return from Hades (179c). Yet there is no suggestion that the relation is anything but onesided. Alkestis loves Admetos—but so does Admetos.

Akhilles, for his love of Patroklos, was "honoured and sent to his place in the Isles of the Blest" (179d), and was given "distinguished honour" (180a) after he got there; however, if any version of that rendering of the myth suggests that Patroklos went along, Phaidros ignores it. The reward is not in the relationship, nor is it even in what Akhilles is. The reward is the opinions that the gods have of him, the "honour" they grant. Thus at most the value of the love relationship is to be found in its capacity to inspire us to do the kinds of things that are admired by the gods.

In accord with this, Eros is described for us as "the most valuable of the gods who has an unsurpassed power to provide" (180b) both excellence ($\dot{\alpha}\varrho\epsilon\tau\acute{\eta}$) and happiness ($\epsilon\dot{v}\delta\alpha\iota\mu o\nu\acute{\iota}\alpha s$). The "excellence" is the socially conventional concept of excellence. The happiness is not found in the relationship between the lovers, but in the rewards they gain because of that relationship. Phaidros' viewpoint comes full circle when we discover that those rewards are the rewards of honor, of the opinions others have of us, rather than of what we are—and they are gained not because of what we are, but because of what others think we are. If, as Diotima is to suggest later,[5] happiness for lovers is to be found in the relationship itself, the fact that Phaidros prostitutes that relationship to other values, values external to the relationship, not only brings him a false (or rather, a vacuous) happiness, it makes genuine happiness impossible. If, as Diotima is to suggest, that relationship is in an important sense a relationship of helping each other to grow, Phaidros' conception of love, being rooted in masks that cannot be put aside, renders such growth impossible. And if, as Diotima says (207c–208b), existence for mortals is growth, such a relationship lessens the reality of the lovers. Instead of being a liberating experience, it is one that stunts.

As Dover[6] has pointed out, the distinction between "lover" (ἐραστής) and "beloved" (ἐρώμενος) or "favorite" (παιδικά) is important in understanding the homosexual relations of the time. The lover was expected to adopt a role commonly associated with the male. He was the pursuer, the agent, the initiator in establishing the relationship, and the initiator of any sexual activity within the relationship. For this reason he was seen as possessed by Eros[7] and, as Phaidros points out (180b), "filled as he is with a god [he] surpasses his favourite in divinity." The beloved, on the other hand, was expected to adopt certain of the characteristics of a role commonly associated with the female. He was to be wooed. He was to submit to his lover's desires. He was the passive member of the pair.

Throughout Phaidros' speech the beloved is praised over the lover, and is seen as the more powerful of the two. The lover is courageous or noble or a good citizen in order to avoid shame in the eyes of the beloved. This theme is elevated still further with the mythological references he gives toward the end of his speech. In the first, Alkestis, the wife and therefore the beloved, is glorified for her courage by being allowed to return to the living. In the second Orpheus, the husband and therefore the lover, is contemned for lacking the courage to die. We are told that he was given only a phantom of Eurydike—and was to lose even that. Phaidros then declares that Orpheus "deserved" to die "at the hands of women."

Phaidros' ambivalence toward women is understandable if now as an adult, and as one whose sexual preference is established, he perceives himself as *eromenos*, beloved, as one who, not being a woman, nevertheless must compete with women for the affection of lovers. (He would be in competition with them only if he were pursuing older, married men, since such relationships with younger men were customary. Although in the ordinary course of things the *eromenos* was the younger of the couple, normally the *erastes* was unmarried.) Moreover, he can compete with them only by emulating them. Thus, on the one hand he can identify himself with Alkestis, and on the other, he can describe death "at the hands of women" with the utmost contempt.

In the third mythological reference Phaidros argues at some length (in opposition to Aiskhylos) that Akhilles, the greatest hero of them all, was not a lover but a beloved. Finally, at the end of his speech, he makes his praise of the beloved over the lover explicit: "For in truth there is no sort of valour more respected by the gods than this which comes of love; yet they are even more admiring and delighted and beneficent [!] when the beloved is fond of the lover than when the lover is fond of his favourite; since a lover, filled as he is with a god, surpasses his favourite in divinity" (180a–b).

I have already suggested that Phaidros and Eryximakhos are lovers. Given the submissiveness of his comment to Eryximakhos (176d–e) that "you know I always obey you, above all in medical matters," the implication seems to be that he is the beloved in their relationship, and Eryximakhos, the lover. If so, then throughout his speech Phaidros appears to be trying to glorify himself by glorifying the beloved.

2 Pausanias

For Pausanias, curiously, there can be no shameful act: "For of every action [πρᾶξις] it may be observed that as acted [πραττομένη] by itself it is neither noble nor [shameful (αἰσχρά)]...each only turns out to be such in the doing [πράξει], as the manner [πραχθῇ] of doing it may be. For when the doing [πραττόμενον] of it is noble and right, the thing itself becomes noble; when wrong, it becomes [shameful (αἰσχρόν)]" (180e–181a, emphasis mine).

He then goes on to apply this to the subject at hand: "So also it is with loving, and Love is not in every case noble or worthy of celebration, but only when he impels us to love in a noble manner" (181a, emphasis mine).

He then adds that "the Love that belongs to the Popular Aphrodite" is found "in the meaner sort of men" who, among other things, "look merely to the accomplishment and care not if the manner be noble or no" (181b, emphasis mine). Again, at 181c–d: "Even in the passion for boys you may note the way of those who are under the single incitement of this Love." And at 182a, "whatsoever is done in an orderly and lawful manner can never justly bring reproach." Finally, at 184a–c, he goes into detail as to what is accepted in Athens as the proper "manner":

> our convention regards a quick capitulation as a disgrace:
> for there ought, first, to be a certain interval—the

generally approved touchstone—of time; and, second, it is disgraceful if the surrender is due to gold or public preferment, or is a mere cowering away from the endurance of ill-treatment, or shows the youth not properly contemptuous of such benefits as he may receive in pelf or political success. . . . One way remains in our custom whereby a favourite may rightly gratify his lover: it is our rule that, just as in the case of the lovers it was counted no flattery or scandal for them to be willingly and utterly enslaved to their favourites, so there is left one sort of voluntary thraldom which is not scandalous; I mean, in the cause of [excellence ($\dot{\alpha}\varrho\epsilon\tau\acute{\eta}\nu$)].

If we overlook the obvious circularity (in the first quote above) of defining "noble" and "shameful" in terms of "noble" and "shameful," the only difference between them that Pausanias will allow is style, and style becomes Pausanias' mask. He symbolizes the difference as the difference between the two Erotes, one being the attendant of the "Heavenly" Aphrodite, the other, of the "Popular" Aphrodite. Mythologically, for Pausanias the difference between the two Aphrodites is that the "Heavenly" Aphrodite, born of Ouranos, although female, "partakes not of the female, but only of the male" (181c),[8] whereas the "Popular" Aphrodite "partakes of both female and male." Actions originating with the Eros associated with the first are always noble actions, whereas those originating with the Popular Eros are matters of "chance" ($\tau\acute{\upsilon}\chi\eta$, 181b), and things done by chance ($\tau\acute{\upsilon}\chi\omega\sigma\iota$) (i.e., without premeditation and therefore without style) may be either "good or its opposite, without distinction." Female stereotypes do not seem to have changed much since the ancients, and perhaps we should not be surprised to find that the major fault of the Popular Eros is "fickleness" (a fault not difficult to explain in those who are compelled by the society to seek their identity through others).

In the end, Pausanias does not seem to differ from Phaidros in any very important way except style. He attacks Phaidros' claim that Eros is a force for conformity in the state, claiming instead that despotic governments such as those in Ionia must forbid homosexual love relations precisely because they create the sort of trust that will make the lovers unafraid of betrayal, and therefore successful conspirators—as was the case with Aristogeiton and Harmodios. Yet throughout his speech he admits that he is merely trying to reflect the customs of Athens, as distinguished from other cities. Since he *is* an Athenian, he is just as conventional as Phaidros—with perhaps equally pathetic consequences.

Next he attacks Phaidros' claim that one should pursue Eros for the sake of rewards (184a–b): "it is disgraceful if the surrender is due to gold or public preferment or is a mere cowering away from the endurance of ill-treatment, or shows the [beloved] not properly contemptuous of such benefits as he may receive in pelf or political success." However, in place of Phaidros' prostitution he puts another of his own which, predictably, has a more socially acceptable appearance. The beloved may "rightly gratify his lover" if he does so for the sake of "excellence" ($\dot{\alpha}\varrho\epsilon\tau\dot{\eta}\nu$, 184c). The relationship thus, once again, is seen as a means, not as an end.

And its real value eludes him.

This displacement of values in turn requires each to play a role, to put on a mask—the lover, that of teacher; the beloved, that of student (184d–e): "the elder of his plenty contributing to intellectual and all other excellence, the younger in his paucity acquiring education and all other arts." And only then, we are told, may the beloved "honourably indulge" his lover.

These roles in turn prevent the emergence of the human individuals behind the masks, thereby preventing the development of any very significant relationship between them. Everything flows from the lover to the beloved, and nothing can move the other way. If the beloved should show (for example) intelligence and respond by making a contribution to what the lover is teaching, she[9] or he will have abandoned the role of beloved as Pausanias defines it, and therefore will have violated the relationship. The beloved must submit.

With Pausanias as with Phaidros, the relation is at its foundation a power relation.

As a result, the beloved can give nothing to the lover but the use of her or his body—and can therefore never be more than a sex object. No dialectic can take place, and despite Pausanias' pious claims that the honorable lover is pursuing not body but soul (181b and 183d), since nothing moves from the beloved to the lover, the soul or mind or individuality of the beloved must remain opaque to the lover, who cannot come in contact "with what abides" (183d–e), still less fall in love with it. As a result, the lover's teaching cannot be personalized or in any way tailored to the needs of the beloved. He will have nothing to teach but the conventions.

Moreover, there is no way in which the beloved can penetrate the mask of the lover and meet her or him as an individual. What comes from the lover is not what or who the lover is, but what the local (in this case Athenian) convention requires the lover to teach. Thus, in the end both must regard the beloved as little more than a receptacle to be filled both mentally and physically by the lover.

Acceptance by the beloved of so degrading a concept of self not only requires subservience to the lover, it precludes the possibility of such a relationship ever resulting in that excellence for the sake of which the beloved entered the relationship in the first place.[10] Still more ironic is the fact that since the beloved is thus reduced to a sex object the lover's actions ultimately must be precisely those actions Pausanias himself condemns in his description of the popular lover (183d–e): "By 'wicked' we mean that popular lover, who craves the body rather than the soul: as he is not in love with what abides, he himself is not abiding. As soon as the bloom of the body he so loved begins to fade he 'flutters off and is gone,' leaving all his speeches and promises dishonoured." The permanent relationship he describes as proper for lovers (181d) has, because of his view of love, become impossible, and what he says of it is reduced to little more than a persuasive line. For Pausanias himself (rather than the generic "lover"), this could at best have been a rather thin promise to Agathon that Pausanias would not leave him.[11]

Small wonder, then, that in his description of the behavior approved for lovers he tells us (183b–c) that "the vow of love-passion. . .is no vow" and can be disregarded; that "both gods and men have given absolute license [πᾶδαν ἐξουδίαν] to the lover." Small wonder, too, that in his description of the popular love the kind of action that horrifies him to the point that he would have it outlawed is that in which the popular lover (181d) "will take advantage of a boy's green thoughtlessness to deceive him and make a mock of him by running straight off to another." This is not, as one might assume, an objection to the immorality of "taking advantage" of an innocent boy and deceiving him. There should be a law against such behavior he says, in order "to prevent the sad waste of attention *paid to* an *object* so uncertain." Then, in case his listeners might have misunderstood his point, he goes on to deny the effectiveness of the lover as teacher, and justifies his proposed law by adding, "for who can tell where a boy will end at last, vicious or virtuous [ἀρετῆς] in body and soul?"

Pausanias makes a point of the fact that what distinguishes the "Heavenly" from the "Popular" Aphrodite—and therefore distinguishes the Eros associated with each—is not only age, but gender. The Heavenly Aphrodite (181c) "[has no portion] of the female, but only of the male." She is "Heavenly" in the sense that she was born of the sperm from the testicles of Ouranos (Sky) when Kronos threw them into the sea. She has no portion of the female since the circumstances of her birth preclude her having a mother.[12] The Popular Aphrodite, on the other hand, is born of Zeus and Dione (180d) and therefore has elements of both female and male. Since the male, according to Pausanias (181c) "has the robuster nature and a larger share of mind," the Eros associated with the Heavenly Aphrodite is seen as more virile, more intelligent, more constant, more concerned with excellence than the Eros of the Popular Aphrodite. The followers of the latter, who is a mix of both male and female, "find themselves doing everything [by chance ($\tau\acute{\upsilon}\chi\omega\sigma\iota$)]"[13] good or its opposite, without distinction." The claim that one of the evils of popular love is that men "love women as well as boys" (181b) follows.

Throughout Pausanias' speech we find the lover glorified over the beloved. Just as Phaidros praised himself through his praise of the beloved, Pausanias seems to be praising himself by praising the lover. If this is the case, since (193c) Pausanias and Agathon are lovers, Agathon might reasonably be expected to show the effects of Pausanias' view of love.

Chapter 3

1 Empedokles

Eryximakhos' mask is his profession. As might be expected its features are more clearcut, more precise. His position will be more comprehensive and more coherent than either Phaidros' or Pausanias'. But it will not be his own. His conventionality will in fact become more and more pedantic and, as one might expect of a physician, more and more prescriptive (or preachy) as his speech progresses.

His source seems to be Empedokles.[1] Kathleen Freeman[2] suggests that Empedokles "may have been the head of a medical school or coterie at Acragas." Diogenes Laertius[3] tells us that Heraklides discussed Empedokles in a medical treatise, *On Diseases;*[4] that Satyros referred to him as a physician;[5] that Pausanias, to whom *On Nature* was addressed, was Empedokles' student and a physician;[6] that Akron was a rival physician;[7] Hermippos claims Empedokles cured a woman named Panthea;[8] and even that Empedokles wrote a *Discourse on Medicine.*[9] Diogenes Laertius was a collector of stories about philosophers and is not always reliable; however, in this case he does give his sources, and since those sources would have been easy enough for his readers at that time to check, the report seems likely to be true. Moreover, certain of the fragments we have of Empedokles' work seem also to suggest that he was a physician. In addition to those that reflect both an interest in and a knowledge of human physiology, at least two make specific medical claims:

> 111. You will learn remedies for ills and help against old age....
> 112. ...they follow me in countless numbers, to ask where their advantage lies,...[some] long pierced by harsh pains, ask to hear the word of healing for all kinds of illnesses.[10]

Thus, although the evidence that Empedokles was a physician is indirect, and the inference from that to the claim that his theories dominated a significant portion of the medical thinking of the period is still less direct, such a thesis nevertheless does seem likely.

Only a few of the many facets of Empedokles' work seem to be relevant here, and although some of those have been controverted,[11] the issues are as yet far from settled. Let me, then, state my interpretations somewhat arbitrarily:

> 1. Love is the binding force of the cosmos. As such it is one of only two dynamic elements in Empedokles' system, the other being strife. (Fr. 16: "They are as they were before and shall be, and never, I think, will endless time be emptied of these two." The "two," according to Hippolytos [*Refutatio Omnium Haeresium*, ed. P. Wendland, Leipzig 1916, 7.29], being "love and strife.")
> 2. Under the rule of love the four material elements (or "roots")—fire, air, water and earth—are equally mixed in all parts of the cosmos, forming an undifferentiated mass. (Fr. 27: "There the swift limbs of the sun are not distinguished [nor the shaggy might of earth, nor sea]; in this way it is held fast in the close covering of [attunement ($\dot{\alpha}\varrho\mu o\nu\acute{\iota}\eta s$)], a rounded sphere, rejoicing in encircling stillness."[12]
> 3. The other dynamic element is strife, and under its rule the four material elements are wholly separated from each other. (Fr. 17: "...And these things never cease their continual exchange of position, at one time all coming together into one through love, at another again being borne away from each other by strife's repulsion.")
> 4. The present epoch is one of transition from the rule of love to the rule of strife. This transition period is a time in which particulars, including living things, are produced and then destroyed by the gradual separation of the elements. (Fr. 17: "A twofold tale I shall tell: at one time it grew to be one only from many, and at another again it divided to be many from one. There is a double birth of what is mortal, and a double passing away; for the uniting of all things brings one generation into being and destroys it, and the other is reared and scattered as they are again divided..." Also fr. 20: "This is well known in the mass of mortal limbs: at one time, in the maturity of a vigorous life, all the limbs that are the body's portion

come into one under love; at another time again, torn asunder by evil strifes, they wander, each apart, on the shore of life. So it is too for plants, and for fish that live in the water, and for wild animals who have their lairs in the hills, and for the wing-sped gulls.'')

5. The survival of individuals, and later of species, rests on the adaptation of those individuals to the environment. (The most startling statement of this thesis comes from Aristotle, *Physics*, 198b 16–33, especially the last few lines: ''wherever then all the parts came about just what they would have been if they had come to be for an end, such things survived, being organized spontaneously in a fitting way; whereas those which grew otherwise perished and continue to perish, as Empedocles says his 'man-faced ox-progeny' did.'' [Oxford trans., Hardie and Gaye.])

6. As this transition continues, highly organized forms gradually give way to less organized forms leading to the formation of the sexes. (Fr. 66: ''the divided meadows of Aphrodite.'' Fr. 71: ''But if your belief about these things in any way lacked assurance, how, from the combining of water, earth, air, and the sun came the forms and color of mortal things which have now arisen, fitted together by Aphrodite.'') This in turn resulted in the natural processes of birth. (Fr. 64: ''And on him desire too.'' Fr. 63: ''But the substance of the limbs is separated, part in [the body of] the man.'' I.e., he saw the woman as having a ''seed'' and contributing ''substance.'' (Cf. ch. 1, n. 5.) Fr. 65: ''They [presumably the female and male seed] were poured in pure places; some met with cold and became women.'' Fr. 67: ''For the male was in the warmer. . .this is the reason why men are dark, more powerfully built, and hairier.'')

7. Since normal birth reproduces the kind of the parents, species are developed which, presumably, would also survive only so long as they were adapted to an environment becoming increasingly disorganized, increasingly random, an entropic environment.

8. Death is separation of the components. (Fr. 9: ''When they have been mixed in the form of a man and come to the air, or in the form of the race of wild animals, or

of plants, or of birds, then people say that this is to be
born, and when they separate they call this again ill-fated
death; these terms are not right, but I follow the custom
and use them myself.")

2 Eryximakhos

Empedokles—at least in the extant fragments[13]—used "φιλότητι"
("love," "friendship," "affection") to refer to what he saw as the
binding force of the cosmos. In the *Symposium* Eryximakhos seems
to be using Ἔρωτα in the same way, substituting the god, Eros, for
Empedokles' dynamic natural force. (This leap may be at least
partially justified by the fact that Empedokles does use "Aphrodite"
[fragments # 17, 22, 66, 71, 86, 87] or "Kupris" [fragments # 73, 95,
98, 128] to refer to his binding force.) Eryximakhos then gives the
"two Erotes" introduced by Pausanias an Empedoklean analysis.
The noble love (unalloyed with female) now is seen as the binding
force of the cosmos. He tells us (186a) medicine has taught him that
Eros is: "the attraction of all creatures to a great variety of things,
which works in the bodies of all animals and all growths upon the
earth, and practically in everything that is; and [he has] learnt how
mighty and wonderful and universal is the sway of this god over
all affairs both human and divine."

The fact that it "works in the bodies of all animals and all
growths upon the earth, and practically in everything that is"
suggests that Eryximakhos sees it as a cosmic force, keeping
earthbound all bodily things (i.e., gravity); holding the heavenly
bodies in their orbits; drawing the roots of plants into the soil as
well as bringing animals together for procreation.

Empedokles' fr. 22 seems to be giving love the same binding
power in the world of particulars: "For all these—sun and earth and
sky and sea—are one with the parts of themselves that have been
separated from them and born in mortal things. In the same way,
those that are more ready to combine are made similar by Aphrodite
and feel mutual affection...."

Eryximakhos' qualification, *"practically* [ἔπος] in everything
that is" is designed to leave room for the baser love (containing both
male and female which comes from Polyhymnia, the "Queen of
Various Song" (187c); that is, which contains difference, or strife.
This reflects the second part of fr. 22: "But such as are most different
from each other in birth and mixture and in the molding of their

forms are most hostile, quite inexperienced in union, and grieving deeply at their generation in strife, in that they were born in wrath."

Eryximakhos' description of medicine follows naturally enough. It is "a knowledge of the love matters of the body in regard to repletion and evacuation" (186c). The successful physician is one who is "able to make friends and happy lovers of the keenest opponents in the body...cold and hot, dry and moist and the rest of them." His task is perhaps rendered more difficult by the fact that, as Empedokles had said (fr. 90): "So sweet seized on sweet, bitter rushed to bitter, sharp came to sharp, and hot coupled with hot."

This latter fragment almost certainly reflects Empedokles' view of the steady inroads of strife into a world from which love is gradually retreating. As things separate, the attraction of like for like[14] brings them together with their various kinds until, in the end, fire, air, water and earth are wholly separated from each other.

If these fragments are put in context with Eryximakhos' speech, a medical theory begins to emerge. Strife functions in two rather different ways to cause illness. The first is internally, by breaking down the organization ("attunement") of the body; the second, externally, by disrupting the mutually supportive relationships ("attunement") between the individual and the environment. Apollo was among other things a god of order.[15] Thus, the function of the physician is to introduce order or "attunement" into both sets of relationships. The physician must therefore view the patient as a whole, both internally and in her or his relations to the environment—a view for which Empedokles was criticized in the Hippokratic treatise *On Ancient Medicine*.[16]

Eryximakhos' discussion of "attunement" appears to originate in the fragment he quotes from Herakleitos (187a). "The one at variance with itself is drawn together, like [the attunement (ἁρμονία)] of bow and lyre." The passage is introduced for the sake of refutation, and although we have no way of knowing whether Empedokles or his followers actually produced such a criticism of Herakleitos, the Empedoklean character of both the "refutation" and the "correction" (187b) is clear: "[attunement (ἁρμονία)] is consonance [συμφωνία], and consonance is a kind of agreement [ὁμολογία]; and agreement of things varying [διαφερομένον], so long as they are at variance [διαφέρωνται], is impossible. On the other hand when a thing varies with no disability of agreement, then it may be [attuned (ἁρμόσαι)]; just as rhythm is produced by fast and slow which, in the beginning were at variance, but later came to agree."

Eryximakhos can now explain how Pausanias' "two Erotes" fit into Empedokles' scheme. When the opposites ("cold and hot, bitter and sweet, dry and moist, and the rest of them," 186d–e) happen to be brought together by the Heavenly Love (he calls it "orderly Love" at 188a) they maintain the orderliness of things (as one might expect of a follower of Apollo). The result is an "attunement," a balance within the individual, in the environment, and between the individual and the environment: "taking on a temperate [attunement ($\dot\alpha\varrho\mu o\nu\dot\iota\alpha\nu$)] as they mingle [they] become bearers of ripe fertility and health to men and animals and plants..." (188a).

When these same opposites are brought together by the Popular Love (which "comes from the Queen of Various Song") then the order of things is broken down, bringing disorder destroying the attunement within the individual, in the environment, and between the individual and the environment: "great destruction and wrong does he wreak. For at these junctures are wont to arise pestilences and many other varieties of disease in beasts and herbs; likewise hoar-frosts, hails and mildews, which spring from mutual encroachments and disturbances in such love-connexions..." (188a–b).

The task of the physician, therefore, is to introduce the orderly Love into the individual, and into the individual's relationships, in such a way as to keep the baser Love under control: "Well-ordered men, [i.e., followers of Apollo like Eryximakhos] and the less regular only so as to bring them to better order, should be indulged in this Love, and this is the sort we should preserve; this is the noble, the Heavenly Love." (197d–e).

Eryximakhos has thus pulled the Apollonian view of the orderliness of things together with the Empedoklean view of Love as the cosmic force binding all things, and subsumed the two under the concept of "attunement." His use of this concept is almost certainly Empedoklean.

In extending it to music[17] Eryximakhos argued that although things that are at variance cannot be drawn together, things that are at variance at one time may be brought together at another. And "attunement" is seen as the result: "just as rhythm is produced by fast and slow, which in the beginning were at variance but later came to agree" (187c).

This seems to illustrate his earlier comment that the "double Love belongs to the nature of all bodies" (186b–d). Although the two forms of Eros are to be found in "all bodies" (186b) the expert physician is one "who is expert in producing [Eros] where it ought to flourish but exists not, and in removing it from where it should not be" (186d). Thus, the physician's task is to "attune" the two loves in the body, not merely to rid the body of the one and replace it with the other. Otherwise there would be no sense to his later comment (187e) regarding the popular love: "in applying him we must proceed with all caution, that no debauchery be implanted with the reaping of his pleasure, just as in our craft we set a high importance on the right use of the appetite for dainties of the table, that we may cull the pleasure without the disease."

Again the two views are brought together. The follower of Apollo saw the god in opposition to Dionysos, order constantly faced with disruption. The Empedoklean view would be that both love and strife are in all things. One cannot therefore rid the body either of strife or of the popular love that contains it.

Eryximakhos chooses to ignore the Empedoklean implication that in the long run strife must win, and the organism must die. And that in the longer run, the increasing entropy of strife will have the same effect on the environment as well, although this will take an enormously longer time (if, as Empedokles suggests in fr. 115, the "daimons to whom life long-lasting is apportioned" can be condemned to reincarnation for "three times countless years"). Instead, Eryximakhos follows out the implications of what he has said thus far and extends his theory of love to the introduction of "attunement" into social life (187c–d)—just as Empedokles did in fr. 17 where he tells us that because of love, mortals' "thoughts are friendly and they work together." And not surprizingly, we find that for Eryximakhos, since here the baser Love sometimes brings together evil combinations, the introduction of "attunement" into social life requires "a good craftsman;" i.e., a craftsman who is the analogue of the physician and is able to introduce the noble Love not only into the social structure, but into the relations among the various states (or societies) as well.

Eryximakhos' next step is to extend this to the natural environment (188a–c):

Note how even the system of the yearly seasons is full of these two forces; how the qualities I mentioned just now, heat and cold, drought and moisture, when brought together by the orderly Eros, and taking on a temperate [attunement ($\dot{\alpha}\varrho\mu o\nu\dot{\iota}\alpha\nu$)] as they mingle, become bearers of ripe fertility and health to men and animals and plants, and are guilty of no wrong. But when the wanton-spirited Eros gains the ascendant in the seasons of the year, great destruction and wrong does he wreak. For at these junctures are wont to arise pestilences and many other varieties of disease in beasts and herbs; likewise hoarfrosts, hails and mildews.

In addition to the resemblance this bears to fr. 22 (quoted above, p. 34–5), this also seems to reflect a statement of Empedokles that quite possibly was intended by him to show the scope of medicine (fr. 111): "You will learn remedies for ills and help against old age, since for you alone shall I accomplish these things. You will check the force of tireless winds, which sweep over land and destroy fields with their blasts; and again, if you wish, you will restore compensating breezes. After black rain you will bring dry weather in season for men, and too after summer dryness you will bring tree-nourishing showers (which live in air), and you will lead from Hades the life-force of a dead man."

Those who study the phenomena of nature, who study the "mutual encroachments and disturbances in such love-connexions as are studied in relation to the motions of the stars and the yearly seasons by what we term astronomy" (188b) are at least analogues of the physician for Eryximakhos. If we take Empedokles' claim seriously then such things come under the purview of medicine, and those who study them would *be* physicians.

From here Eryximakhos moves on to the final logical step (188c): "all means of communication between gods and men are only concerned with either the preservation or the cure of Eros." And (188c–d) "to divination is appointed the task of supervising and treating the health of these loves." The seer, too, must therefore either be, or be an analogue of, the physician—a view that clearly reflects Empedokles' view of himself.

There is science here, even a strong suggestion that love functions as a law of nature. But the science comes from Empedokles. For Eryximakhos it is borrowed science.

Thus, Eryximakhos has not constructed a mask for himself. He has borrowed the Empedoklean mask of his profession. The mask is opaque, and if there is any personality any individual behind the mask he cannot emerge. The pedantic tone of his speech together with his continual references to the authority of medicine suggest that he has in fact become the mask.

Having at this point developed the Empedoklean theme that love is the binding force of the cosmos, Eryximakhos now brings together Pausanias' and Phaidros' views of reward as the reason for pursuing love (188d): "[That love] which is consummated for a good purpose,[18] temperately and justly, both here on earth and in heaven above, wields the mightiest power of all and provides us with a perfect bliss; so that we are able to consort with one another and have friendship also with the gods who are above us." This time, however, the reward is found on a cosmic level as the integration of individuals within themselves and into their world.[19]

But it is the individuals who are so integrated. Somewhere along the line—even though Eryximakhos is Phaidros' lover—the concept of love as a relation between two individuals has disappeared. Eryximakhos is completely absorbed into his profession, and has completely identified himself with it—which is to say that he is completely absorbed in himself. His mask, in other words, is just as opaque from behind as it is from in front. Phaidros had indicated that doing something shameful was not important so long as one is not caught at it, and that the worst thing would be to get caught by one's lover. He seems in little danger of getting caught at anything by a lover who is not in any very important sense aware of him as a person, still less as a person who might do shameful things.

Phaidros, on the other hand, had claimed that the beloved is the one who stimulates action on the part of the lover (as Phaidros stimulated Eryximakhos to propose the speeches in honor of Eros). Eryximakhos admitted (176c) that neither he nor Phaidros can handle very much drinking. Although it is hard to see a self-centered pedant—especially a pompous one like Eryximakhos—out desecrating herms, it is not difficult to see Phaidros, drunk, persuaded by Alkibiades, and in turn persuading a drunken Eryximakhos that so long as they do not get caught there should be no problem.

3 Aristophanes

Throughout Eryximakhos' speech[20] Aristophanes has been hiccoughing, holding his breath, turning red, spluttering, gargling and sneezing—under Eryximakhos' prescription for his hiccoughs. Also,[21] in terms of the Dionysian symbolism of the dialogue, there is reason to believe that the God of Wine has given him the hiccoughs so as to reorder the speeches, putting Aristophanes in a position to satirize Eryximakhos, the follower of Apollo, rather than Pausanias. Aristophanes will in this sense wear a mask of his profession—but with a difference. Satire cannot exist alone, but only in relation to what is being satirized. In this sense, like Dionysos himself, the mask of satire has no character of its own. It can exist only as a distortion of some other mask—although certain types of jokes (both pointed and a little raunchy) and accoutrements (most notably, perhaps, the phallus) as well as certain serious (and often conservative) points could reasonably be expected to appear in any Greek comedy.[22]

Not unexpectedly, we find here a satire not merely of what Eryximakhos says, but of the whole Empedoklean mask that he wears, a satire in which some of the references (e.g., to Pausanias and Agathon at 193b-c) are rather pointed, and much of the humor of which depends upon a certain phallic raunchiness characteristic of Aristophanic comedy. We also find buried there some serious and important points about love—and the most conservative of all claims, the myth of a Golden Age.

Eryximakhos had so strictly limited his speech to the function of love in Empedokles' system that he ignored almost completely the role of strife—and did ignore completely the Empedoklean claim that strife is gradually taking over the cosmos. Aristophanes builds his satire on these omissions.

Like the plays of his real-life counterpart, Plato's Aristophanes is not one to sneak up on his audience with his satire. Eryximakhos yields the floor with the pompous announcement that Aristophanes' hiccoughs are cured, and Aristophanes immediately leaps to the attack. He begins by confirming his cure (189a): "Yes, it has stopped, though not until it was treated with a course of sneezing, such as leaves me wondering that the orderly principle of the body should [yearn for ($\epsilon\pi\iota\theta\upsilon\mu\epsilon\hat{\iota}$)] the noises and titillations involved in sneezing; you see, it stopped the very moment I applied the sneeze to it."

His theme, he tells us, is the power of Eros. He acknowledges Eryximakhos' claims about medicine (189d): "Eros succours mankind and heals those ills whose cure must be the highest happiness of the human race." But the myth he then launches into is designed to show that the healing can take place only in a context produced by strife in a world in which strife is steadily increasing in power.

The three original sexes are described (190b) as the offspring, males of the sun, females of the earth, and androgynes of the moon—"for the moon partakes of both," a position at least consistent with Empedokles' claim that the moon shines by "borrowed light." (Fr. 43, 45: "as the ray, after striking the broad circle of the moon," "a circle of borrowed light moves swiftly round the earth;" fr. 47: "she (the moon) contemplates the bright circle of her lord facing her"). In short, the differentiation of sexes in the original humans was itself the result of the earlier separation of Earth, Sun and Moon. The shape of these primordial humans reflects the shape of "their parents," the Earth, Sun and Moon (190b), which in turn reflect the shape of the original Sphere during the rule of Love (fr. 27: "...it is held fast in the close covering of [attunement], a rounded sphere, rejoicing in encircling stillness." Also fr. 29/28[23] "For two branches do not spring from his back, he has no feet, no swift knees, no organs of reproduction, but he is equal to himself in every direction, without any beginning or end, a rounded sphere, rejoicing in encircling stillness.") Aristophanes completes his description: "the form of each person was round all over, with back and sides encompassing it every way; each had four arms, and legs to match these, and two faces perfectly alike on a cylindrical neck. There was one head to the two faces, which looked opposite ways; there were four ears, two privy members, and all the other parts, as may be imagined, in proportion."

This seems to reflect a description in Empedokles, fr. 61: "Many creatures with a face and breasts on both sides were produced, man-faced bulls arose and again bull-headed men, (others) with male and female nature combined...."

Although they have genitals that differentiate them sexually, the function of the difference in genital structure is by no means clear since they all beget in the same way: "on the earth, like the crickets" (191b).

At this point the humans are powerful enough to believe themselves able to mount an assault on Heaven itself. Thus, strife erupts between them and the gods—just as in an earlier age it had separated the gods and the giants. The gods, however, are themselves incomplete, needing the "honours and observances they had from men" (190c). Empedokles, of course, had argued that the gods were created (fr. 21: "...From them [the elements] comes all that was and is and will be hereafter—trees have sprung from them, and men and women, and animals and birds and water-nourished fish, and long-lived gods too, highest in honor..."); and the suggestion that as strife increased its power in the cosmos the gods would develop needs is compatible with this view. The Empedoklean notion of love as the urge towards unity implies the claim that it also is an urge for reunification of that which has been separated by strife. Thus, the view that in this world of particulars love is known only as a lack follows directly from what is known of Empedokles' position. (This view of love, of course, is to become the basis of Sokrates' thesis later.) In order to satisfy the needs of the gods, then, Zeus cannot destroy humanity as he had previously destroyed the giants. And this, in Aristophanic-Empedoklean terms, can be viewed as the love that gods have for humans.

Zeus next proceeds to control humans by introducing strife among them—not in the way Empedokles might have envisaged, but directly, by dividing each one in half "so that while making them weaker we shall find them more useful by reason of their multiplication" (190d). Bizarre as Aristophanes' myth is at this point, it at least loosely has precedent in Empedokles, fr. 62: "And now hear this—how fire, as it was being separated, brought up by night the shoots of men and pitiable women, for the account is to the point and well informed. First whole-natured forms, having a share of both water and heat,[24] sprang up from the earth; fire, as it tended to reach its like, kept sending them up, when they did not as yet show the lovely shape of limbs, or voice or language native to man."

Moreover, the next step in increasing strife is predicted here: "if they continue turbulent and do not choose to be quiet, I [Zeus] will do it [split them] again..." and let them hop around in bas relief. Appropriately, he has Apollo, god of medicine, heal the wounds from the sectioning. (Aristophanes' way of accounting for the navel and the wrinkles around it may satirize some of the physiological studies going on in medical schools at the time.) Thus, for humans love is clearly now a lack—the lack of one's other half—and having no means of satisfying themselves, they begin to die. Zeus, having failed to foresee this difficulty repairs the damage by inventing sexual reproduction (191b-c). The combinations are random, as one might expect in a satire of Empedokles, but "if in their embracements a man should [chance ($\dot{\epsilon}\nu\tau\dot{\upsilon}\chi o\iota$)][25] on a woman there might be conception and continuation of their kind" (191c).

Any "embracements" of men with men or of women with women would of course be sterile—though the participants would at least "have some satiety of their union and a relief" (191c) and therefore be able to carry on the work of the world. (Cf. Empedokles, fr. 59: "but as [daimon (δαίμονι)] mixed with [daimon (δαίμων)] they fell together as they chanced to meet each other, and many others in addition to these were continually arising.") Sex, therefore, is at this stage a drive, and the object is defined only as human.[26] Sexual preferences are to emerge only as the individuals gain experience, enabling them to discover what their "original form" had been.

Aristophanes has subtly insulted the previous speakers in two ways. By claiming that one of the original forms was androgynous, he has suggested that heterosexuality is at least *as* natural as male homosexuality—as is lesbianism. If Empedokles in fact did hold to an evolutionary theory of sorts based on fitness to the environment, the description at 191c strongly suggests that only heterosexual relationships are adaptive for the species; gay or lesbian relationships yielding only a temporary satisfaction and relief, allowing the participants to go about their business.

He does go on to suggest that those who are sections of androgynes are "adulterers" (μοιχρῶν) and "adulteresses" (μοιχεύτριαι) (191d-e), but this can only reflect the rather curious conventional belief that sexual intercourse with a member of one's own sex does not constitute adultery. Heterosexual males are "woman crazy" (φιλογύναικες) and heterosexual females are "man crazy" (φίλανδροι). Lesbians are quickly brushed aside as "lewd women" (ἑταιρίστριαι). But his description of homosexual men, though couched in more flattering terms, seems to describe precisely the same kind of behavior he condemns in the others: they (191e-192a) "pursue the masculine, and so long as their boyhood lasts they show themselves to be slices of the male by making friends with men and delighting to lie with them and to be clasped in men's embraces." When mature they are "boylovers" (παιδεραστοῦσι) who (192a-b) "have no interest in wiving and getting children," who marry only to satisfy custom, and who would be "quite contented to live together [with their beloveds] unwedded all their days." They also exemplify Empedokles' claims regarding the attraction of like to like, which exerts itself only as strife separates things.

At this point Aristophanes reinforces the earlier suggestion that all three forms of love are natural (192b-c): "Well, when one of them—whether he be a boy-lover or a lover of any other sort—

happens on his own particular half, the two of them are wondrously thrilled with affection and intimacy and love, and are hardly to be induced to leave each other's side for a single moment. These are they who continue together throughout life, though they could not even say what they would have of one another.''

Although sex is an indispensable aspect of this relationship, the joy they take in each other's company cannot be just sex (192c). ''What they would have of one another'' if they could is that they be welded together into a single being ''that so long as [they] live, the pair of [them], being as one, may share a single life; and that when [they] die [they] may also in Hades . . . be one instead of two, having shared a single death.''[27] Even within the framework of the myth this ''welding'' is seen as fanciful. It is what they never again shall be.[28] It is a symbol of the unattainable.

At this point Aristophanes' myth shows a sharply different concept of love than has appeared in the earlier speeches. Love is the sharing of a life. It is growing together—symbolized in the physical growing together of the sex act as expressive of the desire physically to be permanently fused into a single organism, but reaching well beyond the physical in the concept of a shared life, shared experience and therefore shared growth, even a shared death. The concept of sharing ($\varkappa o \iota \nu \hat{\eta}$) immediately eliminates those considerations of relative status or power that figured so large in the first three speeches, replacing them with relations of mutuality— precisely the kind of attitudes that make shared growth possible. Power and sharing are mutually exclusive. To the extent that one is found in a relationship, the other is necessarily to that extent shouldered aside. And just as power relations between halves of a single organism can have no meaning, power relations between two who share a life are equally meaningless.

Aristophanes returns to his myth, explaining that this sort of love is again natural (suggesting, perhaps, that a relationship grounded in power and relative status is not natural, or at any rate is not a love relationship), because it is in its essence an attempt to return to one's original state before the sectioning took place. The reward in such a relationship is the relationship itself—not something else for the sake of which the relationship is established. The reward is to be what is natural for humans to be. The penalty for not pursuing our humanity in this way is, he reminds us, further separation, further alienation from what it is to be human—a separation not only of one person from another, but an internal disintegration as well, that would leave us less than human animals hopping about on one leg. Mythologically this penalty is presented as the result of opposing Eros (193b); i.e., from a separation between humans and the god. Moreover, a separation of humans from other gods ("incur[ring] the hate of Heaven") would constitute a separation of humans from Eros. The greatest "gift" of the god is that "of discovering our proper favourites [παιδικοῖς]"; i.e., of finding the kind of love that properly completes us as human beings. That, because of the increasing power of strife, is rare if not impossible. But "if this be the best thing of all, the nearest approach to it among all acts *open to us* . . . is to find a favourite (παιδικῶν) whose nature is exactly to our mind" (193c–d, emphasis mine).

But Aristophanes had said at the outset that he intended to discuss the power of Eros. We can see now that on one level that is the power to return us to something approximating our primordial state—a state in which humans were powerful enough to threaten the gods themselves. Although Eros might give us such power again we must not exercise it. Power in use is strife, and those who use it will further alienate themselves from their essential humanity. The condition of our establishing a genuine love relationship is—at least within the bounds of that relationship—to give up all aspirations for power and dominance. Once that is accomplished the true power of Eros emerges: the power to make us ever more and more human.

Aristophanes had opened his speech with the claim that Eros "succours mankind and heals those ills whose cure must be the highest happiness of the human race" (189d). He now ends with a similar medical claim that "if we will supply the gods with reverent duty he will restore us to our ancient life and heal and help us into the happiness of the blest" (193d).

He then turns to Eryximakhos with a plea not to make fun of what he has said. Having worked through Eryximakhos' speech the reader might well wonder if Eryximakhos is capable of making fun of anything. This conjecture seems in fact to be confirmed by Aristophanes, who gives as his reason that if Eryximakhos were to try, there might well be no opportunity left to hear Agathon and Sokrates (193d–e). ("There, Eryximakhos, is my discourse on Love. . . make no comic sport of it, for we want to hear what the others will say in their turn—I rather mean the other two, since only Agathon and Socrates are left.") Eryximakhos misses the implied jab and (perhaps because of the medical claims with which Aristophanes' speech is bracketed) tells them that he enjoyed the speech.

4 Agathon

In the banter that follows, the company is confronted with another, different kind of threat to the completion of the evening's entertainment. Sokrates seems about to engage Agathon in a dialectical conversation. Phaidros, as symposiarch, cuts this discussion short, but not before the main outlines have been limned.

Agathon, in claiming that he might get "flustered" in the delivery of his speech,[29] draws a distinction between speaking before "a few men of wit," and before "a host of fools" (194b). Sokrates points out that Agathon has subtly (and unwittingly) insulted his guests because they had all been members of the "host of fools" who witnessed the tragedies of the previous day. "But," says Sokrates (194c–d), "suppose you found yourself with other folk who were clever, you would probably feel *ashamed* that they would *witness* any shameful act you might feel yourself to be doing. . . .Whereas before the multitude you would not be ashamed if you felt you were doing anything shameful?" (emphasis mine). Agathon agrees to the first, but Phaidros does not give him the opportunity to reply to the second.

Thus, although the discussion is interrupted at this point, Sokrates' misgivings are clear. Agathon is not concerned about the possibility of giving a foolish speech. He is not concerned about committing "*any* shameful act." He is only concerned about whether or not anyone catches him at it.[30] He is, in other words, at exactly the same point morally as Phaidros, and even though Phaidros, as symposiarch, has the responsibility of keeping the evening's entertainment on track, the irony of having Phaidros stop the discussion is obvious.[31]

Agathon (195a–b) takes as his point of departure the first statement in Phaidros' speech (178b), that Eros is the oldest of the gods. He makes only one other direct reference to the previous speeches. This is at 196d–e, where he says that Eryximakhos in his speech glorified his profession—a remark so general about a fact so predictable that it does not furnish any evidence that he actually listened to Eryximakhos' speech. There is, in fact, some reason to believe that Agathon heard nothing that was said after Phaidros' initial statement.

At 195c he tells us that "ever since Eros has reigned over the gods" only "amity and peace" have prevailed. Apart from the obvious stupidity of such a remark,[32] it indicates, that he has not heard his own lover, Pausanias, separate the Popular Eros from the Heavenly Eros in order to account for exploitation, prostitution, heterosexuality and other such evils. Still less could he have heard Eryximakhos and Aristophanes develop this theme in terms of strife, alienation, warfare and even attacks on Olympus itself.

A number of other remarks by Agathon reinforce the conclusion that he has not been listening to the other speeches. His claim (196b) that "violence takes not hold of [Eros]" runs counter to what Phaidros says of an army of lovers and beloveds (178e) as well as Phaidros' claim that (179a–b): "no man is such a craven that Love's own influence cannot inspire him with a valour that makes him equal to the bravest born; and without doubt what Homer calls a 'fury inspired' by a god in certain heroes is the effect produced on lovers by [Eros'] peculiar power."

Agathon's assertion that (195a) "not one of [the previous speakers] has told us what is the nature of [Eros]" would seem to ignore Pausanias' central point about one Eros having elements of both male and female, while the other had only the male—to say nothing of Eryximakhos' claim (186a) that Eros is the binding force of the cosmos.[33]

That Agathon might disagree with these points is fair enough. But that he makes no attempt to refute them, and fails even to take cognizance of the fact that they have been raised is an indication that he simply was not listening.

For him to pay no attention to his guests' contributions to the conversation is a not very subtle insult to his guests. As Sokrates had pointed out, he indicated his contempt for them earlier (194c) by referring to the crowd of the previous day, which had included all of those now his guests, as "a host of fools." Agathon now proceeds to insult Sokrates directly by claiming that Eros avoids every trait that Sokrates has,[34] and is attracted only to traits that Sokrates lacks—particularly youth, softness and physical beauty.[35] Next, Agathon insults his own patron, Dionysos, when he substitutes Eros for the god of drama (196d–e): "if I...may dignify our craft as Eryximakhos did his, the god is a composer so accomplished that he is a cause of composing in others."

He then goes on to portray all of the other Olympians as subservient to Eros (197a–b), classifying Apollo, the Muses, Hephaistos, Athene and even Zeus as "disciples" ($\mu\alpha\phi\eta\tau\dot{\eta}s$)—an act which according to Aristophanes (193b) must "incur the hate of Heaven" and therefore be in opposition to Eros. And what seems to be even more pathetic about Agathon's speech is the feeling throughout that all, or at least most, of this is done unwittingly.

Agathon's speech runs from 194e to 197e. From 194e to 195a he outlines his procedure—to "praise [Eros] first for what he is and then for what he gives" (195a). At 195a we are told that Eros is the most blissful, most beautiful and best of the gods. From 195a to 196b we are told that he is most beautiful because he is youngest (195a-c); he is delicate (195c-e); he is "pliant in form" (195e-196a); he has "shapely grace" (196a) and "beauty of hue" (196a-b). Next, Agathon tells of Eros' "excellence" ($\dot{\alpha}\varrho\epsilon\tau\hat{\eta}s$): he is nonviolent, neither giving nor receiving injury (196b-c). He is just and temperate (196c). He is the most courageous of all the gods (196d). He outdoes all in "wisdom" ($\sigma o \phi \iota \alpha$) as poet (in the broad root sense of $\pi o \iota \eta \tau \dot{\eta}s$ as applying to any creative act) (196d-197b) even to the point of giving guidance ($\dot{\eta}\gamma\epsilon\mu o\nu\epsilon\dot{\nu}\sigma\alpha\nu\tau os$) to Apollo, the Muses, Hephaistos, Athene and Zeus in their creative acts (197b). Agathon then (197c) recapitulates his conclusion that Eros is "of surpassing beauty and goodness" and that he is the cause of these in others. (Agathon seems not to notice that he has moved from the claim that through the attraction of like to like Eros is *drawn to* those who happen to *be* beautiful and good, to the assertion here that Eros *causes* them to be beautiful and good.) At this point he launches into verse (197c) followed by a florid peroration into which he manages to slip a pun on his own name—Eros "cares for the good" ($\dot{\epsilon}\pi\iota\mu\epsilon\lambda\dot{\eta}s$ $\dot{\alpha}\gamma\alpha\phi\hat{\omega}\nu$) (197d-e).

Most of it, particularly the peroration, is pap—fitting exactly Sokrates' later accusation (198d-e) that the others all believe that an encomium consists of "the ascription of all the highest and fairest qualities whether the case be so or not; it is really no matter if they are untrue." If there is any meat in Agathon's contribution it is in his assertion that wisdom ($\sigma o \phi \iota \alpha$) is creativity (196d-197b). Here he claims that when people fall in love they become poets, and since Eros can give this power to others, he must have it. Under the influence of Eros all forms of life procreate—thereby depriving Dionysos of his role as life force.[36] He then goes on to say that in "artificial manufacture" ($\tau\dot{\epsilon}\chi\nu\hat{\omega}\nu$ $\delta\epsilon\mu\iota o\nu\varrho\gamma\dot{\iota}\alpha\nu$) those who Eros teaches have "brilliant success" and those who he does not are dark failures (a vacuous claim, saying nothing more than that some are successful and others not). Although these comments might be broadened into a general discussion of creativity in human life, Agathon fails to do so. Instead, he seems to have put it together as groundwork for his subsequent claim that the creative acts of Apollo, the Muses, Hephaistos, Athene and Zeus were all accomplished through the tutelage of Eros. Since these include medicine, music, and governance, he is picking up on themes propounded by Eryximakhos, but that this, too, is unwitting is shown by the fact that he ignores such other themes in Eryximakhos' speech as athletics, agriculture, astronomy and the "communion between gods and men," all of which could have fit rather well into his thesis.

Agathon does claim that all creativity arises through Eros, and that creativity is wisdom ($\sigma o \phi i \alpha$) even though he does not develop either point. His failure to do so supports the suggestion implicit in Lamb's translation of $\sigma o \phi i \alpha$ that for Agathon the word simply meant "skill." Plato, on the other hand, may well have selected the word in order to juxtapose Agathon's and Sokrates' views of creativity (cf. Sokrates' discussion of "poetry" ($\pi o i \eta \sigma \iota s$) as creativity at 205c, his more general discussion of creativity at 208c–209e, and the analysis of these passages below, pp. 70–71 and 77–81). Agathon has, in the course of making his claim, acted out the way in which his attempt to be creative has deprived him of the capacity to say anything wise. The lack of wisdom in his speech defeats the only substantive claim that he makes.

But if Agathon has not been listening to the other speeches, and has not been thinking substantively about his own,[37] it is legitimate to ask just what he has been doing all evening. The answer, curiously, is ready to hand. The only striking thing about Agathon's speech is what Sokrates points out about it (198b): "[It is] a fine assortment of eloquence. The greater part of it was not quite so astounding; but when we drew towards the close, the beauty of the words and phrases could not but take one's breath away."

In short, Agathon has been working on language, the style of his speech. And in so doing he is demonstrating how well his lover teacher has taught him, for it was Pausanias who said (180c–181a): "For of every action it may be observed that as acted by itself it is neither noble nor base....Each only turns out to be such in the doing, as the [style ($\pi \varrho \alpha \chi \phi \hat{\eta}$)] of doing it may be."

This is the "excellence" (184c) that Pausanias has taught to Agathon, and for the sake of which Agathon "gratified his lover." In light of this Agathon's transvestitism[38] is merely the outward manifestation of his submission to Pausanias' dominance. And the vacuity of his speech is the inevitable outcome of their inability to transcend this pattern of dominance. Agathon's mask differs from the others in that it is neither conventional nor professional. It is personal. But it is not his own. It is the mask manufactured for him by Pausanias, and into which he has been assimilated.

His destruction is complete.

Chapter 4

1 Diotima

Sokrates' customary mask is that of the dialectician, the questioner who does not advance beliefs of his own, but who compels those around him critically to examine their own beliefs (and who, through that examination, elicits from them beliefs the reader suspects are Sokrates' own). In this case, however, he is deprived of that mask. At 194d Phaidros, as symposiarch, had cut him short when he started to initiate a dialectic with Agathon. Again, at 199b–c, Phaidros reluctantly granted permission for only a few questions "so as to secure [Agathon's] agreement before [Sokrates] begins [his] speech."

Once Sokrates begins his speech he finds it necessary to put on another mask. This time the mask is Diotima, and he immediately puts the conversation he has just had with Agathon behind the same mask: "For I spoke to her in much the same terms as Agathon addressed just now to me...and she refuted me with the very arguments I have brought against our young friend" (201e).[1]

There seems to be little reason to believe that Diotima is anything but fictional,[2] and there seems to be some reason to believe that Sokrates (rather than Plato) intends for his listeners to regard her as fictional. At 205e there is a clear reference to Aristophanes' speech: "And certainly there runs a story...that all who go seeking their other half are in love; though by my account love is neither for half nor whole, unless, of course, my dear sir, this happens to be something good."

In her defense of this statement she may be referring to Aristophanes' threat of further separation: "For men are prepared to have their own feet and hands cut off if they feel these belongings are harmful."

As Lamb points out (n. 1 to 197a and n. 1 to 205c), at 205c she seems to be picking up on Agathon's remarks on poetry. Agathon had at 196e called Eros "a poet [$\pi o\iota\eta\tau\dot\eta\varsigma$] well skilled...in all composing [$\pi o\acute\iota\eta\sigma\iota\nu$] that has to do with music." He then (197a) expanded the meaning of $\pi o\acute\iota\eta\sigma\iota\nu$ to include the creation of all forms of life, taking it back to its earlier, broader meaning of "maker" or "doer."

At 205b–c Diotima says: "you know that *poetry* [ποίησις] is more than a single thing. For of anything whatever that passes from not being into being the whole cause is composing or poetry; so that the productions of all arts are kinds of poetry, and their craftsmen are all poets."

Again, at 208c–d, there seems clearly to be a reference to Phaidros' speech:

> "Do you suppose," she asked, "that Alcestis would have died for Admetus, or Achilles have sought death on the corpse of Patroclus, or your own Codrus have welcomed it to save the kingdom of his children, if they had not expected to win 'a deathless memory for valour,' which now we keep?"

Her reference to Alkestis is a very poor illustration of her point, and makes sense only as a reply to Phaidros' interpretation of the same myth.[3]

Finally, at 211d–e, she seems to be referring again to Aristophanes' speech: "This [the pure form of beauty], when once beheld, will outshine your gold and your vesture, your beautiful boys and striplings, whose aspect now so astounds you and makes you and many another, at the sight and constant society of your darlings, ready to do without either food or drink if that were any way possible, and only gaze upon them and have their company." Just as for Aristophanes' humans (191a–b): "when our first form had been cut in two, each half in longing for its fellow would come to it again; and then would they fling their arms about each other and in mutual embraces yearn to be grafted together, till they began to perish of hunger and general indolence, through refusing to do anything apart."

At any rate, the reader is told explicitly (212c) that Aristophanes saw at least one of these remarks as an allusion to his own speech, and not as a paraphrase of something said years before by a priest: "After Socrates had thus spoken, there was applause from all the company except Aristophanes, who was beginning to remark on the allusion which Socrates' speech had made to his own."

Finally, there appears to be an "error" in Sokrates' account of Diotima's speech. At 206b Sokrates portrays himself as saying, "[if

I could answer you] I should hardly be. . .sitting at your feet to be enlightened on just these questions." At 207a he says, "All this instruction did I get from her at various times. . .and one time she asked me. . . ." Yet, at 207c he seems to refer back to 206b: "Why it is just for this, I tell you, Diotima—*as I stated a moment ago* [νῦν δέ]—that I have come to see you, because I noted my need for an instructor" (emphasis mine).

Diotima in turn wears at least two masks, that of priest or seer, and that of philosopher—masks that do not always nest too comfortably. The fact that Plato is presenting Diotima as a Sokratic invention suggests that her role as a priest should be examined with some care. Since this implies that her speech originates with Sokrates, it should be treated in the same way we might treat Sokrates' speeches in other dialogues. It cannot be interpreted as excusing any apparent looseness in what she says. On the other hand, the fact that she is presented as a priest, and the relation of this to the mystical elements in the dialogue are taken up below (sections 3 and 4).

Sokrates seems to intend that his listeners be sceptical of what she says. His claim that "by bidding the Athenians offer sacrifices ten years before the plague, she procured for them so much delay in the advent of the sickness" (201d) is vacuous, saying in effect nothing more than that the plague did occur.[4] Moreover, if this claim is taken seriously, the Athenians could hardly have accused Diotima of helping them. The plague started in the second year of the Peloponnesian War and devastated the city for four years, killing thousands of fighting men, and becoming an important factor in the defeat the Athenians ultimately were to suffer.[5] Had the plague struck Athens ten years earlier the course of the war would almost certainly have been different, and the Athenians might have taken steps to avoid the war altogether.

Throughout major portions of her speech, however, Diotima functions not as priest, but as philosopher, taking Sokrates step by step through a dialectical examination of the concept of love. The fact that she from time to time slips into a myth or a mythological treatment of love does not violate this role—or at least violates it no more than does Sokrates in most of Plato's dialogues. As pointed out below,[6] when she does don the mask of priest she does so abruptly, her reasons by no means apparent, and with consequences that may require a rethinking of the entire dialogue.

2 Knowledge

According to the conventional interpretation of Plato's epistemology, the dialectic is seen as a method for arriving at knowledge, and the object of knowledge, at least at the highest level, is an eternal, immutable form. Certain aspects of Sokrates' speech, most notably, of course, the description of the "ladder," seem to support this interpretation (cf. below, pp. 60–64); however, certain other passages seem to be incompatible with it, posing some interesting puzzles for the interpreter of the dialogue.

At 202a Sokrates has Diotima give her definition of knowledge in the guise of a parenthetical remark. She says: "You know, of course, that to have correct opinion, if you can give no reason for it, is neither knowledge—*how can an unreasoned thing be knowledge?*— nor yet ignorance; for what hits on the truth cannot be ignorance" (emphasis mine).

Dover and Nehamas[7] have both noted that although the line appears almost as an afterthought, it nevertheless reflects a characterization of knowledge to be found elsewhere in Plato's work, particularly in *Meno*, 97a–99a (cf. Appendix, esp. pp. 147–149), where it is developed at some length. It ought, therefore, not to be taken lightly.

Although here the phrase is "right opinion" (τὸ ὀρφὰ δοξάζειν), it is immediately reflected against "reality" (ὄντος). In *Meno* "right opinion" (ὀρφὴ δόξα) and "true opinion" (ἀληθὴς δόξα) are used interchangeably (twelve occurrences of the one and six of the other in less than two Stephanus pages from 97b–98d). It would therefore be hazardous to try to draw any philosophically important distinction between the two phrases.

Diotima seems to be giving three necessary conditions of knowledge which together constitute a sufficient condition.[8] For something to be knowledge it must be believed (i.e., it must be an "opinion"), it must be true, and the one who holds it must be able to give reasons in support of it.[9]

Sokrates' use of "true" in this context seems to conflict with his claim that one must be able to give supporting reasons. If, independent of any such reasons, one is aware of the truth of an opinion, then one would not allow the opinion to slip away or be replaced by a less adequate opinion, in which case the reasons would have no function. On the other hand, if the reasons are the *only* ground for retaining an opinion, then the truth or falsity of the opinion would have no function. One would have no grounds apart from those reasons for holding that the opinion is true. Thus either the truth of an opinion or the reasons one has for it are unnecessary. This implies two different (and in the end, incompatible) definitions of knowledge. Either knowledge is an opinion that the holder can support with reasons, or it is simply an opinion that is true.

Yet, both here and in *Meno* Plato seems to want to draw a sharp distinction between knowledge and true opinion on the ground that one can give reasons in support of the one, but not the other. In *Meno* Sokrates states this position strongly: "that there is a difference between right opinion and knowledge is not at all a conjecture with me, but something I would particularly assert that I knew: there are not many things of which I would say that, but this one, at any rate, I will include among those that I know" (98b).[10]

If the distinction is taken seriously, and they are seen as distinguished by the fact that one can give reasons for the one, but not the other, Diotima's claim implies that knowledge is *defined as* being able to give reasons in support of a belief.[11] This allows for the usual distinction that is drawn between knowledge and a belief that happens to be true even though the believer cannot reasonably be said to know that it is true. One might on such grounds say that a child held such a "true opinion" in believing that the earth is spherical. On the other hand, the Pythagorean's claim that the earth is spherical would seem to fit this definition of knowledge since they were able to give a reason in support of that belief: "the sphere is the most beautiful of solid figures."[12]

The reason that they gave, of course, is unacceptable today and as a result, we might be inclined to claim that although the Pythagoreans had a true opinion, since their reason for holding it was not adequate, they did not have knowledge. This in turn might suggest that the definition is flawed: not only should the belief be true, and the believer be able to give reasons in support of it, but those reasons ought in some important sense to be "the right kind of reasons." Moreover, if knowledge is *any* belief that can be supported by reasons, we might find ourselves in the curious position of claiming to know something that is false, simply because we have reasons for believing it.

One way around this might be to maintain (as Diotima appears to) that the truth of the belief is a necessary condition of claiming it as knowledge; however, as pointed out above, that would imply either that we had a method independent of "giving reasons" for determining the truth of a belief, in which case both the dialectical process and the reasons it yields in support of the belief would seem to be superfluous; or we would be left in the uncomfortable position that, lacking any such independent way of determining truth, we could never in any given instance say with finality whether our belief is true or not. This in turn would imply that we have no certainty that there *is* a truth to which our beliefs might conform. But if this is the case, any claim that a belief is "true" becomes meaningless, and we are left with the conclusion that the only distinction between knowledge and opinion is our ability to give reasons in support of the one, but not the other. Knowledge that is "bound by causal reasoning" (*Meno*, 98a) will probably be more difficult to dislodge than an unsupported opinion, but under the right circumstances it, too, will "run away out of the human soul" (ibid.).

The problem with Plato's definition is that if knowledge is nothing more than a belief which the knower can support with reasons, the possibility must be kept open that more reasons for an altered—or completely different—belief might be forthcoming. Any claim that this would not be the case would imply that one *had knowledge* that no other reasons could possibly come forth; i.e., that one had reasons for believing that this was the case. One reason for such a belief might be that one had devised a test which, if met, would be regarded as a sufficient condition for the belief (as the slave in *Meno* (82d–85b) was taught to test his hypotheses by counting the square feet in Sokrates' constructions). But that the test is sufficient would either be an unsupported opinion (i.e., the reasons for its sufficiency would not be known), or the test would be known to be sufficient, in which case the knower would be able to give reasons in support of such knowledge. The same pattern would be repeated with regard to these latter reasons, and in the end the knower would be left either with an infinite regress, or a point at which knowledge rests on mere opinion, and the possibility that the knowledge would change would have to be kept open. The former is humanly impossible. One cannot give an infinite number of reasons for anything in a finite time, and human lives are finite. The latter, however, implies not that the dialectic—the pursuit of reasons—is a means of arriving at knowledge, but that the knowledge itself has a dialectical character, is not discovered but is *created* by the dialectic.[13]

At 207d–208a Diotima, in describing the processive nature of existence for mortals goes on to say: "And here is a yet stranger fact: with regard to the possessions of knowledge, not merely do some of them grow and others perish in us, so that neither in what we know are we ever the same persons; but a like fate attends each single sort of knowledge. What we call [studying (μελετᾶν)] implies that our knowledge is departing; since forgetfulness is an egress of knowledge, while [studying] substitutes a fresh one in place of that which departs, and so preserves our knowledge enough to make it seem the same."

She then adds: "Every mortal thing is preserved in this way; not by keeping it exactly the same forever, like the divine, but by replacing what goes off or is antiquated with something fresh, in the semblance of the original."

Thus, her description of knowledge fits exactly what is implied by her definition of knowledge. As reasons give way to other or better reasons, some of the things we know "grow and others perish in us." Even that which seems the most constant seems so only because "what goes off or is antiquated" is replaced "with something fresh, in the semblance of the original." The semblance cannot be an exact replication. If it were, there would be no accounting for the description of that which is replaced as "antiquated" in contrast with the replacement as "fresh." Neither would the replacement be necessary.

If this is the case with all "the possessions of knowledge," and if the "divine" stays "exactly the same forever," the conclusion seems inescapable that the "divine" cannot be a "possession of knowledge." At most, it could be known only momentarily before it is replaced by something in its "semblance."

Moreover, the pure form of beauty seems to fall heir to the same difficulty. Diotima says that it "is everexistent and neither comes to be nor perishes, neither waxes nor wanes...nor is it such at such a time and other at another." In other words, like the "divine," it is immutable. But since knowledge by its nature must change, knowledge of the immutable must either be momentary or altogether impossible. Thus, Diotima's description of knowledge as processive, like her definition of knowledge, is incompatible with any truth claims for the doctrine of forms.[14]

The doctrine of recollection is not mentioned in the *Symposium*, so any mention of it here might seem out of order. Nevertheless, as pointed out above,[15] the definition of knowledge given in *Meno* seems to be essentially the same as that given by Diotima, and the doctrine of recollection is a central theme of *Meno*. So mention of the doctrine of recollection may not be wholly irrelevant.

The doctrine of recollection in its fully developed form would hold that the soul is created with a knowledge of the eternal, immutable forms; it forgets them because of the trauma of birth, then is reminded of them bit by bit through the experience of things in this world that "participate" in them. This process of "reminding" is facilitated by the dialectic. If the claim that recollection is replacement "with something fresh in the semblance of the original" is put in context with the doctrine of recollection, the implication would be that one's knowledge of the forms is never fully recovered, but deteriorates as one gets older. Between lives the soul might renew this knowledge—as suggested by one of the myths of *Phaidros*—or it might simply continue to deteriorate from one life to the next. In either case the doctrine of recollection could not perform its function and yield knowledge of the forms.[16] Moreover, the concept of knowledge implied by "seeing" the forms does not fit comfortably with Diotima's definition of knowledge.[17]

In short, both Diotima's definition of knowledge, and her description of it, as well as Sokrates' definition of knowledge in *Meno*, seem to run counter to what are generally accepted as the two most fundamental tenets of Plato's philosophy: the doctrine of forms and the doctrine of recollection.

The fact that these incompatibilities occur in no way implies that Plato was aware of them. Still less do they suggest that Plato might have intended them. Such a case, if it is to be built at all, would have to deal with a number of fairly obvious questions: What evidence is there to suggest that he understood the problem? What evidence is there that he intentionally built that problem into Sokrates' speech? Can the problem be resolved without doing violence to the doctrine of forms? If not, did he intend that the doctrine of forms be taken seriously? If the doctrine of forms can be salvaged, what is its place in the metaphysical scheme of the dialogue? If it is not to be taken seriously, why did Plato introduce it in the first place? More generally, what is Plato trying to get across to his reader? And why did he adopt such an apparently devious and misleading way of trying to get it across?[18]

3 The Ladder

Diotima prefaces her introduction to the discussion of the pure form of beauty (209e–210a) by expressing doubt that Sokrates can understand it: " 'Into these love-matters even you, Socrates, might haply be initiated [μνεφείης]; but I doubt if you could approach the rites and revelations [ἐποπτικά] to which these, for the properly instructed, are merely the avenue. However, I will speak of them,' she said, 'and will not stint my best endeavours; only you on your part must try your best to follow.' ''

Her language is clearly religious, reflecting Sokrates' description of her as a ''priest,'' and she describes what she is about to discuss as ἐποπτικά, translated here as ''revelation.'' The word reflects the highest level of the Eleusinian initiation rites, in which the ritual objects were ''shown to'' the initiates. The act of ''showing'' seems to suggest that such knowledge is acquired by ''seeing.'' This in itself does not conflict with Diotima's definition of knowledge. One might reasonably say, ''I saw x'' in reply to the question, ''how do you know x?'' But the next question implied by her definition of knowledge, ''Do you know that you saw x?'' points up both the strength and the weakness of such knowledge.

On the one hand, the answer, ''I saw x'' seems final, and the question, ''Do you know that you saw x?'' merely carping. On the other hand, there is a disturbing ambiguity regarding some of the things one sees. The dream I see might be a message from the god— or even (as in the *Iliad*) a message designed by the god in order to deceive. The sheaves of grain shown to the initiate had their significance not in what the initiate literally saw, but in what they symbolized. What the initiate ''saw''—what was revealed—was not ritual objects in themselves, but ritual objects as concrete referents for cult values. Thus, if the values themselves were unknown, the cult objects would be seen in a much more pedestrian, nonreligious way. In this sense even knowing by ''seeing'' did not qualify as knowledge unless the initiate could ''give reasons'' in support of what was ''seen.''[19] Similarly, if one learns of the pure form of beauty by ''seeing'' it, one must have knowledge of it (be able to give reasons in support of one's claims about it) before one can learn of it. But if knowledge is acquired only through learning, we are caught in a vicious circle.

At any rate, Diotima does not give reasons for what she says of the forms. This, together with the fact that she commits herself to do everything in her power to help Sokrates understand the pure form of beauty (''I will not stint my best endeavours'') implies that she is unable to give reasons for what she says. And that in turn implies that according to her own definition of knowledge, she does not know what she is talking about.

A close look at her description of how one gets to know the pure form of beauty reflects the same difficulty. And her description of that form seems to explain it.

The "ladder" (210a-e) consists of a series of progressive abstractions (using the word "abstraction" in the root sense of "separating out") and generalizations. The first step is abstraction: falling in love with a single beautiful body:[20] "In the first place, indeed, if his conductor guides him aright[21] he must be in love with one particular body, and engender beautiful converse therein."

This is then generalized: "he must remark how the beauty attached to this or that body is cognate to that which is attached to any other. . .[and he must] regard as one and the same the beauty belonging to all; and. . .he must make himself a lover of all beautiful bodies" (210a-b). This will ease his passion for one body by showing it to be only one among many.

The implication of this passage seems to be that although physical beauty is common to many, and is in that sense to be contemned (καταφρονήσαντα), it is not on the same level as ugliness; i.e., beautiful bodies are still beautiful, and are to be loved for their beauty, even though one comes to recognize other rarer kinds of beauty as having higher value.[22]

The next step is abstraction. Having learned to contemn physical beauty as common to many, the next step is to recognize the beauty of souls (abstracted from the beautiful bodies which they animate) as having a higher value than bodily beauty. Here she uses the comparative "higher," implying again that the value of physical beauty is not to be ignored, but is to be regarded as a lesser value than the beauty of souls.

The soul is that which "animates" (ψυχή: "animating force") and differentiates the person—the personality. The recognition of the beauty of souls, therefore, can be generalized by recognizing beauty in the ways that souls interact; i.e., "he may be constrained to contemplate the beautiful as appearing in our observances and our laws, and to behold it all bound together in kinship" (210c). From "observances and laws" and their "kinship" one can abstract the principles upon which they are grounded and the principles of their interactions; i.e., one can move on "to the branches of knowledge" (210c).

At this point, having proceeded step by step up the ladder, encountering beauty in different kinds of things at each step, these different ways in which beauty appears to us can be seen collectively as "the main ocean of the beautiful" (210d), i.e., they can be generalized as the class of all beautiful things.

Thus far there seems to be nothing mysterious in the process. The person "who would proceed rightly in this business" (210a) does have a "guide" or "conductor." Whether the guide is, as Pausanias would have it, the lover (*erastes*) or, as Phaidros had argued, the beloved (*eromenos*) is now ambiguous. The ladder is constructed in such a way that the "guidance" comes from beauty— that which is loved—implying that the "conductor" is the beloved. On the other hand, the beauty at each step seems to be revealed by the process of abstraction and generalization in which both are engaged. Since this is the active pursuit of the beauty, both are in that sense lovers.[23] The couple proceeds together up the ladder. Since each step is a process of abstraction or of generalization, each step arises naturally out of the one preceding. Thus, at any point after the initiation of the process the lovers would be able to "give reasons in support" of what is believed at that step simply by retracing the steps by which they arrived at that belief. In that sense they could claim knowledge at each step after the first, and since the "reasons" are cumulative they could also claim that their knowledge changed and deepened each time another step was taken. Moreover, abstraction and generalization are acts, so at each step the lovers are the agents of the act that leads them to the next step.

4 The Pure Form of Beauty

If the preceding analysis of the ladder is correct, one might expect the last step to be abstraction. Since the penultimate step was generalization to "the class of all beautiful things," the lovers might be expected to abstract from that class that which is common to all the things in the class, which would be the pure form of beauty. Instead, there seems to be a break in the process: "and turning rather towards the main ocean of the beautiful [the lovers] may by contemplation of this bring forth in all their splendour many fair fruits of discourse and meditation in a plenteous crop of philosophy" (210d).

The lovers pause, in other words, contemplate the class of all beautiful things, and "discourse" about them. This appears to be the highest point on the ladder where philosophy occurs, and it is itself treated as a preparatory rite for the initiation to follow: "until

with the strength and increase there acquired he [sees (*κατίδη*)] a
certain single knowledge connected with a beauty which has yet
to be told. . . . When a man has been thus far tutored in the lore of
love, passing from view to view of beautiful things in the right and
regular ascent, suddenly he will have revealed to him as he draws
to the close of his dealings in love, a wondrous vision, beautiful in
its nature; and this, Socrates, is the final object of all his previous
toils" (210e–211a).

Whatever this knowledge (*ἐπιστήμη*) might be, it is placed
beyond philosophy and discourse. It is "seen" (*κατίδη*). It is not
supported by reasons. Moreover, the agency of this perception is
in doubt. What Lamb translates as the passive "will have revealed
to him" is in fact middle voice, but the implication in Lamb's
translation that what occurs is a revelation is supported by other
aspects of Diotima's treatment of it. The break in the progression
up the ladder is clear, and is emphasized by Diotima's description
of the lovers gathering their strength before they can take the next
step. The break is further emphasized by the implication that this
knowledge lies beyond discourse and philosophy. The suddenness
of the encounter together with the description of what is "seen"
(*θεώμεγος*) as a "wondrous vision" (*κατόψεταί τι θαυμαστόν*) support
the view of it as a revelation. In this context the return to religious
language seems entirely in order. The agent of the "revealing"
clearly is no longer the lovers themselves—though exactly what that
agency might be is not revealed.

The reason why Diotima treats knowledge of the pure form of
beauty in this way is not specified, but in fact her description of that
form precludes the possibility of any other treatment of it. Her
description begins with its eternality: "First of all it is everexistent"
(211a). There follows a series of negative statements: "[It] neither
comes to be nor perishes, neither waxes nor wanes [i.e., it is
immutable]." She follows this with a series of statements about what
the pure form of beauty is not. This is not to say that she tries to
enumerate all the things that beauty is not—an infinite process.
Rather does she enumerate ways in which one might confuse what
beauty is with the ways in which it is normally encountered.[24] She
now finishes her description: "but existing ever in singularity of form
independent by itself, while all the multitude of beautiful things
[participate in (*μετέχοντα*)] it in such wise that, though all of them
are coming to be and perishing, it grows neither greater nor less,
and is affected by nothing" (211b).

This is to say that the form is utterly apart from this world, but things in this world participate in it. It is wholly independent of this world, but things in this world participate in it. It is immutable, but not only do the things in this world participate in it, those things themselves are constantly changing. But if things of this world participate in it, it cannot be utterly apart, wholly independent or immutable. In short, the description deteriorates into a series of unresolved contradictions.

The word translated here as "participate" is μετέχοντα. It can also be translated (as Lamb does) as "partake." In either event the word refers to an activity that inescapably involves both the subject and the object in a process. If x participates in y, then y must be the sort of thing that can "be participated in." If x partakes of y then y must be the sort of thing that can "be partaken of." Either translation implies that y must be in process, or at least be such that it can be in process. Yet the few other things Diotima says of the pure form of beauty are designed to deny it any processive character whatsoever. Moreover, although her insistence on the unity and independence of the pure form of beauty would seem to prevent its having any relations to anything outside itself, μετέχοντα, on any translation, would certainly be a kind of relationship. Finally the fact that these contradictions are presented in the framework of a single sentence strongly suggests both that Plato was aware of them, and that he wanted to make the reader aware of them as well.

The problem of participation is, of course, examined in considerable depth in *Parmenides,* and was there presented by Plato as a profound difficulty he found in his doctrine of forms. If *Parmenides* is seen as a transitional dialogue between the middle span of Plato's life and his later works, this treatment of Diotima's speech might be viewed as implying little more than that Plato was aware of the problem when he wrote the *Symposium,* but in an as yet fairly rudimentary way. Such an interpretation would salvage the traditional interpretation of Plato's metaphysics with a minimum of damage—but it would seem not to do full justice to the text.

The expression of the highest form of knowledge as a series of unresolved contradictions, together with the language of the initiation rites of the mystery religions, would suggest that what Diotima is trying to describe is a mystical experience. Her reference to it at 210d as a kind of knowledge (ἐπιστήμην) is incompatible with her own definition of knowledge, but that might now be explained away with the claim that since this is a mystical experience it yields knowledge of a wholly different order, knowledge of a kind that by its nature cannot be likened to any ordinary sort of knowledge. Such knowledge is ultimately inexpressible, and therefore accounts both for Diotima's inability to give reasons in support of it, and for her uncertainty as to whether or not Sokrates can understand what she is saying. Some such interpretation seems to have been adopted by the Neoplatonists, and that such an interpretation is defensible seems at this point beyond a doubt.

The sudden shift away from the dialectical method in Diotima's speech, the adoption of the language of religious initiation and revelation, together with the blatantly self-contradictory description of the pure form of beauty, all suggest not only that Plato was aware of the problem of participation, but that he was also aware that what Diotima said of the pure form of beauty could not fit with her definition of knowledge, and he furthermore was aware of the fact that that contradiction was embedded in her speech. In a sense, then, the problem can be resolved without doing violence to the doctrine of forms if we interpret the experience as a mystical experience, the knowledge as an incommunicable mystery that can be approached in language only through contradiction.[25] Moreover, the very fact that such mysteries are believed to be ''inexpressible'' would explain why Plato wrote of it this way as well as explain Diotima's indirect way of speaking of it. Just as the Zen Master might claim not to be able to give his disciples satori, but to be able nonetheless to lead them to the brink of it by confronting them constantly with contradictions, so might Plato be interpreted here as engaging his reader in a similar confrontation with a similar end in view. One might even adduce in support of this interpretation the statement Plato makes in the *Republic* (523b–c): ''the experiences that do not provoke thought are those that do not at the same time issue in a contradictory perception. Those that do have that effect I set down as provocatives, when the perception no more manifests one thing than its contrary.''[26]

5 Sokrates and Agathon

Although the possibility must be kept open that the Neoplatonic interpretation is correct, that Plato was a mystic, this solution, too, seems a bit facile. I shall argue that it is also inadequate.

In the short dialogue (199c–201c) with Agathon that precedes Sokrates' speech, Sokrates establishes that love requires an object, and therefore cannot have an independent existence—even though such independence is implied in the personification of love as a god. Except for Aristophanes, the previous speakers have all treated love as something apart from the lovers. Phaidros, Pausanias and Agathon treated it as a god. Eryximakhos treated it as a force, but a force which has an independent and separate existence, and which acts on the elements or the particulars of the world from without. Love now is shown by Sokrates to be a relation between a subject and an object; without both it would not exist. Moreover, the fundamental nature of that relation is a lack on the part of the subject which is fulfilled—or is perceived as capable of being fulfilled—by the object.

Sokrates now moves into an analysis of love as a concept. Statements that seem to mean "I desire these present things" (200d) actually reflect the lack of control the individual has over the future. They mean, "I wish these things now present to be present also in the future" (200d). A yet more general conclusion is implied. One cannot love what one does not lack. Thus, although love always drives toward fulfillment, it can exist only as unfulfilled.[27] Loving, therefore, must refer to the future, and must envisage the continued existence of the subject as a necessary condition of fulfillment.

At this point Lamb, following Bury, adds ἀεί to Sokrates' speech and translates the passage: "a man may be said to love a thing not yet provided or possessed, when he would have the presence of certain things secured to him *forever* in the future" (emphasis mine). The argument does not support this conclusion, but supports only the weaker conclusion that "he would have the presence of certain things secured to him in the future." For this reason I follow Dover and Burnet, whose text omits ἀεί and fits the conclusion implied by the argument.[28]

Sokrates now carries these conclusions over to a description of love not as a relation, but as a god, Eros. Since love is a lack, and since, as Agathon had said, love is of beauty, Eros must lack beauty, must not *be* beautiful. This extention to the god of what was said of the relation clearly does not hold. To love the beauty that one has is narcissism and must, like Narkissos' self-love, be objectified in a reflection. Such a reflection need not be in a pool of water, of course, and perhaps the most destructive form of narcissism is that in which one finds in—or makes of—the love-partner a reflection of oneself (as Pausanias has done to Agathon). What one loves in the other, if the love be healthy, is the beauty natural to the other as object. That the lover might also be a beautiful object for someone else is irrelevant. More precisely, when the relation between a subject and an object is a love relation, the objective pole of that relation is beauty; the subjective pole, the particular lack which that particular beauty satisfies. In short (to distort Santayana's definition) beauty is love objectified. But it is not the objectification of self.

As Nussbaum[29] points out, καλῶν, beauty, "is such a broad moral/aesthetic notion that it might be more accurate to [translate] it as 'valuable' and the corresponding noun as 'value'." If this is accepted, then what Sokrates is proposing is a generalized theory of value in terms of which the value is not to be found in the object, nor in the subject. It is only to be found in the relation between a particular subject and a particular object: he is proposing a relational theory of value.[30]

Certainly Sokrates is at pains here to keep the discussion completely general. At 200a he emphasizes that the particular object of love can be whatever Agathon might imagine it to be: "keep carefully in mind what is the object of Love, and only tell me whether he desires the particular thing that is its object." The object, in fact, is whatever one might lack. The examples he gives ("being tall" or "strong" or "swift" or "healthy" or "rich" (200b–c)) are ways of being. Their choice skews the discussion to follow. When Sokrates asks (201b) "he loves what he lacks and has (ἔχει) not?" the word "has" is ambiguous. In Greek, as in English it can refer either to possession ("he has no purple himation") or to a state of being ("he has excellent health"), but the illustrations he uses maneuver the hapless Agathon into the latter interpretation of the question. He fails to see that the beauty one loves is in the object rather than in the subject. Sokrates is also careful to avoid the usual impulse to interpret satisfaction of a desire as nothing more than gaining possession of the desired object, although that seems to be an included meaning. At 200d he refers to the object as "not yet [present (ἕτοιμον)] or possessed (ἔχει)," and at 200e he says more generally that one feels desire for "what is not provided or present; for something they *have* not or *are* not or lack" (emphasis mine). Thus, the object of a love relationship clearly need not be human, and the desire need not be to possess.

The fact that his examples ("tall," "strong," "swift," "healthy," "rich") are ways of being suggests that the love relation, as Aristophanes had implied, is built into the human condition. It results directly from the incompleteness that is part of what being human consists of, and it can be described in a preliminary way as an effort to complete oneself through the object, or, if the object is a person, through that person, a condition symbolized in Aristophanes' speech as two incomplete halves growing together; a condition, precluded by the masking that prevents any genuine contact between people—as acted out by Phaidros and Eryximakhos, by Pausanias and Agathon.

Had Agathon recognized the impossibility of extending to a personified god conclusions drawn about a relation, had he (even out of egotism) claimed that he, being beautiful, is nevertheless capable of loving beautiful men, the discussion quite possibly would have brought out at least some of the main points outlined here. Agathon, however, is too flustered or too self-centered to see even such obvious mistakes, and Sokrates is compelled to develop his position in another way.

Perhaps for this reason, Sokrates is less merciful with Agathon than he might be. After Agathon confesses his "Sokratic ignorance" ("I greatly fear, Socrates, I knew nothing of what I was talking about," 201b) Sokrates again points out the vacuity of Agathon's speech, saying "Ah, your words were beautiful enough..." (also recalling Sokrates' statement (199a–b) that he lacks the ability to speak as Agathon spoke, but will "speak the truth in [his] own way"). At 197d–e Agathon had punned on his own name,[31] claiming that Eros "cared for the good [ἐπιμελὴς ἀγαθῶν]." Sokrates now replies with a similar pun and compels Agathon to admit that Eros lacks the good (ἀγαθῶν ἐνδεής) as well as the beautiful. On Sokrates' framing of the concept of love, the one is implied by the other—i.e., if Eros lacks the good, Eros cares for the good—but Agathon fails to see this, taking Sokrates' pun as a signal of his final defeat. His reply, "I see no means of contradicting you..." shows again his inability to grasp the substance of what Sokrates is saying. The means were there, but he missed them. In this sense Sokrates' comment has a double edge: "No, it is truth, my lovable Agathon, whom you cannot contradict: Socrates you easily may."

6 Mortal Existence

At this point Sokrates begins his speech. After introducing Diotima he picks up the train of thought where he and Agathon broke off. Diotima's definition of knowledge is given in context with a description of true belief as "midway" between knowledge and ignorance—a description that functions as an analogy to love as being between beauty and goodness on the one hand, and ugliness and evil on the other. She then takes up explicitly the question of whether or not love can be a god. Her conclusion is that because love is a relation, love cannot be a god. Mythologically, Eros is described as being a "daimon" or "spirit" instead of a god, and like other such "spirits," he functions primarily *as* a relation; his mission is "interpreting and transporting human things to the gods and divine things to men; entreaties and sacrifices from below, and ordinances and requitals from above: being midway between, it makes each to supplement the other, so that the whole is combined into one" (202e).

This would seem in the mythical view of the cosmos to give to these "daimons" or "spirits" a role analogous to that given to the concept of "participation" in the philosophical view of the cosmos, a role that appears to be reinforced mythologically by the description of them as "between a mortal and an immortal." Seen only mythologically the "immortal" would refer to the gods, the "mortal" to people and things of this world. The invention of a mythical world in which tough problems are solved, however, is not a solution to the tough problems, and when the description of Eros as "between a mortal and an immortal" is applied to the philosophical treatment of the cosmos, it takes on a different, more complex, more profound meaning.

In the passage from 207c–208b Diotima describes "the mortal nature" as inescapably processive:

> The mortal nature ever seeks, as best it can, to be immortal. In one way only can it succeed, and that is by generation; since so it can always leave behind it a new [animal ($\zeta\tilde{\omega}o\nu$)] in place of the old. It is only for a while that each living thing can be described as alive and the same, as a man is said to be the same person from childhood until he is advanced in years: yet though he is called the same he does not at any time possess the same properties; he is continually becoming a new person, and there are things also which he loses, as appears by his hair, his flesh, his bones, and his blood and body altogether. And observe that not only in his body but in his soul besides we find none of his manners or habits, his opinions, desires, pleasures, pains or fears,

ever abiding the same in his particular self; some things grow in him, while others perish...

This is the point at which, as discussed above, she goes on to describe knowledge itself as processive:[32]

And here is a yet stranger fact: with regard to the possessions of knowledge, not merely do some of them grow and others perish in us, so that neither in what we know are we ever the same persons; but a like fate attends each single sort of knowledge. What we call [studying ($\mu\epsilon\lambda\epsilon\tau\hat{\alpha}\nu$)] implies that our knowledge is departing; since forgetfulness is an egress of knowledge, while [studying] substitutes a fresh one in place of that which departs, and so preserves our knowledge enough to make it seem the same (207e–208a).

She now shows how "mortals" can pursue immortality, and contrasts this with the "divine" (which, mythologically at least, is regarded as "immortal"):

Every mortal thing is preserved in this way; not by keeping it exactly the same forever, like the divine, but by replacing what goes off or is antiquated with something fresh, in the semblance of the original. Through this device, Socrates, a mortal thing [participates in ($\mu\epsilon\tau\acute{\epsilon}\chi\epsilon\iota$)] immortality, both in its body and in all other respects; by no other means can it be done (208a–b).

The position that emerges here appears to be radically Herakleitean. For Herakleitos one cannot step twice in the same river (fragments 12, 49a, 91) in the sense that "sameness" or "identity" implies some unchanging character that goes on through time, whereas the waters, the banks, everything else we call "the river"— and the person who steps in it as well—are constantly changing. The only thing that is unchanged is the name, which cannot be uttered twice with the same referent.

Similarly in the passage quoted above, for mortals the nature of being is processive. Whatever identity a person or animal or bit of knowledge might have is not to be found in some one or more aspects of it that remain the same throughout its existence—or even from one moment to another. Its identity is to be found in the continuity of the process itself. There is nothing immutable that is "Sokrates" or "this horse" or even "beauty," rather is there a historical route that has enough continuity, enough internal cohesiveness, to allow us to differentiate it from other, similar historical routes—a concept not too unlike what modern physicists might call a "world line."

At 206a there is a gap in Diotima's argument. Having argued for the conclusion that "we may state unreservedly that men love the good," she then leaps to the conclusion that "love loves the good to be one's own forever [ἀεί]." This extension to infinity is not warranted by the argument, but it is necessary for her next argument, which is designed to show that every act of love is performed for the sake of immortality: "[Love] is of engendering and begetting upon the beautiful...because [engendering] is something everexistent and immortal in our mortal life. From what has been admitted, we needs must yearn for immortality no less than for good, since love loves good to be one's own forever [ἀεί]. And hence it necessarily follows that love is of immortality" (206e–207a).

In arguing for the claim that "love" refers generically to "*all* that desire of good things and of being happy" including such examples as "money-making," "sports," and "philosophy" (205c–d, emphasis mine), she illustrates her argument with the claim that the word "poetry" (ποίησις) is subject to a similar abuse: "For of anything whatever that passes from not being into being the whole cause is composing or poetry; so that the productions of all arts are kinds of poetry, and their craftsmen are all poets" (205b–c).

At 197a Agathon had claimed that Eros is the cause of all poetry—both in nature and in the crafts. He used the word "poetry" (τοιῆσαι) in its root sense, meaning any creative act whatever. In nature, he tells us, Eros causes sexual reproduction; i.e., it is procreative. In the crafts (τεχνῶν δημιουργίαν) Eros teaches those who are successful and does not teach those who are "dark failures." Diotima here separates love from poetry, but points out that both terms are subject to similar abuses. Love refers to "all that desire for good things and being happy," but in ordinary usage is limited to love relations between humans. Similarly, poetry is the cause of "anything whatever that passes from not being into being," but in ordinary usage is limited to "the business of music and meters." Love, then, causes poetry, which in turn produces those things that are instrumentally valuable for the attainment of "good things" and "happiness."[33]

This is the context in which she builds her argument for the conclusion that "what men love is simply and solely the good ($\dot{\alpha}\gamma\alpha\theta o\hat{v}$)" (206a). Thus, Nussbaum's suggestion[34] regarding the breadth of meaning of $\kappa\alpha\lambda\hat{\omega}\nu$, beauty, is here made explicit in the claim that beauty is instrumentally valuable for the attainment of the good which is intrinsically valuable. Love is any desire at all, but since "what men love is simply and solely the good," beauty must be any instrumental value whatever.[35] Thus, the function of "poetry," of all the crafts, is the production of "beauty," which in turn is instrumental for the attainment of the good.[36]

If this part of her argument is seen as being completed by the passage from 207c-208b quoted above,[37] then her reasoning seems to be: Love is desire. Since the satisfaction of a desire cancels the desire, one can only desire what one lacks, from which the conclusion follows that any desire presupposes as included in any object of desire the continued existence of the desiring subject at least to the point at which the desire is satisfied. For mortals existence itself is processive. Thus, the desire for the continued existence of the subject is at its foundation a desire for the continuation of the process that is that subject (that particular "world line" if you will). But the "mortal" *by nature* is incomplete. As a result, that process is in its essence a process of desiring and satisfying desires. In short, love is a fundamental, and therefore necessary component of being for mortals. If love is a necessary component of being for mortals, then so long as the mortal exists it will exist as a lover. Thus, if love necessarily presupposes the continued existence of the lover, then the love of immortality is presupposed in the existence of any mortal.

But this is "immortality" in the sense of the continuation of the process. If to be is to be a process, and if one were to desire to become immortal in the sense of becoming immutable (like the "divine") then what one would desire is the cessation of the process—not immortality, but immolation.

The problem of the philosophical dimension of the assertion that Eros is "between the mortal and the immortal" seems now to be resolved. Love is a relation, and that relation by nature has a necessary reference to the future. As a result, the relata must change, and in that sense love is not "kept exactly the same forever, like the divine." Thus, love is not "immortal" in the sense of being immutable. But that necessary reference to the future also implies that the relation is processive. "It is a divine affair, this engendering and bringing to birth, an immortal element in the [animal (ζῷω)] that is mortal" (206c). That process does not end, and in that sense love is not "mortal."

7 Love and Existence

Love preserves the individual by constantly directing and motivating the individual toward the future. Since the individual is defined as the continuity of the subjective aspect of the love relationship, love also defines the individual.

At 204c Diotima explains Sokrates' "mistake" in believing Eros to be beautiful: "you supposed. . .that the beloved and not the lover was [Eros]." Her meaning should now be clear. The lover pursues the beautiful as a means of attaining the good. As pointed out above,[38] what the lover loves in the beloved is the beauty in the beloved as object. "The lovable, indeed, is truly beautiful, tender, perfect and heaven-blest; but the lover is of a different type" (204c). The lover, however, may in turn be a "beautiful, tender, perfect and heaven-blest" object for the other. Thus, in a love relation each is both lover and beloved.[39] And the relation is therefore necessarily one of complete mutuality and respect, in which each loves the beauty that is found in the other. Moreover, the relation is organic in that each supplements the other in the creation of the good for both. To paraphrase Aristophanes, they "grow together," they complete each other. And Diotima must, therefore, describe love as "a begetting for both" as she does in her description of the love relation (206b–207a): "It is begetting on a beautiful thing by means of both body and soul. . .All men are pregnant, Socrates, both in body and in soul: on reaching a certain age our nature yearns to beget. This it cannot do on an ugly person, but only on the beautiful: the conjunction of man and woman is a begetting for both."

She now goes on to describe the role of beauty in "begetting:"

It is a divine affair, this engendering and bringing to birth, an immortal element in the [animal (ζῷω)] that is mortal; and it cannot occur in the discordant. Thus, Beauty presides over birth as Fate [Μοῖρα] and [Goddess of Childbirth (Ε ἰλείθυια)]; and hence it is that when the pregnant approaches the beautiful it becomes not only gracious but so exhilarate, that it [melts (διαχεῖται)] with begetting and bringing forth; though when it meets the ugly it coils itself close in sullen dismay: rebuffed and repressed, it brings not forth [σκυθρωπόν τε καὶ λυπούμενον συσπειρᾶται καὶ ἀποτρέπεται καὶ ἀνείλλεται καὶ οὐ γεννᾷ], but goes in labour with the burden of its young. Therefore when a person is [swelling (σπαργῶντι)] and teeming ripe he feels himself in a sore flutter for the beautiful, because its possessor can relieve him of his heavy pangs [ὠδῖνος]. For you are wrong, Socrates, in supposing that love is of the beautiful....It is of engendering and begetting on the beautiful.

Diotima's language here is sexually explicit. As Dover points out: "συσπειρᾶται (d6) 'contracts', ἀνείλλεται (d6) 'shrinks', 'curls up' and σπαργῶντι (d8) 'swelling' describe equally the reactions of the male and female genitals to sexual stimulus or revulsion, and διαχεῖται (d4), 'melts', 'relaxes', is more appropriate to the female; ὠδίς (e1), commonly the pains of childbirth, is also a general term for pain and can here denote the tension created in either sex by strong stimulation."[40]

Such language, together with Diotima's claim that love is begetting "by means of both body and soul" imply that here, as in her description of the ladder, physical love is included as a necessary, though perhaps subordinate, aspect of any love relation.

Moreover, the emphasis throughout this passage is on reciprocity. Where possession and dominance of the beloved (eromenos) by the lover (erastes) previously threatened to turn every love relationship into a mutually destructive relationship, the problem is here resolved by displacing "possession." What one wishes to "possess" is not the beautiful, but the good. And the good is attained within the framework of a love relationship in which each participant is both lover and beloved. Because each, as subject, is defined by the relation, each is frighteningly vulnerable to the other, and can be destroyed. Because each, as object is the beloved, whose beauty is cherished by the other, that beauty is protected and nourished so far as possible by the lover. Thus, if the lover finds beauty only on the surface, the deeper aspects of the beloved ("beauty of soul") will not be protected, and the relationship will become destructive. If the lover finds beauty on those deeper levels, the beloved's vulnerability is protected, and becomes the ground of possibility of growth. Since the relationship is seen as reciprocal, in a healthy love relationship each protects the individuality of the other and in the process of the love relationship each nurtures the beauty seen in the other, and thus helps the other to grow within the framework of that individuality.[41]

The view of the individual as process and of the love relationship as a relation of nurturing and growth fits comfortably with what has been said of masks. The first mistake made by Eryximakhos and Phaidros, by Pausanias and Agathon, is in their failure to realize that each party to the relationship must be both lover and beloved. As a result, Eryximakhos and Pausanias don the masks of "lovers" (*erastai*), and Phaidros and Agathon, the masks of "beloveds" (*eromenai*). This in itself would not have been destructive if they had recognized these to be masks. Had they done so the results would have been seen as role playing, a game lovers play without allowing it to become their reality and thereby become destructive—as, for example, lovers might "act out" each other's fantasies.

The mistake in each case is to believe that the mask each wears is not a mask, but the self. Such a belief subtly entrenches the still deeper conviction that there is a self—something that one is, and that remains through all the changes, something permanent. For this reason if, say, Eryximakhos were to be blasted free of his identification of himself with his profession, this would merely set him off on another search for his "real" self. Thus, the belief that there *is* a self is pernicious, and is made more so by being presupposed, and therefore virtually impossible for its victims to discover. The result for the victims of this belief is that at some point the self becomes identified with the mask. The mask becomes permanent because once it is perceived as being permanent any effort to displace it would be seen as self-destructive. Therefore, in a profoundly ironic twist to the argument, the effort to preserve oneself brings to an end the process that the self is—precisely because "keeping it exactly the same forever, like the divine" (208a–b) is contrary to the mortal nature, and necessarily destructive of it. The growth that is indispensable to the mortal nature becomes impossible.

When such a view of the self is carried into a love relationship each is concerned with self-preservation, and must therefore see the other as a threat. Yet, as Pausanias had pointed out, the *role* of the lover is to educate the beloved, and the *role* of the beloved is to be educated by the lover. The appearance of growth is thereby maintained at the same time that each is fundamentally resistant to change. The result, as seen in the analysis of the earlier speeches is that both the lover-beloved aspect of the relationship, and the teacher-student aspect of it are transformed into relations of power and dominance in which neither love nor learning is possible.

Chapter 5

1 Love and Immortality

Diotima was careful to place love between the mortal and the immortal, rather than between the human and the immortal, leaving open its effect on other species. In doing so she also leaves open Agathon's claim that "the composing [ποίησιν] of all forms of life is [Eros'] own craft [σοθίαν], whereby all [animals (ξῷα)] are begotten and produced" (197a). She now makes explicit the implication that love fulfills essentially the same function among other species as it does among humans. It causes both to pursue immortality, to participate in the life process. As a result, she expands her view of love, treating it generically as an inchoate, ubiquitous drive, as the life force:

> What do you suppose, Socrates, to be the cause of this love and desire? For you must have observed the strange state into which all animals are thrown, whether going on earth or winging the air, when they desire to beget: they are sick and amourously disposed, first to have union one with another, and next to find food for the newborn; in whose behalf they are ready to fight hard battles, even the weakest against the strongest, and to sacrifice their lives; to be wracked with starvation themselves if they can but nurture their young, and to be put on any sort of shift. As for men...one might suppose they do these things on the promptings of reason; but what is the cause of this amourous condition in animals? (207a–b).

Her reply to her own question is (207c) that "the mortal nature ever seeks, as best it can, to be immortal." This is the point at which she describes the "mortal nature" as a process (207c–208a), ending with the claim that "through this device [of "replacing what goes off or is antiquated with something fresh, in the semblance of the original"], Socrates, a mortal thing [participates in (μετέχει)] immortality, both in its body and in all other respects; by no other means can it be done." This implies that what one "participates in" is a process, and since the process has its source in the life force itself, the process is "immortal" in the sense that it goes on forever, i.e., in the sense in which Eros is "not mortal." And the nearest that a mortal can approach to immortality is by participating in that process. Her point, however, is not merely that the process goes on forever, and that the individual as part of that process can therefore get a glimpse of that which goes on forever. The drive that is the pursuit of immortality manifests itself on a number of different levels, each of which implies a different level of participation in the life process. What distinguishes humans from other species is the human capacity to participate on multiple and deeper levels.

The first level is mere self-preservation. But this is defeated by the mortal nature. However hard one tries, in the end one will die. The drive then is manifested in a number of different ways in which the "mortal" tries to transcend death, to guarantee that something of itself continues after it dies. The most straightforward way of doing this is through procreation, which is common to all living things—a process through which something of what one is is physically continued into the future beyond one's death. In this sense our participation in the life process continues at least until our descendants die out. And the world is different from what it would have been had we not participated in it in this way.

But humans regard themselves as something more than a genetic code or a part of a gene pool, so for humans procreation will be one way in which we pursue immortality, but a way that in itself is less than satisfactory. Even though our naming conventions ("Plato, son of Ariston," "O'Brien," "Anderson," "Ibn Khaldûn") identify us through our (male) parentage, we regard that as a very minor, perhaps even insignificant, aspect of our identities as persons. In the same way our children go on to develop their own personalities, their own identities, and in the process reject the burden of carrying into the future what we as persons are. Through procreation one may indeed "beget upon the beautiful," but whether the "begotten" be "good" or not is a bit chancy.

Humans therefore go beyond animal procreation and try to participate in the life process in ways that more completely preserve their identities. The next, and beyond mere procreation, the most obvious is "the love of winning a name, and laying up fame immortal for all time to come," (208c) as did Alkestis, Akhilles and

Kodros. But this seems less than satisfactory as well. We know little of Kodros apart from his dedication to Athens and his courage. Apart from Euripides' play, the same is true of Alkestis.[1] What we can say of Alkestis through the play parallels what we can say of Akhilles through Homer. Through Homer's genius Akhilles does emerge as something of an individual, at least up to a point. The Greeks saw his death as heroic proof of his devotion not only to Patroklos, but to honor as well. And the more clearly we see him as a person, the more his personality overshadows his death, and the more clearly his death is seen as an outgrowth of the sort of person he was. Even so, in the end we really do not know him very well. He is less a person than a personification of the ideal warrior. What has survived is the persona, the mask. It is not Akhilles. Thus, even if what is begotten is good, if it is no more than this, it can hardly be seen as a very successful pursuit of immortality, and we should not be surprised to discover in the *Odyssey* that Akhilles would rather be a slave among the living than to rule in Hades.

In the next step (209a) Diotima seems to echo Agathon in describing those who have "pregnancy of soul" as creative people, "all the poets and those craftsmen who are styled *inventors*" (translator's emphasis). They participate in the life process on a deeper level, and in a different way. Akhilles is preserved, insofar as he is preserved at all, by those who remember and repeat for us the verses of Homer. In that sense his memory is dependent first upon the poet, who chose to preserve what is preserved of him, as content, and secondarily upon the willingness of others to preserve the works of Homer. Homer, on the other hand, survives not as content, but as the work itself. He (or she)[2] is the "poet" who selected which actions and which people would be preserved. Homer is the one who delineated their characters for all time to come. And Homer is the one who wove these threads into the rich fabric of the *Iliad* and the *Odyssey*. Akhilles is *described for* us. Homer *acts upon* us.

And these offspring of Homer have been preserved because those who came after Homer deemed them to be good.

As for "those craftsmen who are styled inventors," not only do their offspring as products ("this sword") survive, their offspring as innovations ("this kind of sword," or "this way of producing a sword") if they are also good, survive as well. Moreover, what survives of such a person is wholly independent of such superficial identifying features as a name or physical appearance. We do not have a name, or even a very precise location, for the person who first consciously added tin to copper and produced bronze, but her[3] or his influence on subsequent ages was profound—probably immeasurable. Subsequent generations acted as she or he had taught them to act for thousands of years to follow. Thus, more of that ancient artisan and inventor is preserved in the life process than is preserved of Alkestis, or even Akhilles; and that first metallurgist pursued immortality more successfully than any who sought it through fame.

The next level open to humans to participate in the life process is through "the regulation of cities and habitations" (209a), i.e., through statescraft. Here the participation goes well beyond the physical, and is taken up with structures through which individuals interract. These offspring of love are laws and constitutions, the products of statesmen, and of social and political philosophers.

There is no clear indication in the text whether the individual alone can increase the depth of participation beyond this point. Instead, Diotima turns to the description of a love relationship. Although the text appears to be corrupt at this point (209b),[4] the general import of the passage seems clear. The person who has "been made pregnant with these [i.e., the ideas of statescraft and legislation] from his youth" will wish to bear the offspring and therefore

> goes about seeking the beautiful object whereon he may do his begetting, since he will never beget upon the ugly. Hence it is the beautiful rather than the ugly bodies that he welcomes in his pregnancy, and if he chances[5] also on a soul that is [beautiful ($\kappa\alpha\lambda\hat{\eta}$)] and noble and well-endowed, he gladly cherishes the two combined in one; and straightway in addressing such a person he is resourceful in discoursing of virtue and of what should be the good man's character and what his pursuits; and so he takes in hand the [youth's ($\pi\alpha\iota\delta\epsilon\acute{u}\epsilon\iota\nu$)] education. For I hold that by contact with the fair one and by consorting[6] with him he bears and brings forth his long-felt conception" (209b–c).

The passage implies that the process now requires a love object. Since both are lovers, both beloveds, the relationship is reciprocal. As with the "ladder" (see ch. 4 n. 21), this saves it from becoming a relation of power and dominance. In the first instance, the lover seeks out a beautiful body. The fact that the attraction is purely physical explains why the discovery of a beautiful beloved whose soul also is "[beautiful] and noble and well-endowed" is entirely a matter of chance ($\dot{\epsilon}\nu\tau\dot{\nu}\chi\eta$). Once such a relationship is established, however, there seems to be a stage in which the relationship is educational, followed by the lover begetting "his long-felt conception." If the claim that both are lovers is taken seriously, this would imply that in the initial stages each "takes in hand the other's education," and then that each helps the other to "[bring] forth his long-felt conception" (209c). After this the relationship is more clearly mutual and dialectical: "Equally, too, with him he shares the nurturing of what is begotten, so that men in this condition enjoy a far fuller community with each other than that which comes with children, and a far surer friendship, since the children of their union are fairer and more deathless" (209c). Thus, the deepest level at which one can participate in the life process is the philosophical level.[7]

This is not to say that the participation on other levels ceases. Sokrates is a father and a stonecutter as well as a philosopher. But just as the phrase "begetting on the beautiful with both body and soul" implies a love of the whole person for the whole person, the whole person here participates in the life process. Just as those whose love is limited to procreation do pursue immortality, but do not do so in all the ways they might, the people who fail to engage each other on the philosophical level also pursue immortality, but not as deeply as their humanity permits. And their love relation, because it excludes just that dimension of their being that is central to their nature as humans, is not only less than it might be. It is less than fully human as well.

Thus, not only did Sokrates learn about love from a woman, in doing so he also learned from her both how to become fully human and how to become a philosopher.

The offspring that are born on the philosophical level of a fully human union are "fairer and more deathless" than offspring born of other levels, but Diotima uses the comparative. They are not "eternal" or "immutable." They are not even "fairest and most nearly deathless." Moreover, the comparison is to the offspring of other, lesser loves; it is not to the immutable. She then emphasizes the processive character of these philosophical offspring by maintaining that they procure for the lovers "a glory immortally renewed" rather than "glory immortal."[8]

2 Two Concepts of Immortality

All of what Diotima says regarding the processive character of mortal existence is limited to things in the world that is known by means of the senses, the world of particulars. This would not seem to threaten the traditional view that Plato developed his metaphysics around a world of change, in which each thing has whatever identity it might momentarily retain only because of its participation in pure forms which exist apart from this world and are immutable. One might still without violence to anything said thus far interpret the *Symposium* within the framework of that traditional view. One minor modification might be required: that at the time of writing the *Symposium* he was already aware of the problem of participation, although in a less complete way than when he wrote *Parmenides*. One could even argue that the subordination of beauty to the good implied in the claim that one loves the beautiful in order to beget the good, reflects or foreshadows[9] the hierarchical superiority given to the pure form of the good in the *Republic*, and the later criticism of that hierarchy in *Parmenides*.

If this were the case, however, Diotima might reasonably be expected to maintain that knowledge of the pure form of the good, rather than the pure form of beauty was the highest step of the ladder. Certainly the groundwork has been laid for such an additional step by making beauty instrumentally valuable for the attainment of the good; and—equally certainly—there is no hint of such a step either in her description of the ladder or of the pure form of beauty. This, of course, might simply be an oversight. If so, then since the hierarchical superiority of the good is discussed at length in the *Republic*, the *Republic* must have been written later. The literary genius that shines through the *Symposium* is perhaps less evident in the *Republic*, and this might be seen as detracting from such a claim, though not in any very serious way.

At this point, however, some rather more serious problems with the traditional interpretation begin to emerge. Engaging in any kind of love relationship, including the pursuit of knowledge, is seen as pursuit of immortality. At 208a–b, Diotima says that existence for a mortal is a process of "replacing what goes off or is antiquated with something fresh, in the semblance of the original. Through this device, Socrates, a mortal thing [participates in ($\mu\epsilon\tau\acute{\epsilon}\chi\epsilon\iota$)] immortality, both in its body and in *all* other respects; *by no other means can it be done*" (emphasis mine). Yet at 211d–212a she poses hypothetically the possibility of contemplating the pure form of beauty: "But tell me, what would happen if [someone ($\tau\wp$)] had the fortune to look upon essential beauty entire, pure and unalloyed; not infected with the flesh and colour of humanity and ever so much more of mortal trash? What if he could behold the divine beauty in itself in its unique form? Do you call it a pitiful life for a man to lead—looking that way, observing that vision by the proper means, and having it ever with him?" And she answers her own question: "there only will it befall him,[10] as he sees the beautiful through that which makes it visible, to breed not illusions but true examples of [excellence ($\dot{\alpha}\varrho\epsilon\tau\hat{\eta}s$)], since his contact is not with illusion but with truth [$\dot{\alpha}\lambda\eta\theta\hat{\eta}$]. So when he has begotten a [true excellence ($\dot{\alpha}\varrho\epsilon\tau\grave{\eta}\nu\ \dot{\alpha}\lambda\eta\theta\hat{\eta}$)] and has reared it up he is destined to win the friendship of heaven; *he, above all men, is immortal*" (212a, emphasis mine).

These two ways of pursuing immortality are not the same. In the first case, the more deeply one participates in the ongoing life process, the more difference one makes in that process; and the more difference one makes, the more of what one is is preserved in the process as that difference. Since the process never ends, the process will be forever different from what it would have been without that participation. In that sense, the difference one makes is preserved forever in the process, and since that difference is what one is, through participation in the life process the mortal comes as close to immortality as the mortal nature will allow. The preservation itself is processive, "mortal." One's "offspring" are not immutable, they are "immortally renewed," and the "glory" of the parents is "immortally renewed" through them. "Participation," of course, is no problem when what is being "participated in" is a process. It shows spines only later when Diotima asserts that changing particulars "participate in" immutable forms.

The immortality one encounters at the top of the ladder, on the other hand, seems to rest on the immutability of the pure form of beauty. Only through contemplation of the pure form can one escape illusion—and that is possible only because one is in contact with truth. Yet in any ordinary sense of "truth," contact with it has little or nothing to do with immortality. As I write this the clock in the Ohio Wesleyan Library tells me it is 1:22 P.M. Even if this is true, and I know it, I would hardly have grounds for maintaining that I was therefore any closer to immortality. But Diotima is not talking about what time it is—either in Ohio or in Athens.[11] She is talking about truth in the sense that true beauty is a pure, immutable form.

My incorporating into myself as knowledge some truth about the time of day is unimportant because by the time I have done so it is no longer true—a comment which, if Diotima's description of knowledge is accurate, could be made of my knowledge of anything in the world of particulars. But if I could incorporate into myself—even only as knowledge—that which is by its nature immutable, I would have incorporated into myself that which can never change, and therefore can never cease to be. In that rather odd sense I would have incorporated into myself, made a part of myself, that which is immortal. I could then claim above all who had not had a similar experience, to be immortal—or at least to have come as close to immortality as the mortal nature allows.

One might argue, (as above, pp. 68-71) that this is incompatible with Diotima's claim that the mortal nature is in its entirety processive; i.e., that the mortal nature in fact does not allow even this. But there is a deeper difficulty.

Here the participation problem lies at the heart of the possibility of knowing the pure form of beauty. On one level the beautiful particulars of this world must participate in the pure form of beauty in order to be beautiful, but that participation is also the ground of possibility of our knowing them as beautiful; i.e., we know that they are beautiful because we see beauty "in" them. We then carry this perception of beauty up the ladder with us, finding it in an ever widening category of objects. The beauty is the same at each step even though what we find the beauty in changes from one step to the next.[12] Thus, instead of gaining a deeper and deeper insight into the nature of beauty, we gain a broader and broader view of where to find it. But if this is the case we are not learning more and more about beauty. Rather are we learning more and more about this world of changing, sensible things. And this in turn implies that if the pure form of beauty is "revealed" at any point, it is at the bottom of the ladder, not at the top.

This interpretation yields no difficulty if we assign to Plato some form of the doctrine of recollection. Indeed, considerations of this sort may well have been what led him to develop the doctrine of recollection. Thus, the claim would be that prior to birth the soul already had knowledge of the pure form of beauty. This knowledge was driven out of the mind—or at least out of consciousness—by the trauma of birth. Then, little by little, the soul was reminded of this pure form through experience in this world of things that participate in it, i.e., of beautiful particulars. The ladder, then, would merely describe this gradual process of being "reminded," and the "revelation" at the top would be the full recognition of what one had known all along.

But in this dialogue there seems to be no place for the doctrine of recollection. Not only is it missing from Diotima's description of the ladder and of the pure form of beauty, but as pointed out above[13] it is explicitly rejected in her description of knowledge as processive (208a). Moreover, her description of the pure form of beauty emphasizes its unitary character. It is simple. If it were not simple it would be subject to destruction through the separation of its components (an argument Plato would have been familiar with through the Eleatics, and one that he takes up explicitly in *Phaido*). But if it is simple, it cannot be remembered piecemeal. It cannot have different aspects that we are reminded of through our various experiences of different beautiful things.

For the argument to hold together, Diotima would have to maintain that we have knowledge of the pure form of beauty, and the ladder does not describe the experience of learning about beauty, or of being reminded of it. The ladder can only describe the experience of learning (or being reminded) of the world in which we live. And here again the top step of the ladder, the "revelation," has no place in the scheme.

Moreover, if we ignore all of these difficulties, even the claim that one has knowledge of the pure form of beauty cannot be made to fit with Diotima's description of the "mortal nature." The claim that the pure form of beauty is "contained in" a changing mortal being—even as knowledge—implies a reversal of the notion of participation. The pure form of beauty participates in the knower, becomes, as a particular piece of knowledge, an aspect of the knower's being. Again, how this can be squared with the description of the pure form of beauty remains a mystery.

Finally, if, for mortals, to be is to be a process, for a mortal to desire to be "immortal" in the sense of being immutable would be to desire death.[14] Whatever one might be, one would cease to be when the process came to an end. Since the desire for immortality is built into the process that is the mortal nature, the kind of immortality that is desired is the continuation of the process that is the self as a necessary condition of the satisfaction of any desire, an immortality that is integrated into the life process itself—the kind of immortality implied in Diotima's claim that the mortal can only pursue immortality through the process. It cannot be the kind of immortality that results from immutability.

The pure form of beauty, however, is immortal only because it is immutable. Thus, even if one could incorporate into oneself as knowledge that which is immortal (such as the pure form of beauty) and thereby come as close as mortals can to immortality, this kind of immortality would not satisfy the desire for immortality that is integral to the life process. It is not life-affirming. It is necrophilic.[15]

In sum, the doctrine of forms does not meet the needs Diotima gave as her reasons for introducing it. Those needs are in fact met by a process view of life that Diotima introduces before she gets to the discussion of the pure form of beauty. For Plato to develop an adequate answer to the problem he posed and not be aware that he had done so is patently unacceptable. The more likely conclusion seems to be that he was presenting a process view of the world—though in a fairly rudimentary form—and that he introduced the discussion of the pure form of beauty for some other reason.

3 *Phaidros* and the Written Word

The question of why Plato wrote the way he did opens up the larger question of Plato's view of his own work, and how he saw himself in relation to it. Although there are comments on this in the *Second* and *Seventh Letters*, the one detailed passage whose authenticity is not in dispute[16] is in *Phaidros*. That passage appears at least in part to be self-defeating. In that dialogue Sokrates says:

> The man who thinks that in the written discourse there is necessarily much that is playful, and that no written discourse, whether in metre or in prose, deserves to be treated very seriously (and this applies also to the recitations of the rhapsodes, delivered to sway people's minds, without opportunity for questioning and teaching), but that the best of them really serve only to remind us of what we know; and who thinks that only in words about justice and beauty and goodness spoken by teachers for the sake of instruction and really written in a soul is clearness and perfection and serious value, that such words should be considered the speaker's own legitimate offspring, first the word within himself, if it be found there, and secondly its descendants or brothers which may have sprung up in worthy manner in the souls of others, and who pays no attention to other words,—

that man, Phaedrus, is likely to be such as you and I might pray that we ourselves become. (*Phaidros*, 277e–278b)[17]

As most modern commentators have noted[18] the most obvious fact about this passage is that it comes to us in the form of a "written discourse." More precisely, Plato writes that the written word ought not to be taken seriously. Thus, if we take seriously what the statement asserts, since it is written, we ought not to take seriously what the statement asserts. Logically, the paradox exactly parallels the "Epimenides": "[Epimenides the Cretan says that] 'Cretans are always liars. . .' " (fr. 1, p. 9 of Freeman). In short, if Plato believed it, why did he write it?

This might simply be a mistake on his part. He might have been so absorbed in the dramatic side of his work, the relations between the characters and what they were saying to each other, that he failed to recognize the self-defeating character of what he was doing.

This kind of approach to Plato is hazardous at best, since it functions to bring investigation to a halt and thereby puts one in a position where if the interpretation is wrong it is also incorrigible. Moreover, in addition to the fact that Plato would have been familiar with the "Epimenides," in *Meno* Plato has his characters commit exactly the same kind of error three times: first, when Meno presents in the form of questions an argument against the possibility of asking questions; again, when Sokrates claims to learn by hearing that one cannot learn by hearing, but only by recollection; and finally, when Meno asks Sokrates to teach him that teaching is impossible. Furthermore, in the last instance Sokrates points out to Meno the nature of the fallacy (*Meno*, 80d–82a).[19] There seem, therefore, to be some fairly solid reasons for believing that in this instance Plato knew what he was doing.

There appear to be four reasons for claiming that the written word should not be taken seriously. In the myth of Theuth (Thoth) and Thamos (Ammon), when Theuth presents letters to Thamos, describing them as "an elixir of memory and wisdom" (*Phaidros* 274c), Thamos replies:

"you, who are the father of letters, have been led by your affection to ascribe to them a power the opposite of that which they really possess. For this invention will produce forgetfulness in the minds of those who learn to use it, because they will not practise their memory. Their trust in writing, produced by external characters which are no part of themselves, will discourage the use of their own memory within them. You have invented an elixir not of memory, but of reminding; and you offer your pupils the appearance of wisdom, not true wisdom, for they will read many things without instruction and will therefore seem to know many things, when they are for the most part ignorant and hard to get along with, since they are not wise, but only appear wise." (275a–b)

Theuth's first mistake is in conflating memory and wisdom. They vary independently. Remembering something does not imply understanding of it, so even if the writing did improve memory there is no reason to believe this would make one wiser—even though it might well give one "the appearance of wisdom."[20]

Theuth's second mistake is in his failure to distinguish between memory and being reminded. A reminder is external to the person being reminded, and may or may not actually function to remind one of anything. Whether or not a picture of Simmias will remind me of Simmias will depend upon whether or not I already know and remember Simmias. And whether or not a picture of Simmias will remind me of Kebes will depend upon whether or not I already know and remember Simmias and Kebes, and also know and remember something of the relation between them. Thus, knowledge is a necessary condition of remembering, and remembering in turn is a necessary condition of being reminded. Remembering is thus the link between knowledge and the reminder of knowledge.[21] Although writing can function as a reminder, more often than not, (as Thamos points out) it becomes a substitute for remembering. When this happens, the link is broken, and the knowledge becomes inaccessible.

Thamos' third complaint is the most serious. The written word speaks equally to all and cannot screen its audience. People who have no understanding of what is written can memorize it and regurgitate it at the proper stimulus, giving "the appearance of wisdom, not true wisdom, for they will...seem to know many things, when they are for the most part ignorant." Moreover, believing themselves to be wise when they are not, they will be "hard to get along with;" i.e., they will refuse to pursue wisdom precisely because they believe they have it.[22] Lacking "Sokratic ignorance," they do not know themselves.[23] They believe that they are something (in this case "wise" or "knowledgeable" persons) that they are not. They suffer, therefore, from hubris.

At this point Sokrates voices a fourth criticism of the written word: "Writing, Phaedrus, has this strange quality, and is very like painting; for the creatures of painting stand like living beings, but if one asks them a question, they preserve a solemn silence. And so it is with written words; you might think they spoke as if they had intelligence, but if you question them, wishing to know about their sayings, they always say only one and the same thing" (275d).

Which is to say that one cannot engage the written word in a dialectic. Ask it a question and it will simply repeat what it already says, whereas the dialectic requires not only further explication of what has been said, but a development of knowledge from one level to another. Written words cannot explain or change or deepen their meaning.[24]

On the other hand, Plato does suggest that written words can function as "reminders": "The gardens of letters he [who has knowledge of the just and the good and the beautiful (276c)] will, it seems plant for amusement, and will write, when he writes, to treasure up [memoranda ($\dot{\upsilon}\pi o\mu\nu\dot{\eta}\mu\alpha\tau\alpha$)] for himself, when he comes to the forgetfulness of old age, and for others who follow the same path, and he will be pleased when he sees them putting forth tender leaves."

Such "memoranda" might be of "the just and the good and the beautiful"—although what such memoranda might consist of is by no means clear—or they might instead be of the process by which one arrives at "knowledge of the just and the good and the beautiful." The latter, of course, might account for the fact that Plato wrote in dialogue form. But Plato was not just squirrelling away memoranda to compensate for the forgetfulness he foresaw in his old age. He was writing for publication. And a dialogue written for publication, however faithfully it might record the dialectic that led the author to "knowledge of the just and the good and the beautiful," would not meet the objections Sokrates has raised against the written word. As Griswold points out (*Self-Knowledge in Plato's Phaedrus*, p. 233) even though it is in dialogue form, "as the written text of one author, it is in effect a monologue."

If, as the phrase that follows ("and for others who follow the same path") might suggest, he was publishing them merely as memoranda for his students, he might well be chagrined to discover how seriously they were taken, and how influential they were to become in the millennia to follow—at the same time that just that sort of thing seems to be what he found objectionable about the written word. He did found a school, and he may have believed that the teaching in the Academy would reflect so accurately his own teaching that such writings would for a long time to come serve as "memoranda" for Academy students in their old age. Even that would fail to get around Sokrates' complaint that people who did not have "knowledge of the just and the good and the beautiful" could memorize what is there and give a false appearance of understanding it—even persuade *themselves* that they understand it.

Moreover, this interpretation does not fit at all well with the final phrase, "and [the writer] will be pleased when he sees them [i.e., "others who follow the same path"] putting forth tender leaves." The garden metaphor implies that the "tender leaves" are new plants growing to replace the dead or dying parent plants; i.e., the "others who follow the same path" will not just be reminded of what they already know; they will be stimulated to produce new knowledge in place of the old.[25]

Sokrates now makes this dialectical character of knowledge explicit. Phaidros praises "the pastime of the man who can find amusement in discourse, telling stories about justice, and the other subjects of which you [Sokrates] speak" (276e), and Sokrates rebukes him: "Yes, Phaedrus, so it is; but in my opinion serious discourse about them is far nobler, when one employs the dialectic method and plants and sows in a fitting soul intelligent words which are able to help themselves and him who planted them, which are not fruitless, but yield seed from which there spring up in other minds words capable of continuing the process forever, and which make their possessor happy, to the farthest possible limit of human happiness" (276e–277a).

If on his own terms Plato is to justify his writings, then he must find some way of writing that will bring forth "tender leaves" in his readers. In order to do so, his works must meet the four specific objections raised by Sokrates. They must be able to screen their audience, "offering to the complex soul elaborate and harmonious discourses, and simple talks to simple souls" (277b–c), and they must know "to whom [they] should speak, and before whom to be silent" (276a); i.e., they must somehow be protected from those who, like the written words themselves (or like Phaidros with respect to Lysias' speech, or for that matter, like a tape recorder) simply repeat back what has been written without understanding it (as Phaidros has demonstrated in his attempt to praise Lysias' speech [234e–235b]).

The second requirement his works must satisfy is that they be so constructed that when the right kind of reader asks them a question they do not simply repeat back what they have already said; they must in some significant sense be able not merely to exhibit a dialectic carried out by the characters in them, but to carry on a dialectic directly with the reader.

If these two requirements are satisfied, the other two objections Sokrates raised will be met. Those who are unable to see the difference between memory and wisdom are the people who, if they could, would simply repeat back what is written without understanding it. The written work would perhaps not teach that distinction, but if it can properly screen its audience it would screen out those who do not understand it. If they merely repeat what is written they will not be repeating what is meant.

The distinction between memory and being reminded is preserved in a dialectic by the fact that knowledge (as being able to give reasons in support of a belief) develops and changes as the dialectic progresses, thereby keeping memory, the link between knowledge and the reminder of knowledge, in flux. Any such dialectic will "yield seed from which there spring up in other minds words capable of continuing the process forever" (277a). Thus, if the written work can "put forth tender leaves," can enter into a dialectic with the reader, the processive character of knowledge will be preserved, and with it, the distinction between memory and reminding; i.e., the written work will not be merely an external reminder to the serious reader, but rather will it enter into the learning process as a dialectical partner. At some later date, of course, the written work might still function as a "memorandum" for one who had already gone through the dialectical process—just as Sokrates from time to time "reminds" others in a given dialogue of something that had been previously said or agreed to.[26]

Whether in the final analysis *Phaidros* is subject to an interpretation similar to that being developed here of the *Symposium* is beyond the scope of the present study. The preceding excursion into *Phaidros* has been indulged in order to explicate problems clearly implicit in the foregoing interpretation of the *Symposium*. These problems have to do partly with why Plato wrote in the way he did, but still more with why he wrote anything at all.

If Plato did hold that knowledge is by its nature processive, the most that he can claim for his own position is that he knows that knowledge is by its nature processive. This claim in turn can be no better than the reasons he can give in support of it. This chain of reasons cannot be infinite. It also cannot be anchored in something immutable since that would be self-defeating. One cannot say absolutely that there is nothing immutable, since such a claim would then be regarded as reflecting an absolute and therefore immutable fact. Thus, the most that can legitimately be said of immutables on this interpretation is that if there are any they have yet to be found.

Any attempt to write this down, however, would fix it, present it as if it were an immutable fact. And anyone who read it would be inclined to memorize it *as* an immutable fact rather than arrive at it by means of the dialectic. Such a person would have a belief— perhaps even a true belief—but not knowledge. Knowledge can be arrived at only by way of the reasons supporting that which is known, and that in turn is a dialectical process. Therefore, knowledge is attainable only by way of the dialectic.

Thus, the objections made explicit in *Phaidros* are implicit in the interpretation of the *Symposium* given here.

4 *Symposium* as a Dialectic with Plato

At this point the question is, did Plato's writing deal successfully with the (rather enormous) problems he has Sokrates raise—or at least, does Plato's writing show evidence that he attempted to deal with them? If not, then was he just laying up "memoranda" against his and his students' old age? I shall try to argue that Plato did deal with Sokrates' objections to the written word, and with reasonable success.

Does his work "screen" its audience? And if so, how?

It seems to do so by subtly presenting problems that are by no means obvious to the average reader. As pointed out above,[27] Diotima's description of the pure form of beauty is self-contradictory. The kind of people before whom the work "should be silent" would be unlikely to notice the contradictions. Such readers might well memorize Diotima's description of the pure form of beauty and recite it as the centerpiece of Plato's philosophy.

On the other hand, people who recognized the contradictions would have broken through a "screen." For them the most obvious next question would be, did Plato realize that these contradictions are there? But this is a different kind of question than "what did Plato believe?" and when approached through that question the dialogue does not simply repeat back what has already been said. Rather does such a reader find evidence that Plato was indeed aware of the problem of participation.[28] This in turn leads to the question of whether or not Plato dealt with it. Such a question is too broad to receive an answer at this point, and is likely to push the reader toward the simplistic explanation that Plato was aware of the problem of participation at the time of writing the *Symposium*, rather than only later when he wrote *Parmenides*.

Again, if the reader puts these contradictions together with the fact that Diotima was introduced as a "priestess," and that she uses the language of initiation, such a reader will have broken through another "screen," and will move toward a mystical interpretation of Plato—though again on an as yet very simple level. In seeking to deepen a mystical interpretation of the dialogue, the reader would quite possibly turn to an analysis of Diotima's description of the route by which one reaches knowledge of the pure form of beauty, an analysis of the ladder. Here the reader would discover that the lovers use a straightforward method of abstraction and generalization in order to reach the penultimate step, the class of all beautiful things. This in turn would highlight the break at the top of the ladder, the reintroduction of the language of the mysteries, the fact that the lovers no longer are the agents of discovery, but rather the recipients of a revelation—all of which would serve to strengthen the mystical interpretation. This in turn might lead the reader to a recognition that the word "knowledge" is being used in two different ways.

In one sense, as pointed out above,[29] the investigation might come to a halt at this point. Being able to give reasons in support of a belief would be a kind of knowledge appropriate to this world of changing particulars; and for a world of pure, immutable forms knowledge of an altogether different order would be necessary. This kind of knowledge could not be defined—nor even understood in terms of the other, worldly sense of "knowing." It could only be experienced. And although one can prepare oneself to receive it, one cannot meaningfully pursue it.

Such an interpretation, bringing the investigation to an end as it does, would fail to meet one criterion set forth in *Phaidros*: to "yield seed from which there spring up in other minds other words capable of continuing the process *forever*" (277a, emphasis mine), but such an objection could be dealt with either by limiting discussion to the *Symposium* (claiming, arguably, that statements in *Phaidros* ought to be seen as receiving their meaning in terms of *Phaidros* and not some other dialogue), or even by maintaining that since revelation is at its foundation an individual experience, the "process" that is supposed to "go on forever" is the process by which people as individuals receive their mystical knowledge of the pure form of beauty.

Even so, such a reader might still be challenged to explore the implications of Diotima's definition of knowledge, even though that knowledge be limited to this world of particulars. The particulars of this world are in flux. Therefore, our knowledge of them, if it is to reflect them at all, must also be in flux. Such considerations would easily enough lead to a recognition that Diotima's definition implies that knowledge itself is by nature processive, dialectical.[30] Such an interpretation in turn would lead to Diotima's claim that our knowledge is "mortal" and therefore is preserved by "replacing what goes off or is antiquated with something fresh, in the semblance of the original" (208a–b).

The passage in which this is explained also shows that Diotima is making a strong point of her claim that the *only* way in which a mortal can pursue immortality is through participation in the life process. A reader who had come this far in the analysis of the dialogue would be in a position to contrast this with her later claim (211e–212a) that the one who "had the fortune to look upon essential beauty entire, pure and unalloyed...above all men, is immortal." The reader would then be in a position to ask just how this interpretation of the "mortal nature" could fit with the mystical experience of an immutable form of beauty.

Such a reader would now have broken through yet another "screen," and would be in a position to question the mystical interpretation. Up to this point most readers would have taken the desire for immortality as a given. (Of course. Everyone desires immortality!) And probably would have pictured to themselves an existence not unlike that portrayed of the gods. The reader who had reached this point, however, would be unable to avoid the fact that Diotima had advanced two very different notions of immortality—even to the point of describing Eros as "between a mortal and an immortal" (209e), and describing the glory of Homer and Hesiod as "immortally renewed" (209d). An examination of the two different concepts of "immortality" would lead the reader naturally into a consideration of *why* one pursues it. Since this is a major consideration in the dialogue, that desire would be seen to be embedded in the concept of love.[31] Love in turn would be seen as indispensable to the life process, and the reader would recognize that the kind of "immortality" described in the mystical interpretation cannot satisfy the needs that led to the pursuit of immortality in the first place. The reader will then be in a position to realize that those needs are in fact met by the capacity of mortals, who are in their essence processive, to participate in a life process that goes on forever—with the depth of that participation measured by such different kinds of acts as procreation, pursuit of fame, creativity and invention, statescraft and finally, philosophy—an interpretation that both fits exactly with what Diotima says, and excludes the mystical interpretation.

I do not intend to suggest that the steps outlined above are the only route into what I take to be the deeper levels of the dialogue. (In point of fact, the ground was covered in a somewhat different way in my own exposition of it.) I do not intend to suggest either, that the interpretation offered here is the only way the dialogue can be understood. Still less would I like to suggest that these are the deepest levels that can be reached. (Indeed, I shall in the next section try to suggest at least one more level at which the dialogue can be understood.) What I do intend to suggest is that the dialogue is written in such a way as to screen its audience on a number of different levels, "offering to the complex soul elaborate and harmonious discourses, and simple talks to simple souls" (*Phaidros*, 277b–c). In the process the sensitive reader is driven to ask just those kinds of questions that elicit from the dialogue answers of a different sort from those that lie on the surface.

The first few steps seem to be pretty much the same regardless of the entry point. A contradiction is discovered.[32] This raises the question of whether or not Plato was aware of the contradiction. This question puts one in pursuit of evidence which, if discovered, raises the question of why Plato put the contradiction in the work. And so forth.

Since there are a number of such contradictions, there are also a number of different entry points. If the resolutions of the contradictions all seem to converge on a single interpretation, that looks like reasonably good evidence that one is not off on a wild goose chase.

Clearly, then, if the present approach is correct, Plato's second requirement is met. Not only does the *Symposium* screen its audience, and speak on different levels to souls of different "complexities," it also is so constructed that when the right kind of reader asks it a question in the right way, it does not simply repeat back what it has already said. It leads and guides one step by step into those deeper levels of the dialogue. One finds oneself (to state the case somewhat melodramatically) engaged in a dialectic with Plato— across a span of two and a half millennia!

5 The Same and the Different

Until now the doctrine of forms has been viewed as functioning in the *Symposium* largely as a dialectical foil, leaving untouched the question of why Plato would have gone to such lengths to develop the theory, explain it to his readers, and even show the kinds of problems it is supposed to resolve, how it is supposed to resolve them, and how one encounters them in the first place. That Plato would have taken the trouble to develop a complete and original metaphysical scheme, then carry the development of that scheme through the greater part of his work over a number of years when he did not take it seriously himself would seem to be unacceptable on its face. Any attempt to deal with this problem in terms of the whole of Plato's work is impossible in the framework of the present essay; however, both the steps that might lead to a doctrine of forms, and the elaboration of that doctrine are sufficiently evident in the *Symposium* to require treatment here at least in terms of that dialogue.

Another problem also remains. If Plato's object is to engage the reader in a dialectic that will lead the reader to the knowledge that knowledge (among other things) is essentially processive, once that bit of knowledge is attained the process would come to an end. The claim that knowledge is processive would no longer be subject to change, no longer be processive. As pointed out above,[33] one cannot say absolutely that nothing is immutable, since that is self-defeating. A claim that nothing immutable has ever been discovered would not imply that nothing is immutable. It could at most imply that if there is anything immutable it has yet to be discovered. Thus, the possibility must be kept open that something immutable might be encountered in the future.

More pointedly, the pursuit of knowledge is seen as the highest road by which humans can approach immortality. The reason that is so is that it is the highest way open to humans to participate in a life process that goes on forever. Thus, if that pursuit should be seen as having attained its goal and therefore as having been brought to an end, that level of participation is closed off. That aspect of the life process will not go on forever, and the pursuit of knowledge will not put us in touch with "immortality" in the sense of incorporating ourselves into an unending process.

On the other hand, if the pursuit of knowledge is properly at an end, if one has attained knowledge of a sort that cannot change, then one will be in touch with immortality in the sense of incorporating into oneself as knowledge that which by its nature is unchangeable and therefore eternal; one will be in touch with immortality in the sense in which that word is used with reference to the forms.

At this point the interpetation of the *Symposium* as yielding a process view of the world seems to fall short of its own requirements—and to fall as far short of exhausting what is actually in the dialogue as does the traditional interpretation. Instead, the dialogue itself can be seen as part of an ongoing process that on one level is the development of Plato's thought; on another, engages the reader in a dialectic with Plato; and on yet another, involves the reader in a dialectical clash between two incompatible views of the world. Instead of a world of changing particulars and a world of immutable forms as supplementary aspects of a single cosmos, there is now an ongoing dialectical relationship between a view of the most fundamental reality as consisting of process, and a view of the most fundamental reality as consisting of immutable forms.[34]

In Diotima's description of knowledge as mortal (208a) she tells us that the substitution of something fresh "in place of that which departs. . . preserves our knowledge enough to *make it seem the same*" (emphasis mine). A few lines later she makes the still more general claim for "all mortal things" that "what goes off or is antiquated [is replaced] with something fresh *in the semblance of the original*" (emphasis mine).

Clearly, the only way we can claim that our knowledge is "preserved" or that the replacement "seems the same" as "what goes off" is by comparing our present knowledge with the past knowledge that was lost—in which case it was not lost after all.

We can without difficulty talk meaningfully about replacements being "in the semblance of the original" when we are referring to objects other than ourselves, or even to aspects of ourselves that can be objectified. There does not seem to be any objection to asserting that parts of Sokrates ("his hair, his flesh, his bones, and his blood and body altogether" [207e]) "go off" and are replaced "with something fresh in the semblance of the original." From moment to moment, or even from week to week, if any change takes place it is not likely to be perceptible. But when Plato remembers the Sokrates of, say, ten years before, he can compare the memory with the Sokrates presently before him and recognize the differences. Since the change is observable over long periods, but not over any of the short periods of which the longer periods consist, the change would have to be going on, if not continuously, at least by imperceptible steps. This in turn would require that when something is replaced, the replacement cannot be perceptibly different from that which is replaced; i.e., it must be "in the semblance of the original." Even the claim that the "memories" are also "replaced" and therefore in flux need not lead to any problems so long as the memory is viewed as changing more slowly than Sokrates changes—and that, after all, is why we call it a "memory." We claim that our memory of Sokrates retains something of what Sokrates was, even though Sokrates now is different.

What Diotima says about knowledge, and what she says about other "mortal" things shows that either can be understood only in terms of things that remain at least relatively the same. If *all* things are processive, whatever changes most slowly (call it *A*) would be that against which all other changes are measured. There could not, therefore, be anything against which changes in *A* could be measured. Thus, there could not be any way to show that it, too, is in process. In this way, any attempt to understand change will lead inexorably back to that which, even if mutable, is indistinguishable from the immutable.

In the final analysis even this would not explain what is meant by the claim that the stages in the aging of Sokrates could be described as "imperceptibly different." That requires some ground of similarity, something that must be regarded as the same against which the difference could be regarded as a difference. It requires something very like an immutable form.

Furthermore, if *A* can only be perceived as immutable, even though it might simply change more slowly than all other things, then sameness can be comprehended only when it is reflected against change. Although the doctrine of forms would require that the same beauty be "in" each beautiful thing,[35] at those points where we might expect Diotima to say this, she hedges: "the beauty attached to this or that body is *cognate to* [ἀδεγφόν][36] that which is attached to any other" (210b), "it is *gross folly not to regard as* one and the same the beauty belonging to all" (210b); "he may...contemplate the beautiful as appearing in our observances and our laws, and...behold it all bound together in *kinship* [συγγενές]" (210c, emphases mine). This hedging makes sense only if it is seen as keeping open the possibility that the class of all beautiful things is a collection, the beauty of each thing in the collection being different, though perhaps imperceptibly so, from the beauty of the others—a class of such a nature that a single, pure form of beauty cannot be abstracted from it. Why this possibility should be kept open is explained by the problem of participation, by the fact that the very conditions required by the concept of sameness (its having no parts, its independence, its immutability) separate it completely from, and render it impotent with respect to, the world of change that its existence is supposed to explain.

The argument leads to paradox: change can be understood only in terms of difference, but difference can be understood only in terms of sameness, that which does not change—or at least is perceived as not changing. The application of the concept of difference might reasonably result in abstraction, and the application of the concept of sameness to more than one such abstraction might reasonably result in generalization. Thus, these two together could account for the process of conceptualization that leads up the "ladder." The application of a concept implies that in some sense one "has" it. But there is no way to account for our having either the concept of sameness or of difference.

This, however, is precisely the problem that led Plato to the doctrine of forms in the first place.

Thus, instead of resolving the issue in favor either of a doctrine of forms or of a process view of the world, Plato may now be seen as exploring the problem on ever deepening levels. If he has been successful as well in engaging the reader in his exploration, the dialectic will continue. The two views of the world are not supplementary. They are incompatible. If we make the right choice between them, we shall get as near to immortality as the human condition permits. If we make the wrong choice, we shall fail to fulfill ourselves as human beings. This drives us to continue the dialectic. In this important—and subtly ironic—sense, Plato's work will not on his terms be "fruitless." It will "yield seed from which there will spring up in other minds other words capable of continuing the process forever" (*Phaidros*, 277a).

Chapter 6

1 Sokrates and Eros

The arrival of Alkibiades[1] at this point interrupts Aristophanes' remark ''on the allusion which Socrates' speech made to his own'' (212c), and shambles any structure the partygoers might have planned for the rest of the evening. As pointed out above,[2] Alkibiades enters in the persona of Dionysos—appropriately enough for one whose role is to disrupt. The fact that Plato portrays him as crowned with ivy, the traditional crown of Dionysos, does not seem accidental, since the passage is replete with other Dionysian symbols. Alkibiades himself may well have seen the ivy as a symbol of his dedication to Dionysos on a drunken evening. In view of this, the fact that his crown is not just of ivy, but also of violets is unlikely to be accidental either. Violets were symbolic of Aphrodite. Alkibiades' amours are well known, and he may have seen the violets in his crown as an indication of his vision of himself as beloved, as *eromenos*—a theme to be picked up later in his speech (217a–219e). On the other hand, violets were also a common symbol of Athens, and their inclusion in his crown might also have been seen by him as a demonstration of his devotion to the city (in view of his later defection this possibility would have added a bitter irony for early readers of the dialogue). That there is a double meaning is perfectly in accord with what we know of Alkibiades' personality, and Plato may have intended both readings.

The identification of Eros with Dionysos was pointed out in chapter 1,[3] and that Plato intended some such identification seems clear. But, as many have noted,[4] Diotima's mythological description of Eros is also almost certainly intended as a description of Sokrates:

> [Eros] from the beginning has been attendant and minister to Aphrodite, since he was begotten on the day of her birth, and is, moreover, by nature a lover bent on beauty since Aphrodite is beautiful. Now as the son of Resource and Poverty, [Eros] is in a peculiar case. First, he is ever poor, and far from tender or beautiful as most

suppose him: rather is he hard [σκληρός] and [unwashed (αὐχμηρός)], shoeless and homeless; on the bare ground always he lies with no bedding, and takes his rest on doorsteps and waysides in the open air; true to his mother's nature, he ever dwells with want. But he takes after his father in scheming for all that is beautiful and good; for he is brave [and fervent and intent, a master] hunter, always weaving some stratagem; [longing for (ἐπιθυμητής)][5] and capable of understanding, resourceful, loving wisdom [φιλοσοφῶν] in all things (203c–d).

That Sokrates had always been "attendant and minister to Aphrodite" and "a lover bent on beauty" is attested to by Sokrates himself, who says (177d–e) that "I set up to understand nothing but love-matters," and is confirmed later by Alkibiades, who tells us (216d) that Sokrates "is amorously inclined to [beautiful (καλῶν)] persons; with these he is always busy and enraptured." Although the fact that Sokrates was "ever poor, and far from tender and beautiful" was well enough known to need no mention, Alkibiades refers to Sokrates' poverty elliptically in describing him on campaign in winter as "clad in just such a coat as he was always wont to wear, and [making] his way more easily over the ice unshod than the rest of us did in our shoes" (220b); and he comments directly on Sokrates' physical appearance: "Now as to your likeness, Socrates, to [the satyrs] in figure, I do not suppose even you yourself will dispute it" (215b). That he is "hard" is built into Alkibiades' description of him at Potidaia and Delium ("He surpassed not me only, but everyone else in bearing hardships..." [219e]) together with the long description that follows of how Sokrates bore the hardships of the field. The word αὐχμηρός, which Lamb translates as "parched," also means "unwashed." We have the testimony of Aristodemos (174a) that "being fresh from the bath" and wearing shoes were both "quite rare events with him," and takes this as evidence of something very much out of the ordinary. Although he is not specifically described as "homeless" nothing we know of Sokrates would run counter to the tradition that his home did not play any very important role in his life.[6]

There is no specific mention of him "lying on the bare ground...with no bedding," but such a picture is certainly consistent with the one painted by Alkibiades of Sokrates on campaign, apparently having only one coat. As for his taking "his rest on doorsteps and waysides in the open air," Aristodemos describes him as stopping in the portico of a neighboring house on his way to Agathon's party (175a–d), while Alkibiades describes a similar incident when Sokrates was with the armies (220c–d). On first discovering Sokrates at the party, Alkibiades accused him of scheming "to get a seat beside the [most beautiful ($\varkappa\alpha\lambda\lambda\iota\sigma\tau\omega$)] person in the room" (213c); and later, Alkibiades claims that he, Kharmides, Euthydemos, Diokles and perhaps others have found Sokrates' "way of loving deceitful" (222b),[7] and claims further to be trying to save Agathon from such "deceit," from his "weaving of stratagems."

Sokrates' bravery is expounded at length by Alkibiades (220d–221d); who also interprets his standing in one place from dawn to dawn as evidence of his relentless pursuit of understanding, his love of wisdom. Even Diotima's assertion that "in the selfsame day [Eros] is flourishing and alive at the hour when he is abounding in resource; at another he is dying, and then reviving again" seems to be reflected in Alkibiades' description: "he surpassed not me only, but everyone else in bearing hardships; whenever we were cut off in some place and were compelled, as often on campaigns, to go without food, the rest of us were nowhere in point of endurance. There again, when we had plenty of good cheer, he alone could enjoy it to the full" (219e–220a).

The description of Eros, of course, is part of Sokrates' speech, and his identification of himself with the god picks up on a theme in the other speeches in which, except for Aristophanes, each holds himself up as the kind of person most favored by the god: Phaidros, by glorifying the beloved; Pausanias, by glorifying the lover; Eryximakhos, by claiming that love is a cosmic force, and that every profession that treats of it from music to statescraft to necromancy is but a branch of his own profession of medicine; Agathon, by giving as a description of the kind of person Eros favors most, a description of all the things he fancies himself to be.

2 Sokrates and Silenos

But Sokrates' identification with Eros also stands in contrast to the relationship Alkibiades' speech establishes between Sokrates and Dionysos.

On three different occasions, once (176c) from Eryximakhos, and twice (214a and 220a) from Alkibiades the reader is told that Sokrates is unaffected by drinking. This claim is then acted out at the end of the dialogue where not only is Sokrates the sole survivor of the party, but after he laid the host and the last of the guests to rest, he went to the Lykeion where he washed "and then spent the day in his ordinary fashion [presumably antagonizing people in the marketplace with his questions]; and so, when the day was done, he went home for the evening and [rested]" (223d). The fact that Plato mentioned this three times, then played it out suggests that he intended that it be seen as something more than a display of Sokrates' machismo.

Mythologically, of course, drinking was the province of Dionysos, god of wine, and anyone who was drunk was held literally to be possessed by the god, who then spoke through her or his lips. The (possibly Orphic) dictum, "in wine truth" ($o\hat{\iota}\nu os$ $\varkappa\alpha\grave{\iota}$ $\mathring{\alpha}\lambda\mathring{\eta}\theta\epsilon\iota\alpha$)[8] paraphrased by Alkibiades at 217e reflects this belief. The fact that Sokrates is unaffected by wine, therefore, is (as pointed out in chapter 1, p. 11) at this point open to either of two interpretations: either he is under the protection of Dionysos' traditional opponent, Apollo, and is therefore shielded from Dionysian possession, immune to the effects of wine; or else he is a creature of Dionysos, is always possessed, so that drinking does not cause him to become possessed and thereby change his behavior.

Alkibiades clearly opts for the latter, comparing Sokrates to Silenos and to Marsyas, both of whom are satyrs, creatures of Dionysos. If we take seriously the suggestion that Alkibiades is the persona of Dionysos, this is a case of the god claiming his own.[9]

His first comparison is "to the Silenus-figures that sit in the statuaries' shops; those, I mean, which our craftsmen make with pipes and flutes in their hands: when their two halves are pulled open, they are found to contain [statues of the god ($\mathring{\alpha}\gamma\mathring{\alpha}\lambda\mu\alpha\tau\alpha$ $\mathring{\epsilon}\chi o\nu\tau\epsilon s$ $\theta\epsilon\hat{\omega}\nu$)]" (215a-b). Silenos was Dionysos' tutor and later, his boon companion, portrayed as always drunk—as always possessed by his god. Because he is drunk, he is believed always to tell the truth, but to tell it in riddles. Moreover, Silenos is not consistently associated with any other god. Thus, what were contained in the clay or terracotta statues almost certainly were statues of Dionysos, a graphic portrayal of Dionysos possessing Silenos and speaking through his lips. On another level Dionysos, as god of masks, may now be seen as that which wears the Silenic clay, the life force manifesting itself as Silenos.

That Alkibiades would make the comparison is suggestive in itself. Early readers of the dialogue, however, would have been painfully aware that Alkibiades was the general who persuaded Athens to attack Syracuse, and whose defection to Sparta at the beginning of that campaign was seen as the reason for the catastrophic defeat that in the end was to cost them the war.[10] They would have been equally—and as painfully—aware that the fact that Alkibiades' teacher was Sokrates had raised dark suspicions that Sokrates, or perhaps his kind of thinking, had led Alkibiades both to desecrate the herms and to defect—a suspicion which, despite the amnesty, was believed to have played a significant role in Sokrates' trial and death.[11] Thus, the symbol of Silenos, the teacher, as pregnant with Dionysos, the student, would have been seen as calling for comparison with Sokrates, the teacher, as giving birth to Alkibiades and being in some important sense the parent of his crimes. But the notion of Sokrates as pregnant also reflects the assertion made earlier by Diotima that "all men are pregnant...both in body and soul" (206c). What they are pregnant with, however, varies with the different levels on which they participate in the life process.[12]

At no point does Sokrates portray the lover as being pregnant with the beloved. That view would accord better with Pausanias' concept of love than with Sokrates'. The portrayal of Pausanias as setting forth the conventional Athenian view of love does go a long way toward accounting for the belief among Athenians that Sokrates was responsible for Alkibiades' corruption. Thus, although the symbol invites the comparison, Plato has structured his treatment of "pregnancy" in such a way that anyone trying to find in it grounds for believing that Plato held Sokrates responsible for Alkibiades' defection will be led in another direction. "Beauty," Diotima tells us (206d), "presides over birth as Fate [Μοῖρα] and [Goddess of Childbirth (Εἰλείθυια)]; and hence it is that when the pregnant approaches the beautiful it becomes not only gracious, but so exhilarate that it [melts (διαχεῖται)] with begetting and bringing forth....Therefore when a person is [swelling (σπαργῶντι)] and teeming ripe he feels himself in a sore flutter for the beautiful, because its possessor can relieve him of his heavy pangs" (206d-e).

Later (209c) she makes this explicit: "For I hold that by contact with the fair one and by consorting with him he bears and brings forth his long-felt conception;" i.e., the lover pursues the beautiful in order to give birth to the lover's own thoughts. In this sense, the "golden god" inside Sokrates that speaks through his lips is not Alkibiades, but his own thoughts as they have developed in his relation with the beautiful. And Alkibiades' place in the scheme (if indeed he has one) is as the "beautiful," the love object. His suitability as a love object for Sokrates will rest on what sort of beauty he has.

The symbolism here reflects and expands upon a thesis worked out philosophically in Sokrates' speech. Sokrates identifies himself as Eros, and he also "contains" or "is possessed by" Dionysos. Thus, while Sokrates is the mask through which Dionysos speaks, on another level not Sokrates, but Eros is the mask; love is the vehicle of the life force. Finally, that life force on the most fully human level—as manifested in Sokrates—is that which comes from the lips of the philosopher: the dialectic.[13]

Ironically, Alkibiades unwittingly suggests this theme towards the end of his speech (221e–222a):

> For there is a point I omitted when I began—how his talk most of all resembles the Silenuses that are made to open. If you chose to listen to Socrates' discourses you would feel them at first to be quite ridiculous; on the outside they are clothed with such absurd words and phrases— all, of course, the hide of a mocking satyr. His talk is of pack-asses [Silenos' traditional mount], smiths, cobblers, and tanners, and he seems always to be using the same terms for the same things; so that anyone inexpert and thoughtless might laugh his speeches to scorn. But when these are opened, and you obtain a fresh view of them by getting inside, first of all you will discover that they are the only speeches which have any sense in them; and secondly, that none are so divine, so rich in images of virtue, so largely—nay so completely—intent on all things proper for the study of such as would attain both grace and worth.[14]

3 Sokrates and Marsyas

Alkibiades' second comparison is to Marsyas. According to the myth, Athene fashioned a flute in order to entertain the Olympians. Noticing that Hera and Aphrodite were smiling behind their hands as she played, she went into the forest where she found a quiet pool.

There, she played the flute and studied her reflection. She realized then that the effort forced her to puff out her cheeks and turn purple, presenting an altogether ludicrous picture to anyone who was watching. In rage, she cursed the flute and flung it away.

Later Marsyas, the satyr, found the flute—and discovered it to have the curious and remarkable property that he had but to furnish the breath, and the flute of itself played beautiful music. Not surprisingly, Marsyas acquired a reputation as a great musician— so great, in fact, that his listeners said of him that he was an even finer musician than Apollo, the god of music. Marsyas made the mistake of not correcting them, and Apollo, furious, challenged Marsyas to a contest, to be judged by the Muses. The winner, as prize could do anything he pleased with the loser—a bad bet from the start, since Marsyas was mortal, and Apollo was not.

In the event the contest was a draw. In order to break the tie Apollo challenged Marsyas to do with his instrument what Apollo could do with his: turn it upside down and play it while singing—a feat possible with a lyre, but clearly not possible with a flute. The songs the god sang also flattered the judges (just as Meletos, in the *Apology* flattered the judges by claiming that any Athenian gentleman could teach the youth "excellence"). Having thus won the contest through trickery Apollo demanded as his prize Marsyas' skin, which he subsequently sewed into a waterskin and nailed to a tree in Anatolia, where it became the source of a river.

Exactly how much of this myth Plato might have had in mind is not clear, but that it is more than a casual comparison to Sokrates as ugly and as a charmer seems beyond dispute:

> "Are you not a piper," asks Alkibiades. "Why, yes, and a far more marvelous one than the satyr. His lips indeed had power to entrance mankind by means of instruments; a thing still possible today for anyone who can pipe his tunes: for the music of Olympus's flute belonged, I may tell you, to Marsyas his teacher. So that if anyone, whether a fine flute-player or a paltry flute-girl, can but flute his tunes, they will have no equal for exciting a ravishment, and will indicate by the divinity that is in them who are the apt recipients of the deities and their sanctifications. You differ from him in one point only— that you produce the same effect with simple [words (λόγοις)] unaided by instruments" (215c).

But if, instead of a flute, Sokrates charms (or "excites a ravishment" in) his auditors with words, there is here a fairly obvious allegory of Sokrates, the satyr who by accident, stumbled on the dialectic—an instrument that played by itself when he put it to his lips, and which produced such sweet music that, by its very beauty, it led to his destruction. And just as Apollo tricked Marsyas by an imitation of a musician, so the sophists, through Anytos, Lykon and Meletos, tricked Sokrates with eristic, the imitation of the dialectic, using it to flatter the judges and win them over to the prosecution.

That Sokrates held that the dialectic itself rather than Sokrates, directed his discussions is a recurrent theme in the early and middle dialogues. As early as *Euthyphro* Plato makes the point that neither Euthyphro nor Sokrates is willing to accept responsibility for the fact that Euthyphro's arguments seem not to "remain fixed, but walk about" (*Euth.*, 11c-e, 15b), implying that the moving force is not they, but the process of examination (in this case of the meaning of "piety")—the dialectic.[15] In *Meno* (86d-e) Sokrates complains that he must follow Meno even though he would prefer that the argument go elsewhere. Similar complaints are sprinkled through a number of the early and middle dialogues, culminating, perhaps, in *Theaitetos*, where Sokrates portrays himself as the midwife of other people's ideas—just as here he is portrayed as the vehicle of the dialectic, one who is guided by it rather than one who guides it.

And who is guided by it to his doom.[16]

The fact that the flute came from Athene, a female, fits with the theme in Sokrates' speech that he learned about love—learned the dialectic—from the priest, Diotima.[17]

4 Sokrates and Apollo

On this interpretation of the Marsyas myth Apollo becomes a symbol of eristic, which is indistinguishable from dialectic in form, but which is aimed at victory in debate rather than at genuine understanding. It casts those who engage in it in the role of adversaries rather than partners.[18] The pursuit of understanding requires enormous vitality, sustained effort, the courage to explore and defend unpopular, perhaps unpalatable, even dangerous ideas—all of which Sokrates clearly has. Eristic lacks these, and is reduced therefore to empty rhetoric; the form of the dialectic but perverted to evil ends; vice in the form of virtue. And if the dialectic is seen as the life force, eristic is the embodiment without the anima, death in the form of life.

Such an interpretation of course puts much too much weight on something not included directly in the dialogue at all, and would deserve no mention here were it not consistent with other features of Apollonian themes in the dialogue.

The traditional conflict between Apollo and Dionysos as represented in the relation between their respective devotees, Eryximakhos the physician and Aristophanes the playwright; in the manipulation of the order of the speeches; and in Aristophanes' disruption of Eryximakhos' speech followed by his satire of it—all are treated at length above.[19] Eryximakhos is also portrayed as the one who gives form to the evening's entertainment by proposing first that they not get drunk, then that they give encomia to Eros. Even this latter is formulated not as his own proposal, but as Phaidros'—thereby giving the formal structure of the party by making Phaidros symposiarch, the one whose role is to guarantee that the form agreed to is carried out, that is, until that role is preempted by Alkibiades, the persona of Dionysos.

Even then it is Eryximakhos who makes a futile attempt to give form to the evening after Alkibiades' entrance (214a–c):

"What procedure is this, Alcibiades?" asked Eryximachus. "Are we to have nothing to say or sing over the cup? Are we going to drink just like any thirsty folk?...What are we to do?"

"Whatever you command, for we are bound to obey you:
    One learned leech is worth the multitude.
So prescribe (ἐπίταττε) what you please."

"Then listen," said Eryximachus, "We resolved, before your arrival, that each in order from left to right should make the finest speech he could upon [Eros], and glorify his name. Now all of us here have spoken; so you, since you have made no speech and have drained the cup, must do your duty and speak. This done, you shall prescribe [ἐπιτάξαι] what you like for Socrates, and he for his neighbor on the right, and so on with the rest" (214a–c).

This last was not mentioned in Eryximakhos' original "prescription" for the evening, but may well have been a plan he intended to introduce after the first round of speeches. Such a possibility at any rate would accord with the suggestion apparent from the outset that Eryximakhos hoped the evening might move toward an erotic culmination.[20] The assumption that by "draining the cup" Alkibiades had incurred an obligation to speak seems also to have a formal character.

Alkibiades, of course, continues to dismantle the form Eryximakhos is trying to impose,[21] demanding that he be allowed to praise Sokrates rather than Eros, a proposal to which an apparently exasperated Eryximakhos agrees. Thus, although Alkibiades pretends to allow Eryximakhos to "prescribe," Alkibiades storms ahead and does as he pleases.

In the bantering scene at the end of Alkibiades' speech, Sokrates—now also identified as a creature of Dionysos—collaborates in breaking up Eryximakhos' last proposal for structure, that "you [Alkibiades] shall prescribe [ἐπιτάξαι] what you like for Socrates, and he for his neighbor on the right, and so on with the rest" (214c)—a structure that seems to echo Apollo's proposal for the victor in the contest with Marsyas. Sokrates, however, reformulates "prescribe [ἐπιτάξαι] what you like" as an obligation to praise (ἐπαιγεῖν [222e]), so that when Alkibiades asks that Agathon be allowed to sit between them, Sokrates replies: "That cannot be . . . you have praised [ἐπῆνεσας] me [thus implying that the "second part" of the evening's entertainment has already been initiated by Alkibiades], and so it behooves me to praise [ἐπαινεῖν] my neighbor on the right. Thus if Agathon sits beyond you, he must surely be praising [ἐπαινέσεται] me again, before receiving his due praises [ἐπαινεθῆναι] from me" (222e).

But even this semblance of structure is shattered before it can begin, as the group of drunken revelers bursts upon them.

The whole of the dialogue, of course, is brought to us by Apollodoros, whose name means "beloved of Apollo." He, too, seems more concerned with form than with understanding. His opening remark is, "I believe I have got the story you inquire of pretty well by heart" (172a). He attributes to Glaukon the assertion that Apollodoros is "the most proper [reciter (ἀπαγγέλειν)] of [Sokrates'] discourses" (172b). He next takes Glaukon to task for supposing that he (Apollodoros) might have been present at the party when in fact "it is many a year that Agathon has been away from home and country, and not yet three years that I have been consorting with Socrates..." And he describes his "consorting" as "making it my daily care to [know the form of ($\dot{\epsilon}\iota\delta\dot{\epsilon}\nu\alpha\iota$)] whatever he says or does" (172e).

His concern for formal structures shows itself again in his ability to be quite exact about when the party took place, even though he admits that he was only a child at the time: " 'When you and I were only children,' I told him; 'on the occasion of Agathon's victory with his first tragedy: the day after that of the dedicatory feast which he and his players held for its celebration' " (173a).

Next he admits that he got the story from Aristodemos: "But all the same, I have since questioned Socrates on some details of the story I had from his friend, and he acknowledged them to be in accordance with his account" (173b).

That is, Apollodoros had gone to the trouble to be sure he had the story straight, and now tells his nameless companion that he has recently rehearsed the whole thing to Glaukon "and hence, as I began by saying,[22] I have it pretty well by heart" (173c).

The form, in other words, is guaranteed to be as accurate as Apollodoros can make it. Despite his claim to find delight only in "philosophic discourses," and to consider all other subjects a waste, he does not seem overly concerned about understanding them, so long as he is able strictly to adhere to their original form in recounting them. And despite the Dionysian description of him as a "maniac" ($\mu\alpha\nu\iota\kappa\dot{o}s$) his rage is spent railing futilely at himself and those around him, and his energy is absorbed in memorizing every word. In short, he functions exactly like the written word or the recitations of the rhapsodes as described in *Phaidros* and *Ion*, and if in the process he also functions as a vehicle of Sokrates' thought he does not profess to have any more understanding of that thought than does the scroll upon which it is written. His rigid adherence to form allows his account to function as I have suggested Plato intended the written word to function, but it does not reflect comprehension on the part of the "reciter." The speeches, he says, "were somewhat as follows—but stay, I must try to tell you all in order from the beginning, just as my friend told it to me" (173e–174a).

The only other passage that might be an elliptical reference to Apollo is at the end, when Sokrates and Aristodemos go to the Lykeum to wash before continuing on to the agora. As Brentlinger[23] points out, "they go to wash at the Lyceum, which was adjacent to the temple of Apollo and is named after him ($\Lambda\dot{\nu}\kappa\epsilon\iota\sigma$ being an epithet of Apollo)." Since the Lykeion was also known to be one of Sokrates' haunts (*Euthyphro*, 2a; *Euthydemos*, 271a)—even to the point of being so mentioned by Liddell and Scott—and would be the probable place for Sokrates to go under the circumstances, I am (perhaps mistakenly) reluctant in the face of the evidence adduced above to put much weight on the Apollonian symbolism of the gymnasium.[24]

In general, then, although Apollo's place in the dialogue is shadowy at best, with the sole exception of the reference to the Lykeion, it is consistent. In each case he or his devotees are portrayed as necrophilic; as being ever in pursuit of static, unchanging forms; as denying the beauty of Marsyas' flute, the dialectic; as substituting the lyre for the flute, the eristic for the dialectic, and thus, through deception trying to destroy both Marsyas and Sokrates.

Thus, on this interpretation, Apollo appears to be the mythological symbol of the pursuit of pure, unchangeable forms, a pursuit shown above[25] to be deceptive in that it leads not to life, but to death. Dionysos, on the other hand, appears to be the mythological symbol of the blind, passionate rage to be; that without which form is unchanging, sterile, dead; and that which without form is unguided, chaotic, insane. The only way the two can be brought together is by regarding each form not as an end, but as a step in a process. Thus knowledge, insofar as it is conceptual, insofar as it has form, exists in order to be replaced. Every form, every concept, every order that is imposed, like the masks of Dionysos, must in time be thrown aside as a step toward discovering the form, the concept, the order—the mask—beneath.[26]

And like the masks of Dionysos, if the forms are perceived as immutable they bring the process to a halt. They destroy what life in its essence must be.

As Alkibiades points out, the music survives. Marsyas' tunes, whether played by Olympos (who was associated with Apollo in the contest with Marsyas, and who therefore stole the tunes) or "a paltry flute girl" has "no equal for exciting a ravishment, and will indicate by the divinity that is in them who are apt recipients of the deities and their sanctifications" (215c).

So also for Sokrates: "so soon as we hear you, or your discourses in the mouth of another [as here],—though such person be ever so poor a speaker, and whether the hearer be a woman or a man or a youngster—we are all astounded and entranced" (215d).

Alkibiades will go on to show how Sokrates—and if the present interpretation is accepted, his discourses—selects out those "who are apt recipients of the [deity] and [its] sanctifications." At any rate it will become clear that Alkibiades is not among them.

5 Sokrates and Alkibiades

Alkibiades' description of his own relation with Sokrates is reflected with subtle irony against the view of love developed in Sokrates' speech, which, of course, Alkibiades did not hear.

Silenos by reputation was always so drunk (possessed by his god, the Dionysos within him) that he was unable to distinguish truth from falsehood, and so although he always spoke the truth, he spoke it in riddles. In comparing him to Sokrates, Alkibiades says (216d) that Sokrates affects utter stupidity and ignorance: "Is this not like a Silenus? Exactly. It is an outward casing he wears, similarly to the sculptured Silenus."

This "Sokratic ignorance" is the foundation of the dialectic, the god within who makes it impossible for him to distinguish the true from the false, and which for this reason is the highest human virtue. But if this is so, the highest human virtue would seem to be that set forth in the *Apology* (21d): "I do not think that I know what I do not know," i.e., the refusal to distinguish between the true and the false when reasons cannot be given in support of such a distinction.

The effect this has on Alkibiades is, he says, to be left in a spiritual tumult, and enslaved:

> the influence of our Marsyas has often thrown me into such a state that I thought my life not worth living on these terms. . . . Even now I am still conscious that if I consented to lend him my ear, I could not resist him, but would have the same feeling again. For he compels me to admit that sorely deficient as I am, I neglect myself while I attend to the affairs of Athens. So I withhold my ears perforce as from Sirens, and make off as fast as I can, for fear I should go on sitting beside him till old age was upon me. And there is one experience I have in presence of this man alone, such as nobody would expect of me,— to be made to feel ashamed by anyone; he alone can make me feel it. For he brings home to me that I cannot disown

the duty of doing what he bids me, but that as soon as
I turn away from his company I fall a victim to the favours
of the crowd. So I take a runaway's leave of him and flee
away; when I see him again I think of those former
admissions and am ashamed (215e–216c).

He is attracted and repelled at one and the same time, but in
the end he fails to understand either the attraction or the repulsion.
He believes on some level that Sokrates is right in asking that he
not neglect himself, he even admits this to be a duty; but he does
not seem to have much idea of how to go about it. Ironically, he
sees following Sokrates as a way of neglecting himself. What repels
him, what drives him away from Sokrates is the belief that if he does
not flee he will still be there when old age overtakes him, and he
will have wasted his life—even to the point of comparing Sokrates
to the Sirens, implying that Sokrates would lure him to his doom.
He is "ashamed" of his behavior, but clearly not before "the crowd"
since they are the ones to whom he flees. Neither does he seem to
be shamed in his own eyes. He does not feel that he has really made
a mistake in running away. Although Sokrates "compels [him] to
admit" his neglect of himself, and prevents his "disowning" the
duty of doing Sokrates' bidding, he still sees a life spent in Sokrates'
company as a waste. He is shamed only before Sokrates, and only
because of having admitted to him that he should not neglect
himself. Moreover, since directing someone to do something seems
wholly out of character for Sokrates, even the claim that "I cannot
disown the duty of doing what he bids me" seems to be grounded
in a profound misunderstanding of Sokrates, and in particular, of
his "affectation" of ignorance. We should therefore not be surprised
that in his next remark he reflects the ambivalence of "the crowd"
whose flattery he pursues; the attitude of the demos: "Often I could
wish he had vanished from this world; yet again, should this befall,
I am sure I should be more distressed than ever; so I cannot tell
what to do with the fellow at all" (216c).

Alkibiades' assertion that "sorely deficient as I am, I neglect
myself while I attend to the affairs (πράττω) of Athens" echoes
directly and ironically Sokrates' contention in the *Apology* (31b) that
"I have neglected all my own affairs and have been enduring the
neglect of my concerns all these years, but I am always busy in [the
Athenians'] interest [πράττειν]."

In the *Apology* Sokrates argued that he was "a gift from the god" (31a–b). Whether that god be the dialectic[27] or not, the *Apology* makes clear that Sokrates' service to the god is doing dialectic. Hubris, the basis of sin, is arrogance, the belief that you are something that you are not. In other words, hubris rests on the failure of self-knowledge. The dialectic, on the other hand, is a method of exploring yourself, of discovering your limits at least in the sense of discovering what it is that you do not know; however, knowing what it is that you do not know puts you in a position to correct your ignorance, to discover knowledge. Thus, the dialectic is a process not only of finding, but of transcending limits; a process of self-discovery, but of self-creation as well.[28] It is the surest—perhaps the only sure— way of avoiding hubris. In this sense Sokrates, by doing dialectic, may well be neglecting his "affairs" or his "concerns," but in no way can he be regarded as neglecting himself.

Alkibiades, however, flees Sokrates in order to "attend to the affairs of Athens." The fact is clear in context that what Alkibiades is fleeing is philosophy, the dialectic. And in that sense he is, as he says, neglecting not his "affairs," but "himself." By abandoning philosophy he has forfeited the power to create himself. By yielding to the blandishments of "the crowd," he has given that power to them.

6 Alkibiades and the Dialectic

Before giving the account of his attempts to seduce Sokrates, Alkibiades unwittingly recapitulates reasons some of the earlier speakers gave for engaging in love relationships, and declares Sokrates to be immune to them: "I tell you, all the beauty a man may have is nothing to him; he despises it more than any of you can believe; nor does wealth attract him, nor any sort of honour that is the envied prize of the crowd. All these possessions he counts as nothing worth..."

Wealth as the reward of love was expounded by Phaidros; honor, by Pausanias. That Alkibiades, like Agathon, limits beauty to physical attractiveness is clear evidence of his failure to understand either Sokrates, or beauty as Sokrates understands it—a failure made still more ironic by the fact that Alkibiades himself will give an account of Sokrates' attempts to help him deepen his understanding of both.

Alkibiades is very inexact regarding what attracted him to Sokrates. He claims to have seen the "images" inside Sokrates, and to have "thought them...divine and golden...perfectly fair and wondrous" (216e–217a), but he says nothing of why he thought so or even of what they might be. The foregoing analysis (chapters 4 and 5) implies that what actually was "in" Sokrates was the dialectic, but nothing in Alkibiades' speech suggests that this was what he perceived. In fact, he goes on at this point to say that what he saw caused him to think "I simply had to do as Socrates bade me," implying the same misunderstanding of Sokrates' character as before, but this time in a context suggesting that Alkibiades misunderstood the dialectic as well. This is confirmed in the next sentence, where Alkibiades admits that his needs would be met if he could but "*hear* [ἀκοῦσαι] all that our Socrates knew" (217a, emphasis mine).

Major portions of Sokrates' speech were taken up with an attack on learning as a process merely of hearing and remembering, and with advancing the thesis that learning is a dialectical process.[29] Moreover, Alkibiades' suggestion that one learns by hearing and remembering is also rendered impotent both by Sokrates' definition of knowledge as being able to give reasons in support of a belief, and by his characterization of knowing as "replacement."

Sokrates had also commented on this kind of learning when he first arrived at the party and Agathon invited him to share his couch: "Here, Socrates, come sit by me, so that by contact with you I may have some benefit from that piece of wisdom that occurred to you there in the porch" (175c–d).

To which Sokrates replies: "How fine it would be, Agathon...if wisdom were a sort of thing that could flow out of one of us who is fuller into him who is emptier, by our mere contact with each other, as water will flow through wool from the fuller into the emptier" (175d).

Moreover, Alkibiades, like Agathon, sees his own physical attractiveness as the bait, and as Pausanias had recommended, blandly expresses his willingness to prostitute himself for the sake of learning. Having already noted (216d) "how Socrates is amorously inclined to handsome persons," Alkibiades goes on to say: "And believing he had a serious affection for my youthful bloom, I supposed I had here a godsend and a rare stroke of luck, thinking myself free at any time by gratifying his desires to hear all that our Socrates knew; for I was enormously proud of my youthful charms" (217a).

His mistake was not in his assessment of his own beauty—that had been confirmed to him many times. It was in his failure to recognize that gratifying Sokrates' desires would require that he go beyond the physical, and beyond the conception of knowledge as information. As a result, Alkibiades fails also to comprehend Sokrates' reaction to his initial attempts at seduction: "Yes, gentlemen, I went and met him, and the two of us would be alone; and I thought he would seize the chance of talking to me as a lover does to his [beloved (παιδικοῖς)] in private, and I was glad. But nothing of the sort occurred at all: he would merely converse [διαλεχθεὶς] with me in his usual manner, and when he had spent the day with me he would leave and go his way" (217b).

For Sokrates a love relationship, if it is to be fully human, is dialectical as well as physical; it is "begetting on a beautiful thing by means of *both* body and soul" (206b, emphasis mine). In Diotima's description of the ladder, she had claimed that in the beginning of a relationship, "if his conductor guides him aright, he must be in love with one particular body, and engender beautiful converse [γενιᾶν λόγους καλούς] therein" (210a-b). Thus, that Sokrates spent whole days in conversation with Alkibiades can be seen as an attempt to establish the kind of relationship in which love can grow. Alkibiades in turn should have recognized that Sokrates would not spend that much time with people who did not interest him,[30] and he should have seen this as a compliment.

Sokrates had every reason to approach Alkibiades with a certain amount of circumspection. A moment before, Alkibiades had told Agathon and his guests that the reason he wanted to seduce Sokrates was so Sokrates would be willing to spend time with him and he could "hear all that. . . Socrates knew." Now it becomes clear that Alkibiades' actual values were the reverse of this. He wanted to spend time and have long conversations with Sokrates in order to seduce him. As a result, instead of seeing Sokrates' behavior as a compliment, he sees it as an insult to his "youthful charms."

Earlier[31] Pausanias, reflecting the Athenian custom, had held that youth must be protected from "that popular lover, who craves the body rather than the soul" (183d-e). Athens, he tells us requires "ordeals and tests" (184a) in order to screen out such "popular lovers," and allow love only to those who pursue love as a means to excellence (ἀρετήν) (184c). Thus, in professing to want to seduce Sokrates in order to learn from him, Alkibiades is offering just that rationalization for a seduction that is acceptable to "the crowd" in

Athens—those to whom he flees, and who he allows to control him. By showing through his actions that his real motive is not learning (which for Sokrates comprises human excellence) but seduction, he has revealed that even by the criteria of "the crowd" he is a "popular lover" whose eye is not on excellence, but on the score; he has been tested by Sokrates, and has been shown to be unworthy of love not only by the standards set by Sokrates, but by conventional Athenian standards as well.

Alkibiades' next move is to try bodily contact as a way of turning Sokrates on: "I proposed he should go with me to the trainer's, and I trained with him, expecting to gain my point there. So he trained and wrestled with me many a time when no one was there. The same story! I got no further with the affair" (217c).

With increasing frustration at this point Alkibiades is moving away from the learning he professes to be pursuing rather than toward it. Sokrates' reaction, again, is to go along with what Alkibiades professes, and ignore what his professions, in an increasingly obvious way, are intended to communicate. If there is anything odd about Sokrates' response it is that he would bother— and this probably is explained by the fact that Sokrates sees in Alkibiades one who will become an excellent person, an excellent philosopher, if he can learn control, in which case he also will become a person worthy of love.[32]

Having failed to achieve his end by indirection, Alkibiades now decides upon a more direct approach: "Then, as I made no progress that way, I resolved to charge full tilt at the man, and not throw up the contest once I had entered upon it: I felt I must clear up the situation. Accordingly I invited him to dine with me, for all the world like a lover [ἐραστής] scheming to ensnare his favourite [παιδικοῖς]. Even this he was backward to accept; however, he was eventually persuaded. The first time he came, he wanted to leave as soon as he had dined. On that occasion I was ashamed and let him go" (217c–d).

The shame in this case is not because of what he had admitted to Sokrates (as he had said earlier), but because he recognizes that Sokrates would not approve of his motives—a tacit admission that his values had somehow gotten inverted. Since Alkibiades' pride, his sense of self, is so clearly bound up with his perception of himself as the beloved who can seduce anyone, he sets aside these reservations next time, in the belief that by speaking directly, Sokrates can be persuaded to yield. Ironically, he still uses conversation as bait: "The second time I devised a scheme: when we had dined I went on talking with him far into the night, and when he wanted to go I made a pretext of the lateness of the hour and constrained him to stay. So he sought repose on the couch next to me, on which he had been sitting at dinner, and no one was sleeping in the room but ourselves" (217d).

By now Alkibiades' preoccupation with sex has become so infused with his sense of self that it has been transformed into a compulsion to conquer. That what he hoped for might in some other context be called an act of love is by this time irrelevant. He sees Sokrates as an adversary, and he becomes increasingly absorbed in plotting tactics for victory. In short, that in Alkibiades' character that made him a superb military commander has now taken over. He is portrayed as the strategist, the general.

At this point Plato subtly has Alkibiades unwittingly provide the contrast for his increasing fixation on sexual conquest, and his dwindling interest in philosophy. He does so at the outset by having Alkibiades characterize Sokrates' rejection of Alkibiades' advances as a "deed of lofty disdain" (217e, but repeated later at 219c), whereas in fact Alkibiades' elevated view of the importance of his own physical charms has caused him to act out (though he does not express) his disdain for philosophy.

The contrast now is heightened by Alkibiades' claim to have been "stung" by Sokrates' "philosophic discourses" which force one to "do or say whatever they will." But Alkibiades seems to realize that the sting comes from the "philosophic discourses," not from Sokrates, who is as much a victim of the sting as anyone else:

> I share the plight of the man who was bitten by the snake. . . . I have been bitten by a more painful creature, in the most painful way that one can be bitten: in my heart, or my soul, or whatever one is to call it, I am stricken and stung by his philosophic discourses, which adhere more fiercely than any adder when once they lay hold of a young and not ungifted soul, and force it to do or say whatever they will; I have only to look around me, and there is a Phaedrus, an Agathon, an Eryximachus, a Pausanias, an Aristodemus, and an Aristophanes—*I need not mention Socrates himself*—and all the rest of them; every one of you has had his share of philosophic [mania and bacchic frenzy (φιλοσόφου μανίας τε καὶ βαχχείας)]. (217e–218b, emphasis mine).

The "sting" that is delivered by the "philosophic discourses" seems on one level to be "Sokratic ignorance," the recognition that one does not know what one thought one knew, the stimulus to the pursuit of knowledge; but on Alkibiades' lips the reference is also ironic. The "sting" of philosophy is by the nature of the philosophic enterprise the sting that is the necessary part of any search: the sting of realizing that the answers—if indeed there are any—have yet to be found. This is the sting of realizing one's own shortcomings, the kind of realization that will drive Sokrates to search for what is better, but will drive a self-centered person like Alkibiades to do whatever is necessary to conceal those shortcomings from others and, in the end, from himself; a process that is a natural outgrowth of a "shame culture," of allowing oneself to be defined by "the crowd," but a process, too, that is the precise antithesis of philosophy. Thus again, Plato seems to suggest that Alkibiades has failed to grasp the real nature of the dialectic, that he has failed ultimately to know himself.

7 The Failed Seduction

At this point yet another layer of irony is introduced. Some years before, Alkibiades had been accused of sacrilege: specifically, of revealing the Eleusinian mysteries to the uninitiated by satirizing them in the presence of his servants. Not long after the present dialogue is supposed to have taken place, when the herms were desecrated, this incident was to be recalled by Alkibiades' enemies in order to lend credence to the accusation that he was involved. Here, Alkibiades himself jokingly refers to that earlier incident while invoking the air of an initiation rite. The guests, having suffered the "snakebite" are given the role of the initiates, and are to hear the revelation: "You shall stand up alike for what then was done and for what now is spoken. But the domestics, and all else profane and clownish, must clap the heaviest of doors on their ears" (218b).[33]

Alkibiades now tells of his final attempt to seduce Sokrates. The frustration and urgency he felt at the time, and his less than successful attempt to conceal them are illustrated at the outset when he says that he shook Sokrates awake, then solicitously asked, "...are you awake?" (218c). Next, he stated his intention with the same mixture of urgency and arrogance: "I consider...that you are the only worthy lover I have had, and it looks to me as if you were shy of mentioning it to me. My position is this: I count it sheer folly not to gratify you in this as in any other need you may have of either my property or that of my friends'' (218b).

He then hastily tries to conceal both the urgency and the arrogance behind a mask of calm reasonableness: "To me nothing is more important than the attainment of the highest possible excellence, and in this aim I believe I can find no abler ally than you. So, I should feel a far worse shame before sensible people for not gratifying such a friend than I should before the senseless multitude for gratifying him'' (218c–d).

The argument from shame parallels exactly the position set forth by Agathon just before his speech in the bantering interchange with Sokrates that was cut short by Phaidros ("I hope you do not always fancy me so puffed up with the playhouse as to forget that an intelligent speaker is more alarmed at a few men of wit than at a host of fools,'' 194b–e). That argument in turn, as pointed out above,[34] echoes Phaidros' contention that there is nothing much objectionable in doing wrong so long as one is not caught at it. Similarly, despite Alkibiades' declaration that he was trying to attain "the highest possible excellence," he seems more concerned with what "sensible people" would think of him than with attainment of excellence. For this reason even this declaration of his intent was given more for its expected effect on Sokrates than because of any commitment to it. And it is included in his speech at the party because of its expected effect in persuading those at the party that his motives were for self-improvement. The phrase "sensible people" in a statement like this (as had been the case with Agathon's) functions only as a way of flattering whoever one is addressing, and giving them the impression of being separated off from "the multitude." Thus, there is little here to suggest that Alkibiades was immune to the opinions of "the crowd."[35]

Sokrates' reply appears to fasten on that part of Alkibiades' speech that had been put in for effect, and which was not seriously intended. As a result, Alkibiades misinterpreted Sokrates' reply as "put[ting] on that innocent air which habit has made so characteristic of him" (218d). Because of this Alkibiades can repeat, but he cannot understand what Sokrates said. Sokrates in fact pointed out that Alkibiades was prostituting himself, and that, like many prostitutes, he hoped to exact an exorbitant price: "My dear Alcibiades, I daresay you are not really a dolt, if what you say of me is the actual truth, and there is a certain power in me that could help you be better; for then what a stupendous beauty you must see in me, vastly superior to your comeliness! And if on espying this you are trying for a mutual exchange of beauty for beauty, it is no slight advantage you are counting on—you are trying to get genuine in return for reputed beauties, and in fact are designing to fetch off the old bargain of *gold for bronze''* (218d–219a, emphasis the translator's).

The ''gold'' that Sokrates offers is a love relation through which they will jointly produce the good for themselves and each other. The ''bronze'' that Alkibiades offers is his physical attractiveness. Love is ''begetting upon the beautiful'' (206e), but Alkibiades' beauty is not genuine. In a love relation each is both lover and beloved,[36] ''a begetting for both'' (206c) requiring mutual effort, mutual growth; but Alkibiades' offer of sex as coin for the purchase of Sokrates' knowledge precludes the possibility of such a relation. Although Alkibiades compares himself to the ''lover'' ($\dot{\epsilon}\varrho\alpha\sigma\tau\dot{\eta}s$), and Sokrates to the ''favorite'' ($\pi\alpha\iota\delta\iota\varkappa o\hat{\iota}s$) (217c–d) he sees that comparison as ironic. He remains oblivious to the fact that love is at its foundation a dialectical relationship.

Yet all of these misapprehensions are corrigible. All that is required to put Alkibiades on track is that he concern himself with Sokrates' beauty rather than his own; that he see the ''begetting'' of the good as a joint and reciprocal effort; all of which add up to the recognition of the dialectical center of any human love relation.

Sokrates' next comment is designed to show just that; he invites Alkibiades to join him in a dialectical examination of what constitutes worth for a human:

> But be more wary, my gifted friend: you may be deceived
> and I may be worthless. Remember, the intellectual sight
> begins to be keen when the visual is entering on its wane:
> but you are a long way yet from that time (219a).

Alkibiades, however, sees this not as an invitation, but as a tactic for postponement:

> To this I answered, ''you have heard what I have to say;
> not a word differed from the feeling in my mind: it is for
> you now to consider what *you* judge to be best for you
> and me'' (219a, emphasis mine).

Sokrates, in his reply ignores the submissiveness of the *eromenos* implied in Alkibiades' request that Sokrates judge for both of them what is best. At the same time he repeats his invitation to the kind of dialectic that would make a love relation possible:

> Ah, there you speak to some purpose...for in the days to come *we* shall consider and do what appears to be best for *the two of us* in this and our other affairs (219a–b, emphasis mine).

Certainly nothing in what Sokrates had said would justify Alkibiades' assertion that having "let fly my shafts, I fancied he felt the wound" (219b). The fact that he can repeat what Sokrates said implies that he heard it. But his statement also implies that he ignored the meaning of what Sokrates said. Alkibiades seems in fact to have started with, and never abandoned, the assumption that his physical charms are irresistible. This has caused him to interpret everything Sokrates has said as "shyness," as gentle demurrers presented pro forma as a preliminary to seduction. This accounts for the fact that the only reason he gives for believing Sokrates had "felt the wound" is that he had "let fly [his] shafts."

> So up I got, and without suffering the man to say a word more I wrapped my own coat about him—it was wintertime; drew myself under his cloak...;[37] wound my arms about this truly spiritual and miraculous [being]; and lay thus all night long (219b–c).

Strictly speaking, Sokrates does not reject Alkibiades—although Alkibiades would be hard put to recognize this. He does not kick Alkibiades out of bed, nor does he leave the bed himself. Instead he does the one thing that is wholly devastating to Alkibiades' ego: he just lies there: "you may be sure, by gods—and goddesses—that when I arose I had in no more particular sense slept a night with Socrates than if it had been with my father or my elder brother" (219d–e).

Had Sokrates rejected Alkibiades such a rejection could have been taken to mean that Sokrates was attracted, and was fighting his own desire to have sex with Alkibiades. This would have left Alkibiades' ego more or less intact, and he would have been able to deal with the situation by angrily cutting off the friendship. Sokrates, by neither rejecting him nor accepting him forced Alkibiades to the shattering recognition that Sokrates might not even be attracted. It also kept open the possibility of a sexual relationship at the same time that it prevented that relationship from developing, leaving Alkibiades in the curious position of having no excuse to break the relationship at the same time that he failed to understand how to advance it.

> After that, you can well imagine what a state of mind I was in, feeling myself affronted, yet marvelling at the sobriety and integrity of his nature: for I had lighted on a man such as I never would have dreamt of meeting— so sensible and so resolute. Hence I could find neither a reason for being angry and depriving myself of his society nor a ready means of enticing him (219d–e).

The means were there, but Alkibiades failed to understand what they were, just as he failed to understand Sokrates himself. This failure is pathetically exposed in his next comments, putting his understanding on a level with Phaidros': "For I was well aware that he was far more proof against money on every side than Ajax against a spear; and in what I thought was my sole means of catching him he had eluded me. So I was at a loss, and wandered about in the most abject thraldom to this man that ever was known" (219e).

He can neither understand Sokrates, nor get free of him. The very fact that he describes his feeling as "abject thraldom" accentuates what might be called his "*eromenic* failure," the failure to realize that a love partner must be both *erastes* and *eromenos*, both lover and beloved—but not in the conventional sense of devising deceptive strategies for conquest or entrapment. What Alkibiades has failed to recognize is that love is fundamentally dialectical. Thus Alkibiades fails—not because Sokrates is (as claimed by Aristoxenos)[38] a dedicated (and avid!) heterosexual; nor (as Rosen would have it)[39] because he is "abstinent or defective erotically;" nor more broadly (as argued by Nussbaum)[40] because he has no interest in, or even contemns sex. Sokrates is not stone, and Alkibiades does not fail because of his particularity. Alkibiades fails because of his own duplicity, his own unworthiness. He fails because he is offering philosophy as an inducement to sex; he is offering that which is the essence of humanity for that which humans share with other animals.

He is offering bronze for gold.

Appendix

Plato's *Meno*

The purpose of this Appendix is to suggest that there are some striking similarities between the *Symposium* and *Meno*, similarities striking enough to indicate that they arose out of the same period in the development of Plato's thought and reflect similar concerns. In particular, they are parallel in method, in the treatment of the concept of "being human," and in the treatment of knowledge. There is no reason to believe that Plato intended the two dialogues to be read together; nevertheless, the fact that they revolve around the same center suggests that they will prove to be mutually illuminating.[1] Although I shall argue that in *Meno* the "Doctrine of Recollection" is not intended to be taken as a serious attempt to explain learning, I do not intend to suggest that this would necessarily apply to other dialogues, least of all to *Phaido*, where the case is argued in a significantly different way.

1

The way that *Meno* is written seems designed to direct the reader's attention to Meno's paradox. Not only is it the most interesting point philosophically, it is also the fulcrum that gives leverage to the major themes of the dialogue. The paradox as Meno states it is: "Why, on what lines will you [inquire (ζητήσεις)], Socrates, for a thing of whose nature you know nothing at all [τὸ παράπαν]? Pray what sort of thing, amongst those that you know not, will you treat as the object of your [inquiry (ζητήσεις)]? Or even supposing, at the best, that you hit upon it, how will you know it is the thing you did not know?" (80d)[2]

The argument has as its conclusion that one cannot meaningfully ask any question at all. Yet the argument is presented in the form of three questions. Thus, the form in which the argument is presented defeats the conclusion.[3]

One might think Plato slipped, but immediately afterwards (81a), Sokrates apparently commits the same fallacy when he claims to have learned the doctrine of recollection by hearing it ("I have heard [ἀκήκοα] from wise men and women who told of things divine that—"); i.e., he claims to have learned by hearing that one does not learn by hearing.[4]

Perhaps Plato slipped again.

This fallacy is then committed a third time when Meno asks (81e) Sokrates to "teach" (διδάξαι) him the doctrine of recollection. This time, however, Sokrates explains the fallacy: "I remarked just now, Meno, that you are a rogue; and so here you are asking if I can [teach (διδάξαι)] you, when I say there is no teaching [διδαξήν] but only recollection: you hope that I may be caught contradicting myself forthwith" (81e–82a).

Thus, between 80d and 82a—a little over one Stephanus page— the same fallacy is committed three times, and the third time Sokrates explains the nature of the fallacy. Clearly, then, Plato, the author, also understood the fallacy, and must have understood it in the other two occurrences as well. This in turn implies that Plato intended for us to see Meno, the character, as not understanding either the fallacy or the paradox.[5]

The fact that Meno presents the paradox at all can best be understood in terms of the dramatic side of the dialogue—what is being acted out. Earlier (75a–76e) when Meno began to sense that he was getting into deep water, he had tried to steer the discussion away from "excellence" (ἀρετή) by pushing Sokrates first to define "figure," then, when Sokrates defined it in terms of "color," to define "color."[6] It seems probable that had Sokrates done so, Meno would have then asked him to define the terms in the definition, and so on ad infinitum. Sokrates prevents this by giving him a circular definition: "Figure [σχῆμα]. . .is the only existing thing that is found always following color" (75b); and "color is an effluence of figures [σχημάτων] commensurate with sight and sensible" (76d). Between these two (76a) Sokrates ventured another definition of "figure" as "limit of the solid." The definition appears at first to be a technical one that will work out; however, had Meno made the same move here, and demanded that Sokrates give him a definition of "solid" he would have discovered that this definition of "figure" is also circular, since the definition could work only if the "solid" in question is a "solid figure," and not an "unlimited solid." There is, of course, no reason to believe that Meno foresaw this, and the fact that he ignores this definition demanding instead that Sokrates give him a definition of "color" suggests that he is not in pursuit of a good definition. Rather does he want to give Sokrates an endless procession of terms to define before he can get back to the subject at hand, and thereby bring to a halt a discussion Meno can no longer control.

In this framework, Sokrates' circular definition functions to prevent Meno from keeping the discussion off course. Meno apparently does not even realize he has been outmaneuvered: he praises Sokrates' definition of "color" as excellent in itself, and also as the sort of thing that would keep him in Athens if Sokrates would but promise to continue to produce more like it—perhaps in the vague hope that such flattery might lead Sokrates off track in another way.

Sokrates then, somewhat sardonically, points out that the definition fails yet again, in that it does not define: "I fancy you observe that it enables you to tell what sound and smell are, and numerous other things of the kind" (76d–e).

Meno misses the significance of Sokrates' comment, and Sokrates then goes on to point out (76e) that what appeals to Meno is not the content of the definition, but its dramatic style. Thus Meno is portrayed as one who is convinced that learning consists of remembering things and being able to produce them at the proper stimulus. The more resounding the phrasing of what one remembers, the better it is, implying that the goal is not to know, but to impress others with what one appears to know.

This accords with a comment made by Sokrates at the beginning of the dialogue, (70b–c) to the effect that Gorgias had given the Thessalians "the regular habit[7] of answering any chance question in a fearless, magnificent manner, as *befits* [ὥσπερ εἰκός] those who know" (emphasis mine). In other words, he had taught them not how to acquire knowledge, but how to simulate it. We should therefore not be surprised that Meno overlooked the circularity, but was drawn to the resounding phrasing of Sokrates' definition of "color." Nor should we be surprised that Meno believes knowledge to consist of remembering what one has heard. Such a definition of knowledge is vapid on its face—the sort of thing any rhapsode, even one like Ion, (or any tape recorder) can do. Nevertheless, that is exactly the concept of knowledge Meno acts out for us here.[8]

There is, of course, a significant difference between defining *knowledge* as "recalling and being able to reproduce what one has heard," and defining *learning* as recollection. The contrast between these two must be understood in order to understand the contradiction implied by Sokrates' claim to have learned the doctrine of recollection by "hearing" it. Meno's failure to pick up on that contradiction explains in a measure his failure to understand some of the major difficulties in the doctrine of recollection.[9]

These moves by Sokrates show the reader much about Meno, and at the same time serve to get the discussion back on track.

At 80a–b Meno admits to "Sokratic ignorance," the realization that he does not know what excellence is: "For in truth I feel my soul and my tongue benumbed, and I am at a loss what answer to give you. And yet on countless occasions I have made abundant speeches on [excellence ($\alpha\varrho\epsilon\tau\hat{\eta}s$)] to [many people ($\pi\varrho\dot{o}s$ $\pi o\lambda\lambda o\acute{v}s$)]—and very good speeches they were, so I thought—but now I cannot say one word as to what it is."

This is an admission that his simulation of knowledge was unsuccessful. As a result, there now will be no getting the discussion back on track. First, he insults Sokrates by comparing him to the stingray (80a). When that fails to stop the questioning he presents his paradox (80d–e). Sokrates outmaneuvers him this time by presenting the doctrine of recollection (81a–e), but when he then tries to get back to the question of what excellence is (81e), Meno instead demands that Sokrates "teach" him the doctrine of recollection. When Sokrates points out the fallacy in that, he asks Sokrates to demonstrate the doctrine (82a). After Sokrates obliges (in the slave dialogue 82b–85b) and again asks him to return to the question of what excellence is (86c), Meno insists that they return to his original question regarding not the nature, but the genesis of virtue (86c–d), a question they appear still to be pursuing at the end of the dialogue.

Thus, from the moment Meno admitted he did not know what human excellence is his major concern was not to find out what it is, but either to bring the discussion to a halt, or failing that, to get it onto another track where he felt more comfortable.

In this context, Meno's paradox is presented as a conversation stopper. He does not understand it, so he must have heard it— probably from Gorgias[10]—and remembered it. On these terms Sokrates' presentation of the doctrine of recollection can be seen at least in part as a move that keeps the dialectic going. If Meno accepts it, he will thereby have granted that meaningful questions are possible, and they can get on with the question of what "excellence" is. If he rejects it the burden will be on him to show why he rejects it, and the dialectic will continue anyway—although in a different direction, since it would now turn to the question of what knowledge is and how it is acquired.[11]

2

Another passage that seems to be critical to an understanding of the dialogue comes in as an aside. Meno asks: "If someone said he did not know color, and was in the same difficulty about it as about figure, what answer do you suppose would have come from you?" (75c).

In reply, Sokrates explains the difference between how he would deal with an eristic philosopher, and how he would deal with one who would be willing to carry on a dialectic:

> The truth from me; and if my questioner were a professor of the eristic [ἐριστικῶν] and contentious sort, I should say to him: I have made my statement; if it is wrong, your business is to examine and refute it. But if, like you and me on this occasion, we were friends and chose to have a [dialectic (διαλεγέσθαι)] together, I should have to reply in some milder tone more suited to dialectic [διαλεκτικώτερον]. The more dialectical [διαλεκτικώτερον] way, I suppose, is not merely to answer what is true, but also to make use of those points which the questioned person[12] [*concedes* (προσομολογῇ)] that he knows. And this is the way I shall now try to argue with you [emphasis mine] (75c–d).

This explains why Sokrates made the move he made at the outset of the dialogue. Meno had asked him (70a) "whether [excellence (ἀρετή)] can be taught, or is acquired by practice, not teaching?" In asking this he has asked what rhetoricians would call a "complex question." If his concern is to know whether or not excellence can be taught, then he has tacitly "conceded" that he does know what excellence is. This "concession" then allows Sokrates to pursue the question of the nature of excellence rather than of its genesis.

Such a "concession," of course, does not entail that the person being questioned actually have such knowledge, and in Meno's case the "concession," leads ultimately to "Sokratic ignorance," to the realization that he does not know what excellence is, but only thought he knew; that is, he believed he knew something that he does not know. In that sense he believed himself to be something that he is not. He is guilty of hubris.[13]

The same passage says that when Sokrates is confronted by an eristic philosopher, he would "say to him: I have made my statement; if it is wrong, your business is to examine and refute it." After Meno presents his paradox, Sokrates characterizes it as "an eristic argument:" "Do you see what [an eristic (ἐριστικόν)] argument you are introducing...?" (80e). This passage is followed immediately by Sokrates' presentation of the doctrine of recollection, after which Sokrates repeats the characterization: "So we must not hearken to that [eristic (ἐριστικῷ)] argument: it would make us idle, and is pleasing only to the indolent ear, whereas the other makes us energetic and inquiring" (81d-e). Thus, if the doctrine of recollection is wrong, Meno's "business is to examine and refute it."

At this point Sokrates' claim (81a) to have learned the doctrine of recollection by "hearing" it begins to look like a broad hint both to Meno and to the reader that the doctrine of recollection should be examined closely—a challenge made explicit at 81b where Sokrates says, "As to their words, they are these: mark now, if you judge them to be true."

In point of fact, there are good reasons for questioning the doctrine of recollection. In presenting it Sokrates begins with a strong suggestion that those from whom he heard the doctrine[14] had a vested interest in propagating it: "[The speakers] were certain priests and priestesses [ἱερέων τε καὶ ἱερειῶν] who have *studied so as to be able to give a reasoned account of their ministry*; and Pindar also and many another poet of heavenly gifts. As to their words, they are these: mark now, if you judge them to be true. They say the soul of man is immortal, and at one time comes to an end, which is called dying, and at another is born again, but never perishes. Consequently *one ought to live all one's life in the utmost holiness*" (81a-b, emphases mine). He then quotes a passage—perhaps from Pindar—designed to reinforce this thesis: "For from whomsoever Persephone shall accept requital for ancient wrong, the souls of these she restores in the ninth year to the upper sun again; from them arise glorious kings and men of splendid might and surpassing wisdom, and for all remaining time are they called holy heroes amongst mankind" (81b-c).

The interpretation of these passages as suggesting a vested interest on the part of the "priests and priestesses" receives support, too, from the fact that they wish to give an account of their ministry (μεταχειρίζονται) rather than of their beliefs, suggesting that they are more interested in justifying than in understanding what they are doing.

The doctrine of recollection itself is stated thus:

> Seeing then that the soul is immortal and has been born many times, and has [seen (ἑωρακυῖα)] all things both in this world and in the nether realms, she has [learned (μεμάθηκεν)] of all and everything; so that it is no wonder that she should be able to recollect all that she knew before about [excellence (ἀρετῆς)] and other things. For as all nature is akin, and the soul has learned [μεμαθηκυίας] all things, there is no reason why we should not, by remembering but one single thing—an act which men call learning (μάθησιν)—discover everything else, if we have courage and faint not in the [inquiry (ζητῶν)]; since, it would seem, [inquiry (ζητεῖν)] and learning [μανθάνειν] are wholly [ὅλον ἐστίν] recollection (81c-d).

But if learning consists *wholly* (ὅλον ἐστίν) of recollection, and one can only recall what has previously been *learned* (μεμάθηκεν), then the soul learns by recalling what it has previously learned by recalling...and so on to infinity. The question of how initial learning took place has been moved infinitely into the past, but it has not been answered. In this sense the doctrine of recollection fails to accomplish what it supposedly was introduced to accomplish.[15]

Moreover, his claim that the soul "has [learned] of *all and everything*" implies that the soul has learned of all falsehoods as well as all truths. If this is the case, then the fact that one recalls something is no guarantee of its truth. To recall *x* and to recall *that x is true* would be two separate acts of recollection, and there is no reason to believe they could not arise independently.[16]

After Meno posed his paradox, Sokrates rephrased it: "I understand the point you would make, Meno. Do you see what [an eristic] argument you are introducing—that, forsooth, a man cannot inquire either about what he knows or what he does not know? For he cannot inquire about what he knows, because he knows it, and in that case is in no need of inquiry; nor again can he inquire about what he does not know, since he does not know about what he is to inquire" (80d–e).

In posing his paradox, Meno had asked, "Why, on what lines will you [inquire (ζητήσεις)], Sokrates, for a thing of whose nature you know *nothing at all* [τὸ παράπαν]?" (80d). This qualification is dropped in Sokrates' rephrasing, but Meno's attention is diverted by the fact that Sokrates adds to what Meno had said the other possible case: "he cannot inquire about what he knows, because he knows it, and in that case is in no need of inquiry."[17] The change, of course, is slight, and one would not expect Meno to notice, or to make anything of it if he did. Nevertheless, this phrasing allows for two very different interpretations of the paradox. The first would be as it was stated by Meno, but the second would be the much easier problem of how Sokrates might ask a meaningful question about something he happened not to know, even though it occurred in a framework of other things he did know. In the case as Meno stated it, no such context of relevant knowledge would be allowed.[18] Thus, if Sokrates is found to be dealing with the latter interpretation, and ignoring the paradox as Meno presented it, Meno's failure to object would be further evidence that Meno did not understand the paradox, but had borrowed it.

This seems to be exactly what Sokrates does: the problem he pretends to deal with is the latter, easier problem. In describing the doctrine of recollection, he says, "there is no reason why we should not, by remembering but one single thing...discover everything else" (81d). In other words, that thing would serve as a "reminder" of other things, and, "because all nature is akin," with proper dialectical guidance one could be led step by step from one thing to another until everything else is discovered.

Had Meno understood his paradox he would at this point have challenged Sokrates to explain how one can learn that first thing. One cannot be "reminded" of it, since whatever the "reminder" might be would then be "first." This difficulty, of course, parallels the problem of initial learning. There cannot be an infinite series of "reminders."

Here again, even if the doctrine of recollection should be taken seriously, it fails to deal with Meno's paradox as Meno stated it.

3

The slave dialogue, Sokrates' "demonstration" of the doctrine of recollection, begins with Sokrates apparently trying to give Meno another hint that he is dealing not with the paradox as Meno stated it, but with the question of how one can acquire knowledge within a framework of other knowledge. At any rate, this seems to be the best explanation of the otherwise weird formality of the scene that opens the slave dialogue, when, with the slave standing in front of him Sokrates asks not the slave, but Meno, whether or not the slave speaks Greek (82b)—thereby establishing in a highly formal way that he and the slave share a common language, and that his questions will therefore be understood.[19]

Sokrates' first question seems to be designed to establish another, narrower and more pertinent framework of common knowledge: "Do you know that a square is a figure like this?" (82b). From this point on the most that Sokrates can claim is that the slave has acquired new knowledge within a framework of other knowledge. Yet to suggest that the slave did not know what a square is not only seems improbable on its face, but also runs counter to the slave's own response to Sokrates' question, "I do" [Ἔγωγε)[20].

Sokrates now leads the slave by a series of easy questions into a deeper understanding of the figure they are dealing with. The sides are all of equal length. If the sides are equal, then the bisecting lines parallel to the sides must also be equal (82c).

There is no geometrical reason for Sokrates to divide the square in this way, since the square of double the area would in any event be produced by squaring the diagonal. There are, however, a number of pedagogical reasons for the division. First, by dividing the square this way, and recognizing that each line bisects the square, the slave will be in a position to understand more readily the later bisection of the square by the diagonal. Secondly, the division of the square into four quarters allows Sokrates to show the slave that he can test his answers by constructing them and counting the square feet they contain. Thirdly, since the first solution the slave will offer is to double the side, starting with a side of two feet enables the slave to move easily to the idea of three feet as dividing the difference between two and four.[21] Finally, this kind of division directs the slave's attention to the length of the side of the square, and predisposes him to try to answer Sokrates' question about the side of the square of double area in terms of some multiple of the foot. Such an answer is impossible, of course: the ratio between the side and diagonal of a square is one to the square root of two—an irrational number—so there cannot be any "number" the slave can give that will yield the length Sokrates requests.

Nevertheless, Sokrates asks his questions in such a way as to push the slave in this direction: "Come now, try and tell me how long will each side of that figure be. This one is two feet long: what will be the side of the other, which is double in size?" (82d-e).

The slave's reply, "Clearly, Socrates, double," is exactly what Sokrates has led him to say. This now allows Sokrates to point out to Meno that the slave believes he has knowledge when he does not (82e). It also allows Sokrates to show the slave how to test his answer by constructing the square with sides of double length, dividing it into square feet, and then counting up the square feet it contains (82e-83c).[22]

Once the slave realizes his answer is incorrect, Sokrates again leads him toward trying to find a length commensurable with the side that will yield the correct answer:

> SOC. Very well, and is not a space of eight feet double the size of this one, and half the size of this other?
> BOY. Yes.
> SOC. Will it not be made from a line longer than the one of these, and shorter than the other?
> BOY. I think so.
> SOC. Excellent; always answer just what you think. Now tell me, did we not draw this line two feet, and that four?
> BOY. Yes.
> SOC. Then the line on the side of the eight foot figure should be more than this of two feet, and less than the other of four?
> BOY. It should.
> SOC. Try and tell me how much you would say it is. (83c-e)

After an exchange like this, no one should be surprised that the slave says it should be three feet; i.e., half the difference between the side of two feet and the side of four feet—just as eight square feet, the area he wants, is between the square of four feet and the square of sixteen. Sokrates has him test his answer in the same way as before, and he discovers that although he is closer to the correct answer, he is still wrong. At this juncture, Sokrates tacitly admits he has been misleading the slave when he says (84a), "if you would rather not *reckon it out* [ἀριθμεῖν]" and in the rest of that sentence gives the slave the first hint that his method might be wrong: "just *show* [δεῖξον] what line it is."

At this point the slave admits to "Sokratic ignorance:" "Well on my word, Socrates, I for one do not know" (84a).

Thus, in the first part of the slave dialogue the elenchus is achieved through careful, and highly manipulative questioning by Sokrates.[23] If it has any connection with recollection, that connection is by no means obvious. Sokrates admits as much when he explains the effect of his questioning: "Now do you imagine he would have attempted to inquire or learn what he thought he knew, when he did not know it, until he had been reduced to the perplexity of realizing that he did not know, and had felt a craving to know?" (84c).

Sokrates then challenges Meno to "be on the watch to see if at any point you find me teaching him or expounding to him, instead of questioning him on his opinions" (84d). Although Meno raises no such challenge, what Sokrates in fact does is construct the figure for the slave, and at the same time give him information in a step-by-step manner. Each step is thinly disguised by a question mark at the end—which functions not to indicate that the slave recalls or believes what Sokrates has said, but rather functions only to elicit from the slave a confirmation that he understands what Sokrates has said. Although this latter part of the slave dialogue is claimed to "demonstrate" or "prove" the doctrine of recollection, it clearly fails to do so. Moreover, the failure seems transparent enough that we might well suspect that Plato intended that it be less than persuasive. Such an interpretation would at any rate fit both with the fact that the doctrine of recollection as presented in this dialogue is seriously flawed, and with the broad hints that the reader should approach that doctrine with a certain amount of scepticism. It would also account for the fact that after five and a half Stephanus pages (81a–85c) devoted to an apparent attempt to substitute "recollection" for "learning," Sokrates would ask at 87b–c: "is [excellence] taught [διδακτόν] or not—or, as we were saying just now, remembered [ἀναμνηστόν]? *Let us have no disputing about the choice of a name*" (emphasis mine)—after which he continues for the rest of the dialogue to refer to the subject of their discussion as "teaching" (διδακτόν).

All of this seems to suggest that Plato did not intend that the doctrine of recollection be taken seriously—at least not in this dialogue.[24]

4

When outlining how he would deal with an eristic philosopher (75c–d) Sokrates had said that his answer would be "a true one." In presenting the doctrine of recollection, he also claims truth for what he had "heard" (81a):

> MEN. What was it they said?
> SOC. Something true [ἀληθῆ], as I thought, and admirable.

Thus, if the doctrine of recollection does not function and is not acceptable as an answer to Meno's "eristic argument," then in what sense is Sokrates' answer "true"?

Sokrates ends his presentation of the doctrine of recollection by saying: "So we must not hearken to that [eristic (ἐριστιχῷ)] argument: it would make us idle, and is pleasing only to the indolent ear, whereas the other makes us energetic and inquiring" (81d–e).

He then adds, "putting my *trust* [πιστεύων] in [rather than "knowing" or "remembering"] its truth, I am ready to inquire with you into the nature of [excellence (ἀρετή)]" (81e).

Sokrates makes the same point again after the slave dialogue, and this time, uncharacteristically, he does not hedge: "Most of the points I have made in support of my argument are not such as I can confidently assert; but that the belief in the duty of inquiring after what we do not know will make us better [βελτίους] and braver and less helpless than the notion that there is not even a possibility of discovering what we do not know, nor any duty of inquiring after it—this is a point for which I am determined to do battle, so far as I am able, both in word and deed" (86b–c).

In both passages the implication is not that there is any certainty that one will learn something, but rather that one is a better person, more fully human, if one pursues learning than if one does not.

Meno can believe that learning is possible, or that it is impossible; and learning in fact can be possible, or impossible. If Meno believes that it is impossible, and it is impossible, he will never have the satisfaction of knowing that he is right, since it would be impossible for him to learn that he is. If he believes that it is possible, and it is impossible, he will never have the frustration of knowing he is wrong, since he would not be able to learn that either. In short, if learning is impossible that fact cannot affect our lives in any way.

On the other hand, if he believes that learning is impossible, but it is in fact possible, he will then, by following the "indolent" path, have missed the opportunity to learn anything. Finally, if he believes that learning is possible, and it should be possible, then he might learn something—*or he might not.* (If the fact that learning is possible and the fact that Meno believed it to be possible were a guarantee that learning would take place, then learning would necessarily *be* possible, since by attempting to learn Meno would of necessity either learn what he was attempting to learn, or he would learn that he could not learn it.) Thus, for Sokrates the *pursuit* of learning is more important than learning itself.

Although the Greek word ἀρετή is frequently translated as "virtue," it refers to virtue in the sense of "essential excellence" (as a character in a Victorian novel might ask, "What is the *virtue* of this medicine?"). In this sense the subject of *Meno* is "human excellence," that which distinguishes humans from other animals and things, and which distinguishes the best humans from those not the best. If this is the case, then the apparent conclusion Sokrates and Meno reach—that such excellence is a gift of the gods, and comes only to the few—seems particularly odd, since it implies that human excellence is not something humans can acquire, and is something that only a very small number of humans have. On the other hand, the import of these passages seems to be that the ἀρετή, the "essential excellence," of the human is to seek knowledge—although not necessarily to attain it. It is "doing dialectic."

At 80a Meno compares Sokrates to the stingray. The comparison, aimed at Sokrates' legendary ugliness, is intended as an insult, and as pointed out above (p. 128) was probably spoken in the vague hope that Sokrates might give up the conversation. In reply, Sokrates pretends to miss both the insult and its apparent intent (80c): "[Your aim in thus comparing me was] that I might compare you in return. One thing I know about handsome people is this—they delight in being compared to something. They do well over it, since fine features, I suppose, must have fine similes. But I am not for playing your game" (80c).

The game Sokrates refuses to play is that of comparing Meno's physical appearance with anything at all. Nevertheless, in the slave dialogue he clearly does make a comparison between Meno and his slave, although the comparison has nothing to do with Meno's physical beauty.[25] Moreover, he makes the comparison pointed enough that it should be obvious not only to the reader, but to Meno as well.

Once the slave admits he does not know how to answer Sokrates' question (84a), Sokrates breaks off the discussion temporarily. Turning to Meno, he refers to the process of trapping the slave into that admission as "[numbing him as the torpedo does (ναρκᾶν ὥσπερ ἡ νάρκη)]" (84b), just as previously (80a–b) Meno had compared Sokrates to the "flat torpedo sea-fish [πλατεία νάρκη τῇ θαλαττίᾳ]; for it benumbs [ναρκᾶν] anyone who approaches and touches it," adding that he has been thus benumbed by Sokrates. Here, Sokrates points out that the slave is now better able to pursue an answer precisely because he realizes that he does not know the answer. In other words, he now understands the question. Once Meno agrees that the slave is better off knowing what it is that he does not know, Sokrates drives home the comparison: "And we have certainly given him some assistance, it would seem, towards finding out the truth of the matter: for now he will push on in the [inquiry (ζητήσειεν)] gladly, as lacking knowledge; whereas then he would have been only too ready to suppose he was right in saying, before any number of people (πρὸς πολλούς) any number of times, that the double space must have a line of double length for its side" (84b–c)—just as Meno had "on countless occasions...made abundant speeches on [excellence] to [any number of people (πρὸς πολλούς)]—and very good speeches they were, so [he] thought" (80b).

From this point on the significance of the comparison becomes increasingly clear.

When Meno admitted he did not know what human excellence is, he moved immediately to cut off discussion, and had adamantly refused to pursue the question. His slave, however, makes no such move, but allows Sokrates to continue the discussion until the slave learns the answer. The basis of the difference is clearly stated in the discussion of the torpedo's effect, when Sokrates says to Meno: "Now do you imagine he would have attempted to inquire [ζητεῖν] or learn [μανθάνειν][26] what he thought he knew, when he did not know it, *until he had been reduced to the perplexity of realizing that he did not know, and had felt a craving to know?*" (84c, emphasis mine).

In short, there are two requirements for learning: knowledge of one's ignorance, and a "craving to know," i.e., a desire to learn. Meno's persistent dodging of the question after "having been reduced to the perplexity of realizing that he did not know" shows clearly that he did not have "a craving to know." Meno's comparison of Sokrates with the stingray points up the fact that

Sokrates is not pretty (no news either to Sokrates, or to anyone else who might be listening). Since the pursuit of learning is what distinguishes humans from other animals and things, and distinguishes the best humans from those not the best, Sokrates' comparison of Meno with his slave shows Meno to be less than fully human in a much more significant sense. The slave has the "craving to know." Meno does not.

Meno's paradox as Sokrates reinterpreted it had in fact been resolved before Meno presented it. As soon as Meno admitted he did not know what excellence is (80b), the question, "what is excellence?" not only was at hand, but clearly was understood by Meno—just as the slave's admission that he did not know constituted an admission that he understood the question of how to construct a square double the area of a given square.

Sokrates makes the latter point explicit in his interchange with Meno at 84b–c. Meno, in stating his paradox, had built his argument around the possibility of inquiry (ζητήσεις):

> "Why, on what lines will you [inquire (ζητήσεις)], Socrates...? Pray, what sort of thing, amongst those that you know not, will you treat us to as the object of your [inquiry (ζητήσεις)]?" (80d).

Sokrates now (84b–c) uses the same word in addressing Meno—though Meno doesn't seem to notice:

> soc. And we have certainly given him some assistance, it would seem, towards finding out the truth of the matter: for now he will push on in the [inquiry (ζητήσειεν)] gladly, as lacking knowledge; whereas then he would have been only too ready to suppose he was right in saying, before any number of people any number of times, that the double space must have a line of double length for its side.
> MEN. It seems so.
> soc. Now do you imagine he would have attempted to *inquire* [ζητεῖν] or learn [μανθάνειν] what he thought he knew, when he did not know it, until he had been reduced to the perplexity of realizing that he did not know, and had felt a craving to know? (84b–c)

Thus, the resolution of the paradox is "Sokratic ignorance," the realization that one does not know what one thought one knew. It is achieved by starting with what the person being questioned concedes (75d) (as Sokrates had started with Meno's implicit concession that he knew what excellence is) and subjecting that "concession" to critical, dialectical examination. The paradox that is resolved, therefore, is not how it is possible to inquire about "a thing of whose nature you know *nothing at all* [τὸ παράπαν]" (80d).[27] It is the easier paradox allowed by Sokrates' restatement of Meno's paradox.

The dialectic cannot be carried beyond the elenchus, however, without the "craving to know." This is what the slave has, and Meno lacks.

And this is how Meno fails to achieve human excellence.

Any ancient reader of the dialogue would probably[28] have been familiar with Xenophon's account of Meno as the person who sold out the Ten Thousand Greek mercenaries fifteen hundred miles inside hostile territory and on the wrong side of the Euphrates (*Anabasis*, II.6.21–65). Such a reader would also have been familiar with Xenophon's description of Meno as an avaricious psychopath. In these terms having the dialogue open with Meno asking whether or not excellence (ἀρετή) can be taught is heavily ironic. Whatever human excellence is, Meno does not have it.

Plato has now shown in precise and explicit terms why this is the case. In doing so he has also shown the deep irony in the meaning of Meno's name: "he who stays where he is."

5

After the slave dialogue, when Meno demands that Sokrates return to the original question regarding not the nature, but the genesis of excellence, Sokrates proposes what he calls a "hypothetical approach" to the question. The comparison between his "example" of such an approach and his own proposed "hypothesis" seems odd. He states his proposal thus: "what kind of thing must [excellence] be in the class of mental properties, so as to be [taught (διδακτόν)][29] or not? In the first place if it is something dissimilar or similar to knowledge, is it [to be taught (διδακτόν)] or not—or as we were saying just now, remembered? Let us have no disputing about the name: is it [to be taught (διδακτόν)]?" (87b).

Sokrates' "geometrical example" of a hypothesis is: "if this area is such that when you apply it to the given line of the circle you find it falls short by a space similar to that which you have just applied, then I take it you have one consequence, and if it is impossible for it to fall so, then you have some other" (87a). Thus, Sokrates' example is a conditional proposition.

But his own "hypothesis" is not. Although his statement, "if it is something dissimilar or similar to knowledge, is it [to be taught] or not" (87b), has the appearance of a conditional proposition, the antecedent ("dissimilar *or* similar [ἀλλοῖον ἤ οἷον] to knowledge") is universal, and there is no consequent. Instead of giving Meno a conditional proposition, he has simply restated a part of Meno's question, "is excellence to be taught or not?" He immediately masks this by inserting the comment, "or as we were saying just now, remembered? Let us have no disputing about the name: is it [to be taught]?"

His next statement he calls "a fact plain to everyone" (87c), and presents it as an answer to the question he has just asked. This "fact" is "that the one and only thing taught [διδάσκεται] to men is knowledge"; and he appears to draw from this the conclusion that "if [excellence (ἀρετή)] is a kind of knowledge, clearly it [is to be taught (διδακτόν)]" (87c) (thereby subtly reintroducing the question, "what is excellence?").

If this is an inference it does not work. The argument would be: all things that are taught are knowledge, therefore, if excellence is a kind of knowledge it is taught. Such an argument would rest on a suppressed immediate inference that is invalid: all things that are taught are knowledge, therefore all knowledge consists of things that are taught.[30]

The non sequitur (if it is one)[31] is obvious to us, and we could reasonably expect it to be obvious to Plato as well, since much of the early part of the dialogue is taken up with a discussion of precisely the same fallacy. At 73d Meno asserts that "justice is [excellence (ἀρετή)]," to which Sokrates replies, "[Excellence], Meno, or an [excellence]?" (73e) pointing up the fact that the predicate of a universal affirmative proposition can include more than the subject. When Meno fails to understand the question, Sokrates gives him an illustration: "To take roundness, for instance; I should call it a figure, and not figure pure and simple. And I should name it so because there are other figures as well." Similarly (74c-d), "white" is not color, but a color.

The point is not inconsequential, since Sokrates is later (87c) to use this proposition ("if [excellence] is a kind of knowledge . . . it [is to be taught]'' as one premise in his argument for the claim that excellence is not a kind of knowledge. Although this argument is scattered over the pages to follow, it seems to have the following form: ''The one and only thing taught to men is knowledge'' (87c). ''If [excellence] is a kind of knowledge clearly it [is to be taught]'' (87c). ''If anything at all, not merely [excellence], is [to be taught (διδακτόν)],'' there must be teachers of it (89d). There are no teachers of excellence (96c). ''And if no teachers then no [learners (μαθηταί)]. . . .Hence [excellence] is not [to be taught]'' (96c). The conclusion, though unstated, follows clearly by *modus tollens*: therefore, excellence is not a kind of knowledge.

Although this argument seems to arrive at the conclusion that excellence is not a kind of knowledge, it brackets another argument that seems to imply that it is.

At 87d Sokrates says: ''Then if there is some good apart and separable from knowledge, it may be that [excellence] is not a kind of knowledge; but if there is nothing good that is not [encompassed (περιέχει)] by knowledge, our suspicion that [excellence] is a kind of knowledge would be [a right suspicion (ὀρθῶς ὑποπτεύοιμεν)].''

At 87e Sokrates argues that ''all good things are profitable [ὠφέλιμοι].'' The word, as in English, also has the broader meaning of ''beneficial,'' but its choice here is a satirical reminder to the reader of Meno's avarice—which in turn is so much a part of Meno's system of values that he appears to be oblivious to the different shades of meaning.

Physical things (health, strength, beauty, wealth) are ''profitable when the use is right, and harmful when it is not.'' Their use can be ''right'' consistently only if guided by knowledge of what ''right use''[32] is: ''[These things are] made profitable or harmful by the soul according as she uses them rightly or wrongly: just as in the case of the soul generally, we found that the guidance of [prudence (φρόνησις)][33] makes profitable the properties of the soul, while that of folly makes them harmful'' (88d-e).

In turning to ''goods of the soul,'' Sokrates attributes to Meno (''by these *you* understand'') the belief that these include such things as ''[moderation (σωφροσύνην)], justice, courage, [quickness to learn (εὐμαφίαν)],[34] memory, magnanimity'' (88a).

The inclusion of memory in this list points up the hazard of Meno's failure to distinguish between memory and knowledge. Sokrates says, ''Now tell me; such of these as *you* think are not knowledge, but different from knowledge—do they not sometimes harm us and sometimes profit us?" (88b, emphasis mine). Thus, if memory is different from knowledge and not guided by knowledge it can become harmful, and if Meno believes memory and knowledge to be the same he is at risk, although the precise nature of the risk is not yet clear.

Sokrates' major point is evident: "all the undertakings and endurances of the soul, when guided by [prudence (φρονήσεως)] end in happiness, but when folly guides, in the opposite" (88c).

He illustrates his point, using courage:

> For example, courage, if it is courage apart from prudence, and only a sort of boldness: when a man is bold without [mind (νοῦ)], he is harmed; but when he has [mind (νῷ)] at the same time, he is profited (88b).

So also with "moderation" and "quickness of learning":

> And the same holds for [moderation (σωφροσύνη)] and [quickness of learning (εὐμαφία)]: things learnt and coordinated with the aid of [mind (νοῦ)] are profitable, but without [mind] they are harmful (88b).

Thus:

> we may assert this as a universal rule, that in man all other things depend upon the soul, while the things of the soul herself depend upon [prudence (φρόνησιν)], if they are to be good; and so by this account the profitable will be [prudence (φρόνησις)], and [excellence], we say, is profitable (88e–89a).

Sokrates now draws the strongest conclusion his premises will allow, that "[excellence] is either wholly *or partly* [prudence]" (89a, emphasis mine).

Thus, this part of his argument clearly leaves open the possibility that excellence is partly knowledge and partly something else. This being the case, the two conclusions are not incompatible. The claim that excellence is knowledge would be false if excellence is only partly so.

The conclusion Sokrates actually draws at this point is more modest. Meno's opening question had been: "Can you tell me,

Socrates, whether [excellence is a thing to be taught (διδακτὸν ἡ ἀρετή)] or is acquired by practice, not teaching? Or if neither by practice nor by learning, whether it comes to mankind by nature or in some other way?'' (70a).

Sokrates concludes that at least one part of Meno's question has been answered: ''good men cannot be good by nature'' (89a), for ''if good men were so by nature, we surely should have had men able to discern who of the young were good by nature, and on their pointing them out we should have taken them over and kept them safe in the [acropolis (αχροπόλει)], having set our mark on them far rather than on our gold treasure, in order that none might have [corrupted (διέφθειρεν)] them.''

6

This is the point at which Sokrates returns to the question of whether or not excellence is knowledge: ''I do not withdraw as incorrect the statement that it is [to be taught (διδακτόν)] if it is knowledge, but as to its being knowledge, consider if you think I have grounds for misgiving'' (89d).

Two premises have been laid down at the time of Anytos' arrival. The first is that ''if anything at all, not merely [excellence], is [to be taught (διδακτόν) there must]...be teachers and learners of it'' (89d). The second (which may be inferred[35] from the first, since ''οὐκοῦν'' could be inviting assent either ''to an inference, or to an addition to what has already received assent'' [LSJ]) that ''if a thing had neither teachers nor learners, we should be right in surmising that it could not be taught'' (89e).

After Anytos joins them Sokrates pursues the question of how excellence is acquired in terms of who the teachers of excellence might be,[36] suggesting that: ''[One] should go to these men who profess to be teachers of [excellence (ἀρετῆs διδασκάλους)] and advertise themselves as the common teachers of the Greeks, and are ready to instruct anyone who chooses in return for fees charged on a fixed scale'' (91b); i.e., the sophists.

Anytos calls this suggestion insanity (μανία), claiming that the sophists are a ''[ruin (λώβη)] and corruption [διαφθορά] to those who frequent them.'' Anytos' claim contains a number of subtle ironies. ''Corruption of the youth,'' of course, is to be one of the charges he will bring against Sokrates in court. When dealing with this charge, Sokrates is to argue that knowingly to corrupt those around him would be foolish since the result would be to surround himself with corrupt people, and thereby endanger himself (*Apol.*, 25d–26a). This argument is foreshadowed in Sokrates' questions to Anytos here (92a): "Now are we to take it, according to you, that they wittingly deceived and [ruined (λωβᾶσθαι)] the youth, or that they were themselves unconscious of it? Are we to conclude those who are frequently termed the wisest of mankind to have been so [insane (μαίνεσθαι)] as that?"

On the other hand, Gorgias is portrayed here as the one who corrupted Meno and his "fellow Thessalians" by teaching them not how to acquire, but how to simulate wisdom; and who did so by persuading them that they have learned something if they can but remember it and repeat it at the proper stimulus (cf. above, p. 127). Thus, at least on this one point Anytos seems to be right, even though he does not know why.

Anytos, on the other hand, has protected himself from corruption by the sophists (92b): "I have never in my life had dealings with any of them, nor would I let any of my people have to do with them either." At this point Sokrates challenges Anytos to deal with the point Sokrates himself refused to deal with in Meno's paradox:

> soc. Then you have absolutely [ἄπειρος] no experience of those persons?
> an. And trust I never may.
> soc. How then, my good sir, can you tell whether a thing has any good or evil in it if you are [absolutely (ἄπειρος)] without experience of it?

When Anytos replies by merely repeating his claim to know without any experience of the sophists that they are corrupters of the youth, Sokrates raises the question of who else might teach excellence to Meno. Anytos replies "Why mention a particular one? Any Athenian gentleman he comes across, without exception, will do him more good, if he will do as he is bid, than the sophists" (92e) (just as, at Sokrates' trial, Meletos was to argue [*Apol.*, 24d–25a] that the young can learn to be good from anyone in Athens except Sokrates).

Thus, yet another possible way of acquiring excellence is being proposed. The source of excellence is "Athenian gentlemen," and the process by which it is acquired is "to do as one is bid."[37]

In reply to this, Sokrates elicits from Anytos the further claim that the Athenian gentlemen "must have learnt in their turn from the older generation, who were gentlemen" (93a). Thus, this new way is subject, ironically, to the same objection raised above[38] concerning the doctrine of recollection. Just as that doctrine had been stated in such a way as to imply an infinite regress of recollections that cannot account for learning, those "Athenian gentlemen" (92e) must also have learned from an earlier generation of "Athenian gentlemen," and so on to infinity. In this case, however, even if one should accept the idea of an infinite number of previous lives there can be no suggestion that there has been an infinite number of generations of "Athenian gentlemen." On the other hand, if those "Athenian gentlemen" learned excellence by some other method, then some other more direct method is possible, and Meno should not look to the "Athenian gentlemen" as a way of gaining excellence, since that would give it to him at second hand and might be subject to error. Rather should he look to the way in which they learned it so as to learn it directly for himself.[39] But that raises the issue of what such a method might be, bringing them back to "whether [excellence is a thing to be taught] or is acquired by practice, not teaching? Or if neither by practice nor by learning, whether it comes to mankind by nature or in some other way" (70a). In short, Anytos' advice as to the source from which one might acquire excellence fails in precisely the same way that the doctrine of recollection fails to furnish a source for learning of any kind.

Sokrates now turns to the Athenian gentlemen themselves: "And our inquiry into this problem resolves itself into the question: Did the good men of our own and of former times know how to transmit to another man the [excellence] in respect of which they were good, or is it something not to be transmitted or taken over from one human being to another?"

Anytos admits that Themistokles, Aristeides, Perikles and Thukydides were all Athenian gentlemen of the highest rank and principles, and that they did everything in their power to educate their sons, yet failed to pass on to them their own excellence. Their sons learned such arts as horsemanship, music, gymnastics "and all else that comes under the heading of the arts" (94b) because the fathers, who were excellent, told them to do so. Therefore, Anytos' method—doing as Athenian gentlemen tell them to do—also fails.

At this point another of the possibilities raised in Meno's initial question has been dealt with: if excellence cannot be acquired by doing as one is told, even by people who themselves have excellence, then excellence cannot be acquired by practice.

When Sokrates states the conclusion these examples suggest ("it looks as though virtue were not a teachable thing"), Anytos' response is to hurl a thinly veiled threat at Sokrates and leave (94e): "Socrates, I consider you are too apt to speak ill of people. I, for one, if you will take my advice, would warn you to be careful: in most cities it is probably easier to do people harm than good, and particularly in this one; I think you know that yourself" (94e–95a).

Any ancient reader would have known that Anytos was to lead the prosecution resulting in Sokrates' execution. By stating the threat in this way Plato has reflected it against Meno's earlier statement to Sokrates that: "You are well advised, I consider, in not voyaging or taking a trip away from home; for if you went on like this as a stranger in any other city you would very likely be taken up for a wizard" (80b).

The implication, of course, is that there is no place where one such as Sokrates can expect to be safe.

By leaving, Anytos demonstrates that he will no more expose his opinions to Sokrates than he will to those he calls "sophists," that in fact he is incapable of distinguishing between Sokrates and the sophists—a failure that explains his prosecution of Sokrates.

Meno was shown above[40] to be less than fully human because he lacked the desire to learn. Now it may be seen that Anytos is in a still worse case. Whereas Meno could be brought, however reluctantly, to Sokratic ignorance, Anytos not only lacks the desire to learn, he refuses to be taught that he does not know what he thinks he knows. In that sense he is even less human than Meno.

After Anytos' departure, Sokrates and Meno agree that "neither the sophists nor the men who are themselves good and honourable are teachers of [excellence]," and that if this is the case, "clearly no others can be" (96b). But as they have already agreed, if there are no teachers of excellence, then it is not to be taught. This leads Meno to restate his question: "And that makes me wonder, I must say, Socrates, whether perhaps there are no good men at all, or by what possible sort of process good people can come to exist" (96d).

Sokrates' apparent answer to this is that since "true opinion" is as good a guide to action as knowledge, those who are good are so because they have a true opinion of excellence, even though they do not have knowledge of it. The difficulty with true opinions, however, is that like Daidalos' statues, so long as they stay with us, [they] are a fine possession, and effect all that is good; but they do not care to stay for long, and run away out of the human soul" (97e–98a). Thus, if those who are excellent are so because they have a true opinion of excellence, this opinion will not stay with them, and they will cease to be excellent. Those who were described as having excellence—Themistokles, Aristeides and the rest—were also viewed as being men of excellence throughout their lives, not just fleetingly. Therefore, true opinion cannot account for the excellence of such people.

At 98a Sokrates argues that the difference between knowledge and true opinion is that knowledge is tied down "with causal reasoning [αἰτίασ λογισμῷ]." This, as pointed out above,[41] parallels the definition of knowledge given in the *Symposium* (202a). In both cases the implication is that knowledge can be no better than the reasons one can give in support of it. Thus, any given item of knowledge would necessarily have to give way before more reasons for another, different belief.[42] The more reasons one can give in support of a belief, the firmer that belief will be, but no belief can be regarded as wholly unshakable. In other words here, as in the *Symposium*, knowledge is in its essence dialectical. And any given instance of knowledge must be viewed as open to the possibility of change.

On the other hand, the doctrine of recollection implies that once something has been learned, one needs only to recall it in order to have knowledge of it. This in turn implies that that which is known cannot change over time. It must be the same now when it is recalled as it was in the past, the time from which it is recalled. Thus, Sokrates' definition of knowledge is incompatible with the doctrine of recollection—just as, in the *Symposium* the same definition of knowledge was incompatible with the doctrine of forms as presented in that dialogue, and for essentially the same reasons. Even if the doctrine of recollection should not entail the doctrine of forms, it does entail the immutability of knowledge.

This is not to say that such information as how to double the area of a given square will change—although better methods might be discovered. The kind of knowledge Sokrates and Meno tied to excellence was φρόνησις, prudence, that practical wisdom that leads to the "right use" that "makes profitable the properties of soul" (88d–e). In that sense knowing how to double the area of a given square is in itself of little worth. It becomes "profitable" only when one knows how to use it.

Once the slave learns how to double the area of a given square, he is in a position to discover that he does not know what to do with his knowledge. If he pursues his ignorance in one direction, he might ask himself if this method would work with other plane figures such as rectangles, triangles or circles. He might thus be led into an exploration bit by bit of the whole of plane geometry. From that, he might ask what "shape" in general is, a question that could lead him to Sokrates' definition of it as "limit of the solid" (76a)—which in turn would take him into the intricacies of solid geometry.

At any point he might realize that he could branch off in another direction and look for applications of what he was learning to other aspects of his life. This might lead him into anything from surveying to measuring the heights of the pyramids and the distances of ships at sea, to navigation.[43]

At each point, the process would be the same. He would discover his ignorance. That discovery would point the way to a significant question, the answer to which would lead him to another question. In this way each piece of knowledge, as the antecedent of an unknown consequent, would function as a signpost to the next question. And if "all nature is akin," each answer, by showing another link in the interconnectedness of things, would add more reasons in support of the knowledge the slave has.

And this may be the underlying meaning of Sokrates' statement (85c–d) that "at this moment those opinions have just been stirred up in him, like a dream; but if he were repeatedly asked these same questions in a variety of forms, you know he will have in the end as exact an understanding of them as anyone."

After giving his definition of knowedge, Sokrates goes on to say (98b): "And indeed I . . . speak as one who does not know, but only conjectures: yet that there is a difference between right opinion and knowledge is not at all a conjecture with me but something I would particularly assert that I knew.

In other words, even though Sokrates does not give reasons in support of this belief, he is claiming that he can. (That Meno does not challenge him to do so, though unfortunate, cannot at this point come as a surprise to the reader.) Earlier (86b–c), he had expressed the determination "to do battle, so far as [he was] able, both in word and deed" for his "belief in the duty of inquiring after what we do not know." That, however, was a belief. Now he is making a still stronger claim to know that there is a difference between knowledge and "right opinion [ὀρθὴ δόξα]." This conviction in turn would seem to be a pretty good "reason for believing" that we have a duty to inquire—in which case the latter would qualify as knowledge whether the first did or not.

These claims fit with the earlier implication that the pursuit of knowledge is more important than the attainment of it, and they can only make sense in terms of that implication.

Any reason Sokrates might give for his claim that there is a difference between right opinion and knowledge would seem to rest on some sort of metaphysical claim which would free him of the kind of radical relativism asserted by the sophists.[44] Any absolute metaphysical claims, however, would run counter to the definition of knowledge propounded here.

In point of fact there seems to be only one clearly metaphysical claim in Meno. This is at 81d, where he says that "all nature is akin." If taken in context with the doctrine of recollection, this explains how the dialectic leads one from one "reminder" to another in the pursuit of knowledge. On the other hand, if taken in the present context, it points toward (but does not fully commit him to)[45] an organic metaphysics—which, since it entails degrees of truth and falsity, makes Sokrates' definition of knowledge possible. Sokrates "knows" that there is a difference between right opinion and knowledge because each "reason" that is added to and deepens any given belief adds also to the "reasons for believing" the underlying implication that all nature is organically interlinked.

When Meno first posed the question of how excellence is to be acquired (70a), he raised three possibilities: that it can be taught, that it is acquired by practice, or by nature. All three of these have now been rejected, and in their place, the apparent conclusion of the dialogue is that "[excellence] comes to us by a divine dispensation, when it does come" (100b); i.e., it is a gift from the gods.

Sokrates' "hypothesis," ended with the conclusion (89a) "that [excellence] is either wholly or partly [prudence ($\phi\varrho\acute{o}\nu\eta\sigma\iota\nu$)]." The reason for this qualification should now be apparent. Sokrates had been arguing that human excellence consists of the pursuit of knowledge, the human capacity to carry on dialectic. But the dialectic has two components, one of which is knowledge of one's ignorance. This is a kind of knowledge, and can be taught—even to one as flawed as Meno.

The other requirement is that having discovered one's ignorance, one have the desire to correct it. But the desire to learn cannot be taught, since one would have to have it in order to learn it. In this sense the desire to learn is "a gift of the gods," but by no means one reserved to the few. It is one thing that every infant brings into the world at birth, and could not survive without, since the infant would not otherwise be able to learn such necessities of survival as language, the sources of food, etc.[46]

Plato's point can be reframed in a slightly different way: Sokratic ignorance is the discovery of one of a person's limits. To know oneself is to know one's limits. Thus the elenchus, by which one arrives at Sokratic ignorance, is a process of exploring oneself, of arriving at self-knowledge. Now, however, it is clear that self-knowledge is not enough. Meno, a man of profound vice, can be taught his ignorance and thus can arrive at self-knowledge. What is needed in order to acquire human excellence, to complete oneself as a human being, is Sokratic ignorance together with the desire to learn. But just as the one leads to knowledge of one's limits, and therefore to knowledge of oneself, the other results in moving those limits back, if only so far as one has reasons to support the movement. To move one's limits, to thus enlarge oneself, is to create oneself. In this important sense, human excellence is a process of self-creation.

But the desire to learn is also the one thing that can be destroyed by a bad education, by persuading one, as Gorgias had persuaded Meno, that one has knowledge if one can at the proper stimulus repeat what one has heard. This is the corruption of one's humanity. In that sense human excellence, ἀρετή, is to reserve to oneself the power to create oneself.

The risk Meno runs[47] in confusing memory with knowledge is the risk that one will fail to become fully human.

Thus both of the apparent conclusions are correct, and they are not, as they appear to be, contradictory. Excellence is a kind of knowledge—knowledge of one's ignorance—together with a gift of the gods—the desire to learn. And this is the deeper irony in Sokrates' parting comment: "But the certainty of this we shall only know when, before asking in what way [excellence] comes to mankind, we set about inquiring what [excellence] is, in and of itself."

Notes

Introduction

1. New Haven: Yale University Press, 1968 (second edition, with notes, 1987).

2. I did hear once of a spiritualist institution, supposedly in Florida, where the faculty consisted entirely of mediums. They claimed that their Plato course was taught by Plato himself.

3. G. R. F. Ferrari, *Listening to the Cicadas* (Cambridge: Cambridge University Press, 1987), p. 86. I would add that despite my criticisms this work in my opinion contains some of the most important work that has been done on *Phaidros* in recent years and is indispensable to any attempt to understand that dialogue.

4. *De Senect.* §5.

5. Despite Rosen's promise (p. lxii) to limit his references to other dialogues to instances in which "these references are indicated within the *Symposium* by Plato himself," Rosen seems peculiarly susceptible to this temptation, making such connections when the references to the *Symposium* are either nebulous or nonexistent—or at any rate if they do exist he fails to point them out—and even referring to dialogues that almost certainly were written later, perhaps much later. (E.g. the excursion into the *Republic* and *Laws* beginning on page 69, taking as its point of departure that for Plato "wisdom alone is good in itself"—a statement denied by Diotima and Sokrates at 204e–205a—and continuing into a discussion of the Athenian Stranger's objections to homosexuality.) Such straightforward references would seem to be particularly hazardous for one who, like Rosen, believes much of Plato's philosophy to be concealed beneath the surface.

6. An exception to this is in "Socrates' Concept of Piety," *Jo. of Hist. of Phil.*, vol. 5, no. 1, where I tried to build a case that *Euthyphro*, the *Apology*, and *Krito* were intended to be read together. Other dialogues, of course, (e.g., *Parmenides*, *Theaitetos*, the *Sophist* and the *Statesman*) may also have been intended to be read together, but such questions are beyond the scope of the present essay.

Chapter 1.

1. The Dionysian aspects of the *Symposium* have been discussed in a number of studies—Rosen (*Plato's Symposium*), Brentlinger (in his

introduction to *The Symposium of Plato*, Groden, Brentlinger and Baskin, U. of Massachusetts Press, 1970), and Diskin Clay ("The Tragic and Comic Poet of the *Symposium*," in *Essays in Ancient Greek Philosophy*, vol. II edited by John Anton and Anthony Preus, SUNY Press, Albany, 1983, pp. 186–202), to mention only three. Clay in particular points out much of the material dealt with here, and although he handles it differently and ends up in a somewhat different place, for the most part those differences are in emphasis rather than in content. Clay's conclusion that "it is Socrates, or Eros, or whatever name it is right to call this *daimon*, who fills the gap between the high and the low, gods and men, and makes a whole of tragedy and comedy, binding this whole to himself" strikes me as somewhat overblown, but his major point about the unity of tragedy, comedy and philosophy seems undeniable. What unites them, and is missing in Clay's treatment, is Dionysos in his role as the life force.

2. Although some of these sources are late, Aristophanes' identification of Phanes with Eros suggests that at least in that case the later sources reflect a tradition going back to the fifth century B.C.E. For an analysis of the identification of Phanes, Eros and Dionysos as an Orphic doctrine, see W. K. C. Guthrie, *Orpheus and Greek Religion* (London: Methuen, 1935, 1952), pp. 84–127. Guthrie also portrays Phanes/Eros/Dionysos as the life force: "[Phanes] is Eros, because the usual Greek mythological substitute for evolution was not simply creation but procreation. Life springs from Love, and so Love has to be there before life in order to provide the vital force which will mingle or marry two beings that further beings may be produced. . . . Phanes again is Zeus, or rather Zeus became Phanes by the process of swallowing him, and finally Phanes is Dionysos because in that form he was reborn from Zeus" (pp. 100–101). Although Plato draws freely on this tradition this should not be taken to imply either that an Orphic cult existed in the fifth century, or if it did, that Plato was narrowly committed to such a view. For a brief account of some of the scholarly controversy surrounding Orpheus and the Orphic cult, see Emmet Robbins, "Famous Orpheus," in *Orpheus, the Metamorphosis of a Myth*, ed. John Warden (Toronto: University of Toronto Press, 1982), pp. 11–21.

3. Martha C. Nussbaum, *The Fragility of Goodness* (Cambridge: Cambridge Univ. Press, 1986), pp. 194–5.

4. See chapter 4 for my attempt to unpack this rather turgid phrase.

5. This portrayal of Dionysos as the life force is another instance of the assimilation to a male of the power of giving life, a move similar to that of Athene as well as Dionysos being born of Zeus—or Eve of Adam. The fact that the Greeks (and later, the Romans) portrayed Dionysos as effeminate, and even as a transvestite, is perhaps a tacit admission that the

life force ought not to be gendered. That he, too, was born of Zeus seems to be another reaffirmation of his male lineage, possibly a riposte to his alleged effeminacy. Medicine of the time was divided on the question of the male role in conception. Hippokratic physicians, to be followed by Aristotle, viewed the mother as no more than a receptacle, supplying nutriment to the sperm until it was mature enough for birth. Empedokles, on the other hand, claimed that both the mother and the father contributed both to the substance and to the structure of the embryo (cf. Empedokles fr. 63, quoted p. 33 and Aristotle, *Generation of Animals*, 764b4–20, 722b7–17).

6. At 207c–208b. The implications of this are taken up in chapter 4, sections 6 and 7 (as well as in the Appendix, pp. 147–151), where this passage is discussed at some length.

7. The question of where to place *Meno* in relation to the *Symposium* in the development of Plato's thought can only be answered in terms of internal evidence. That both dialogues contain the same definition of knowledge is beyond dispute (see ch. 4, sec. 2). The theme discussed here of "being human" as a process of self-creation by means of the dialectic may be found in Plato's earliest dialogues (cf. "Socrates' Concept of Piety," *Jour. of the Hist. of Philosophy*, vol. 5, no. 1), but in both *Meno* and the *Symposium* it is also tied to the definition of knowledge (cf. Appendix, *passim*). Moreover, there is reason to believe that both are so written as to engage the reader in a dialectic with Plato (cf. ch. 5, sec. 3 and 4, as well as the Appendix). Such evidence is by no means conclusive, but it does suggest strongly that both dialogues were written at a time when these themes occupied a central place in Plato's thought. An analysis of *Meno* is included as an appendix in the belief that the two will be mutually illuminating.

8. This is acted out in a very explicit way in *Oedipos Rex*, for example, where the hero literally does not know who he is. The theme is handled more subtly, but equally clearly in *Antigone*, where Kreon attempts to find his identity in his office rather than in his family relationships. Other Greek tragedies can be seen to develop the concept of hubris in essentially similar ways.

9. The implications of this for knowledge are central to the considerations of chapters 4 and 5.

10. This theme is developed at length in the chapters to follow.

11. The question of Diotima's existence is discussed below, ch. 4, sec. 1, and notes 2 and 18 to that chapter. There is no need to compare this to the treatment of poetry in the *Republic* in order to see that Plato has taken care to keep the discussion of forms at a considerable remove from his reader.

12. Except as noted I follow the Lamb translation in the Loeb Library ed., vol. V (London and Cambridge, 1925).

13. Cf. the analysis of Alkibiades' speech, ch. 6, sec. 2.

14. Literally, "wine and truth."

15. Cf. pp. 14–15. Also ch. 6, sec. 2.

16. Cf. ch. 6, sec. 2 and 3.

17. K. J. Dover, *Greek Popular Morality in the Time of Plato and Aristotle* (Oxford: Basil Blackwell, 1974), p. 210. Also Dover, *Symposium* (Cambridge: Cambridge Univ. Press, 1980), commentary to 176e6, p. 87.

18. Since (see ch. 6, sec. 4) Eryximakhos seems to view the conversation he is proposing as preliminary to sexual activity among the guests, the fact that Apollo is credited with introducing homosexuality to the Greeks may not be irrelevant at this point.

19. Ch. 3, sec. 3. As Nussbaum *The Fragility of Goodness*, (n., p. 466) points out, Aristophanes' hiccoughs have been discussed at some length by Plochmann, Guthrie, Rosen and others. Clay, who understands their significance in manipulating the order of the speeches, sees the direct manipulator as Plato rather than Dionysos, and sees the hiccoughs portrayed as "an accident" ("The Tragic and Comic Poet," p. 188). He goes on to argue that "[Plato's] apparent arrangement is to separate Aristophanes and Agathon by Eryximachus and Aristodemus. But when the sequence of praise that moves toward Socrates from left to right is dislocated by Aristophanes' hiccough, the underlying plan of the dialogue is revealed. Comic and tragic poet are brought together" (p. 189). Although I see the significance of this move differently, the two interpretations are not mutually exclusive. The move functions both to put Aristophanes' speech after Eryximakhos' and before Agathon's.

20. Clay suggests that "if Aristophanes has any cue for these eruptions it must be Eryximachus' repetition of the word *kosmion* [order]" (p. 188). (His reference to 189c seems to be a misprint. He is probably referring to Aristophanes' comment at 189a that "the orderly [κόσμιον] principle of the body should call for [ἐπιθυμεῖ] the noises and titillations involved in sneezing.")

21. Nussbaum (*The Fragility of Goodness*, p. 194) points out, but does not analyze the connection between Agathon's request that Dionysos judge between them (175e) and Alkibiades, ivy-wreathed, appearing and seeming to make such a judgment.

22. Clay comments that "under the influence of Dionysos [Alkibiades] has placed a crown on the head of the κάλλιστος [i.e., Agathon] and

σοφώτατος—σοφώτατος not in the sense of poetic skill, but in another sense of this word which describes the wisest and most eloquent of all men" (p. 190).

23. The most notable example of this, perhaps being in Euripides' *Bakkhai*.

24. Cf. sec. 3 of this chapter.

25. These identifications are discussed at length in ch. 6, sec. 2 and 3.

26. That the dialectic is one way that Dionysos speaks through Sokrates is discussed in ch. 6.

27. I find myself in disagreement here with Rosen (*Plato's Symposium*, p. 290), who gives this office to Eryximakhos, and also with Dover (*Symposium*, p. 11), who, although he does not commit himself, leans toward Eryximakhos as occupying that role.

28. This interruption might be seen as motivated by self-protection, since Sokrates is about to attack Agathon at a point where what he says reflects a position adopted by Phaidros (cf. ch. 2, sec. 1). Such an interpretation, however, would imply that Phaidros has a much clearer understanding of his own statements than seems to be the case. In any event, if Phaidros did not have considerable authority over the others Sokrates would not be likely to submit without question, as he does here.

Chapter 2.

1. In some cases, although I shall end up with a very different interpretation, my analysis of these earlier speeches—particularly those of Phaidros and Pausanias—owes a fairly obvious debt to Stanley Rosen, *Plato's Symposium*, chapters 2 and 3.

2. Kenneth Dover, *Symposium*, (Cambridge: Cambridge University Press, 1980), p. 91. This theme is also developed at length in his *Greek Popular Morality in the Time of Plato and Aristotle*, (Oxford: Blackwell, 1974), 230–242.

3. As pointed out above (ch. 1, n. 7), Plato may have held this view even in his earliest writings. Cf. "Socrates' Concept of Piety," *Jour. of the Hist. of Philosophy*, vol. 5, no. 1. (Jan. 1967).

4. Phaidros perceives as the norm that one lover (ἄνδρα ὅστις ἐρᾷ) would have one "favorite" (παιδικῶν), but that one "beloved" (ἐρώμενον) would have more than one lover (ἐραστάς). This fits with his perception of the beloved as the stimulus to all the lover's actions.

5. This theme is developed at length in chapters 4 and 5.

6. Kenneth Dover, *Greek Homosexuality* (Cambridge, Mass.: Harvard University Press, 1978), passim.

7. The claim presented here mythologically (and not clearly understood by Phaidros) that Eros is in the lover rather than the beloved is to form the center of Sokrates' view of love. Cf. below, pp. 61, 72-75.

8. Yet another instance of the male god portrayed as giving birth to the goddess (cf. ch. 1, n. 5). In this case Plato clearly sees the situation as grotesque. On one level he is using it to reveal the extent to which Pausanias' view of love is distorted, but since Pausanias is portrayed as reflecting the Athenian view of love, Plato is also showing the extent to which the Athenian view is distorted.

9. Although the characters—at least in the earlier parts of the dialogue—are males speaking about male love relationships, what Plato, the author, is saying about them is intended to apply to any love relationship whatever—as implied in Sokrates' claim that he learned about love from a woman.

10. That this was nevertheless the prevalent view in Athens, as Pausanias says, is attested to by the fact that Alkibiades expected to establish just such a relationship with Sokrates (217a and 218c-d). Cf. ch. 6, pp. 115-117, 121.

11. Although there seems to be little evidence, as Rosen would have it (*Plato's Symposium*, p. 73ff.), that Pausanias was physically unattractive, he may well have felt the terrors of inadequacy. At any rate I tend to agree with Rosen's claim that Pausanias presents this argument for constancy in hopes of preventing the flight of the beloved. There is no evidence that his relationship with Agathon broke up, and there is some reason (cf. Dover, *Symposium*, note to 177d8, p. 89; Aelian, *Varia historia*, 2.21) to believe that Pausanias even followed Agathon to Macedon (at the least indicating that he valued his relationship with Agathon more than his relationship with Athens). I lean toward an explanation of this in terms of Pausanias developing a power relation with Agathon, then using it to destroy Agathon's will (cf. pp. 49-50). Having gained such ascendancy, once his victim was compelled to leave Athens Pausanias found it it easier to follow than to go through the apprehensions and the difficulties of trying to establish another such relationship.

12. Although disputed by Empedokles and his school, (cf. ch. 1, n. 5; ch. 3, p. 33) this myth reflects the popular belief at the time that the role of the woman in procreation was solely that of a receptacle where the sperm of the male developed into an infant ready for birth. In this case that role was taken over by the sea.

13. The view of procreation as resulting from "chance" encounters reflects Empedokles' view, and is played upon briefly both by Eryximakhos and Aristophanes. Cf. ch. 3, esp. pp. 42–43.

Chapter 3.

1. Rosen (*Plato's Symposium*, p. 66, n. 18; p. 94f.; 109ff.) notes, but discounts the possibility that Eryximakhos' speech is built on an Empedoklean foundation. He relegates to a footnote (p. 139, n. 48) the only connection he notes between Empedokles and Aristophanes' speech. There is danger in the argument that follows that what I have done is develop an interpretation of Empedokles from Eryximakhos' speech, and then interpreted Eryximakhos' speech in terms of that interpretation of Empedokles. What I have tried to do is show that the medical theory propounded by Eryximakhos is wholly consistent with one common interpretation of Empedokles' "cosmic cycle." This is suggestive, considering the fact that much of what Eryximakhos says of love and strife almost certainly comes from Empedokles.

The purpose of the present essay is to explore the *Symposium*. Any exploration of Empedokles must remain subsidiary to that. For that reason I cannot here pursue the controversies that have arisen over the interpretation of Empedokles' work. I do not therefore suggest that this interpretation should be viewed as more than an interesting possibility resting on a more or less traditional interpretation.

2. Kathleen Freeman, *The Pre-Socratic Philosophers* (Oxford: Basil Blackwell and Mott, Ltd., 1946), p. 177, n. 4.

3. *Lives of the Philosophers.* I have relied primarily on Caponigri's translation (Chicago: Henry Regnery Co., 1969). Empedokles is the subject of chapter VIII, pp. 57–66.

4. Ibid., p. 57.

5. Ibid., p. 59.

6. Ibid., p. 60.

7. Ibid., p. 61.

8. Ibid., p. 63.

9. Ibid., p. 66.

10. Unless otherwise noted, all translations of Empedokles are from M. R. Wright, *Empedocles: The Extant Fragments*, (New Haven and London: Yale University Press, 1981). These are from pp. 261 and 264. I have used the Diehls-Kranz numbering of the Fragments.

160   THE MASKS OF DIONYSOS

11. Most (but not all) of the interpetations adopted here are consistent with those of David O'Brien, *Empedocles' Cosmic Cycle* (Cambridge: Cambridge University Press, 1969). For an introductory summary of a few of the issues, cf. A. A. Long, "Empedocles' Cosmic Cycle in the 'Sixties,'" in *The Pre-Socratics*, ed. P. D. Mourelatos, (Garden City, N.Y.: Doubleday, 1974). *The Poem of Empedocles, A Text and Translation With an Introduction,* by Brad Inwood (Toronto: University of Toronto Press, 1992) contains an excellent up-to-date bibliography.

12. The internal brackets mark where Wright has broken the fragment into two parts. I am indebted to Professor Robert Turnbull for pointing out that since "harmony" in any modern understanding of that term was unknown in the music of the Greeks, "attunement" is probably a less misleading translation of ἁρμονίαν than is "harmony."

13. Except for a number of references to Aphrodite (or Kupris), the only exception to this seems to be in fr. 109, where he used στοργήν.

14. Nothing in the available fragments seems to suggest that Empedokles recognized that his use of the attraction of like for like makes his use of strife redundant.

15. On Apollo as god of order, cf. ch. 6, sec. 5.

16. Freeman, *Pre-Socratic Philosophers*, p. 200. (Just as today the advocates of "holistic medicine" are likely to be under attack from modern followers of Hippokrates.)

17. This might be taken as a reference to Pythagoras rather than Empedokles; however, there is considerable evidence that Pythagoreanism was well known in Akragas in Empedokles' time. (This has received support from archeological evidence of Pythagorean influence on the design of the Olympieion. Cf. Malcom Bell, "Stylobate and Roof in the Olympieion at Akragas," *Am. Jour. of Arch.*, vol. 84, no. 3.) More directly, the tradition strongly suggests that Empedokles was at least well acquainted with Pythagoreanism, and may at one time have been a member of the cult. (Cf. Diogenes Laertius, p. 58.) Thus, although the extant fragments do not touch on musical "attunements," Empedokles' use of the concept, together with his knowledge of Pythagoreanism make it unlikely that he would have omitted this from his consideration of the role of love in his system.

18. Although Eryximakhos leaves open the question of what the purpose might be, that purpose still seems to lie outside the love relationship. Thus again, although his view is not made explicit, like Phaidros and Pausanias, Eryximakhos sees the relationship between lover and beloved as essentially prostitutional.

19. This theme is picked up later by Sokrates. Cf. ch. 5, sec. 1.

20. Cf. ch. 1, p. 12.

21. Ibid.

22. For a particularly thorough analysis of Aristophanes' myth as a satire of the human condition, see Nussbaum, *The Fragility of Goodness*, pp. 172–73.

23. Following Wright in the conflation of these two fragments.

24. This may in part reflect the claim that after sexual differentiation cold produces female (fr. 65) while warmth produces male (fr. 67).

25. Cf. Pausanias' description of the "baser" love, ch. 2, p. 27 above.

26. Jeffrey Henderson (*The Maculate Muse* Yale, New Haven, 1975 pp. 52–53) points out "the pronounced tendency of the Greeks to lay more stress on the sexual *instinct* itself than on the *object*; in glorifying the former they were much freer than we are to vary sexual objects on their relative merits. . . . The only kinds of perversion remarked by the comic poets are cases in which sexual acts other than vaginal intercourse, otherwise perfectly proper, are carried to excess or practiced in an inappropriate setting."

27. Significantly, Aristophanes puts this healing power in the hands of Hephaistos, god of the crafts, rather than giving it to Apollo, who had been given the task of sewing them up in such a way as to make permanent their separation.

28. Cf. Nussbaum, *The Fragility of Goodness*, p. 175.

29. Agathon's purpose in saying this is not to apologize in advance for a poor delivery, but rather (as Sokrates' comments suggest) to call attention to what he expects to be an outstanding performance—thereby pointing out even before he begins his speech the importance he places on appearance, on style.

30. Rosen, mistakenly, I believe, interprets this interchange (*Plato's Symposium*, p. 167) as developing the contrast between shame and nobility, rather than between shame and guilt.

31. A yet deeper irony appears later in Alkibiades' speech (cf. below, p. 121). Agathon had said, "I hope you do not always fancy me so puffed up with the playhouse as to forget that an intelligent speaker is more alarmed at a few men of wit than at a host of fools." Alkibiades, replicating the position voiced by Pausanias (Agathon's lover) that by having sex with Sokrates he can improve his soul, also reflects this statement of Agathon's (218d): "So I should feel a far worse shame before sensible people for not gratifying such a friend than I should before the senseless multitude for gratifying him."

32. Such a statement would ignore, for example, the discord resulting from Medea's love of Jason or Helen's love of Paris, both of which were caused by Eros, and both of which came long after the creation of humans. This is to say nothing of wars among humans, or of the hostility the gods show for each other during the Trojan War, or even in competing for human sex partners.

33. Although Sokrates later (199c) compliments Agathon for drawing this distinction between "display[ing] the character" of Eros and "treat[ing] of his acts," this does not indicate that Sokrates concurs either in the claim that none of the others has said anything about Eros' character, or in the character that Agathon attributes to Eros. The latter, of course, is clear in Sokrates' opening discussion with Agathon.

34. Lamb goes so far as to suggest in a footnote to 195e that as Agathon speaks he "smiles at or touches the bald head of Socrates."

35. Rosen (*Plato's Symposium*, p. 176) sees this passage (195b) as an attempt on Agathon's part to drive a wedge between Phaidros and Eryximakhos as part of a strategy for seducing Phaidros. Since both Phaidros and Agathon are *eromenoi* (and, presumably, even Agathon would not want to extend the attraction of "like to like" that far), it seems more likely that Agathon would see Phaidros as a rival.

36. Later Sokrates, then Alkibiades, will identify Eros with Dionysos, but there is no reason to believe that Agathon is making any such identification here. Rather is he contrasting Eros with the other gods in order to show their subservience to him.

37. Clearly I list myself among those commentators who, according to Rosen (*Plato's Symposium*, pp. 159–60) have failed to "discern the importance of Agathon's speech," and "can say that it has almost no content."

38. Cf. his portrayal in *Thesmophoriazusai*. Dover (*Greek Homosexuality*, p. 144) rightly points out that "whether he declined an active heterosexual role, and whether he wore feminine clothing, we do not know." Agathon himself would have been absent from Athens for a generation or more by the time the *Symposium* was published. Aristophanes' play, however, would have been known to Plato's readers, and whether the accusation was true or not would have had little significant effect on the way he was viewed by the Athenians.

Chapter 4.

1. Although this appears to soften Sokrates' otherwise rather rough treatment of Agathon by having Sokrates in effect adopt Agathon's role,

the fact that he puts his speech into the mouth of a woman would have at least irked most of the previous speakers. That he claimed to have used a woman's argument to defeat Agathon would have been still more irksome. The fact that he goes on to claim that he learned about love from a woman (201d) would have been seen by them as a direct challenge to their assertions regarding the superiority of male homosexual relations over all others.

2. The question, of course, has been much debated over the years. (Cf. Andrea Nye, "The Hidden Host: Irigaray and Diotima at Plato's *Symposium*," *Hypatia*, vol. 3, no. 3 [Winter 1989] for a recent differing opinion.) There is no independent evidence of her existence, so any such argument must come to rest primarily on what is in the dialogue itself. Rosen (*Plato's Symposium*, pp. 223–24) plays on the resemblance between Diotima in the *Symposium* and Aspasia, as protrayed in *Menexenos*, suggesting that "we may playfully but instructively regard Diotima, Anaxagoras, and Aspasia as Socrates' early teachers concerning beauty, truth and goodness respectively." He limits his discussion to the "Socrates who is a persona in the Platonic dialogues" (p. 221), who he seems to regard as the same through all the dialogues, and specifically rejects any attempt to correlate that character with the historical Sokrates. On the other hand Aiskhines of Sphettos, a member of the historical Sokrates' circle, apparently wrote a play called *Aspasia*, in which he claimed that she taught Sokrates philosophy just as the *Menexenos* (235e) has her teaching him rhetoric. If true, then since in this dialogue Sokrates appears to have learned philosophy from Diotima (cf. p. 81), she may in fact be a surrogate for Aspasia. Although such questions are not directly relevant to the concerns of the present essay, the possibility that the historical Aspasia taught philosophy to the historical Sokrates raises the fascinating possibility that the main stream of Western philosophy was of a woman born.

3. Cf. above, ch. 2, pp. 25–26. A reference to Orpheus would in this context be inappropriate, and Kodros' sacrifice is substituted in its stead. Rosen (*Plato's Symposium*, p. 257) also sees this passage as a reference to Phaidros' speech. He interprets the passage as having a deeper significance as well.

4. At most this can be taken to mean that she postponed the plague. It does not, as Nussbaum claims (*The Fragility of Goodness*, p. 177) indicate that she has the power to *avert* the plague.

5. The dialogue is supposed to take place before that defeat, but the effect of the plague on Athens' capacity to wage war would nevertheless have been obvious to those present. They would in all probability be convinced that but for the plague the war would long since have been won. The dialogue was written, of course, many years after the defeat, and the readers of the dialogue would have seen this effect of the plague clearly—

THE MASKS OF DIONYSOS

even though the appearance of Alkibiades in the dialogue would have called even more clearly to mind the effect of his defection at the time of the attack on Syracuse.

6. Pp. 61–64.

7. *Symposium*, ed. Kenneth Dover (Cambridge: Cambridge University Press, 1980), pp. 138–39; Alexander Nehamas, "Episteme, Logos and Essence in Plato's Later Thought," paper given before the Society for Ancient Greek Philosophy, December 1982.

8. I am indebted to Professor Lawrence Powers of Wayne State University, and to one of my anonymous readers for pointing out two different aspects of this problem.

9. Diotima does not discuss this concept of knowledge directly; nevertheless, what she says of knowledge later (207d–208a) not only fits with this passage, it also fits the more amplified discussion in *Meno*. The two passages, in fact, are open to interpretations so similar as to suggest that both dialogues were written at a time when Plato was developing a serious concern with the relations of knowledge, truth and opinion. For this reason I have taken the liberty of using the one in the interpretation of the other. *Meno* is analyzed in detail in the Appendix.

10. Sokrates is explicit in *Meno* (98c–d) about asserting that neither knowledge nor true opinion is "a natural property of mankind" (i.e., innate), but that both are "acquired" (ἐπίκτητα). He does not examine the question of how a true opinion might be acquired, but given the way he attacks Meno's belief that he has acquired knowledge by remembering what others have told him, Sokrates might well be interpreted as holding that such remembering was a means of acquiring not knowledge, but opinion— either true or (as acted out by Meno) false. Cf. Appendix, pp. 126–127.

11. Later (cf. pp. 63–64) the possibility will be examined that there are two different kinds of knowledge, one of which requires reasons, and one of which does not. These in turn seem to be required only if there are two different kinds of objects to be known.

12. Following Heath, *Aristarchus of Samos* (Oxford, 1913), reprinted 1959 and 1966, p. 48f.

13. For a treatment of this in *Meno*, see Appendix, also n. 39 of the same.

14. For a different interpretation of the problems raised by this passage, see Rosen (*Plato's Symposium*, p. 254f.). He points out (p. 255) that "even if we assume that [the first instance of memory] arises from the vision of an Idea, this initial vision is instantly replaced by a transient replica. At

each moment. . . we would be moving farther away from the Idea." He does not connect this passage with Diotima's definition of knowledge, but sees it as pointing toward an imitation of immortality, rather than toward a different kind of immortality. Cf. pp. 82–86.

15. P. 54. Cf. also Appendix.

16. Cf. Appendix, pp. 147–150.

17. Cf. p. 59.

18. One solution to these puzzles is to hold that Diotima was a real person; that her speech reflects her own philosophical position rather than Sokrates' or Plato's; and that the doctrine of forms is not actually part of that position at all. I have indicated above (pp. 51–53) on the basis of internal evidence my reservations regarding the likelihood of her reality. Since she is presented to us as a "priest," such an explanation of the *Symposium* would appear to require some additional external evidence that her speech parallels the doctrine of at least one cult of the time. Such evidence seems not to be forthcoming. As for the claim that the doctrine of forms has no place in the *Symposium*, not only does the description of the "pure form of beauty" seem to preclude this (cf. pp. 61–64), but the question of just what that "form" might otherwise be, and its place in Plato's thought, would appear to present nearly insurmountable difficulties. Rosen, who perhaps has faced this problem more directly than many others, sees the pure form of beauty described here as the unity of "beautiful particulars of the highest kind" (268). He also seems to see it as a precursor of the doctrine of forms: "Diotima's description of beauty does not presuppose the theory of Ideas, but may be understood as part of the preparation for its subsequent development [presumably in other dialogues] by Socrates. Her prophesy shows us how genesis points toward ousia" (pp. 270–71).

19. This is one reason that today much of the meaning of the Eleusinian mysteries remains cloudy to us. Even though we have some evidence suggesting that, for example, sheaves of grain were included among the cult objects shown to the initiates, precisely what that might have meant to the initiate remains open to interpretation.

20. Although Diotima does not make the sex act explicit, there is nothing in the passage to suggest that it does not take place. Whether or not love reaches physical consumation in *Phaidros* (cf. Ferrari's careful analysis in chapter 6 of *Listening to the Cicadas*, also his n. 47 on pp. 268–69), here the sex act seems clearly to be an important—perhaps even essential— part of the "ladder." Although its importance shrinks as the lovers mount higher, there does not seem to be any reason to believe that it is abandoned.

21. Although this phrase ὀρθῶς ἡγῆται ὁ ἡγούμενος seems to imply a relationship of leader to follower, which would introduce an element of

power into the relationship, Diotima has previously (204c) established that Love is the lover (ἐραστόν), not the beloved (ἐρώμενον). I have argued below (pp. 72–75) this implies that in a healthy relationship both partners are lovers. If so, the present passage implies that each is the "guide" of the other, though perhaps in different ways.

22. Nothing in this passage suggests that Diotima was advocating celibacy. Rather does it suggest that, like physical beauty, sex should be kept in perspective. Although, as here, promiscuity might help exhaust our passions, sex should not be allowed to become so dominant in our lives as to push aside those higher values that distinguish humans from other animals.

23. Thus, that Diotima here has the role of *erastes* to Sokrates' *eromenos* is to be explained in terms of Diotima's treatment of the difference between the two (204c). Cf. pp. 72–75; n. 39, p. 167.

24. Whether this distinction is drawn successfully or not is another question. Cf. pp. 98–99.

25. As is common in Western religions, where such apparent contradictions as that the god is both three and one, or is wholly immanent in the world and wholly transcendent of it, etc., are "resolved" by branding them as "mysteries."

26. Shorey's translation.

27. My treatment of this aspect of love ought, perhaps, to be contrasted with Nussbaum's (*The Fragility of Goodness*, p. 176): "Eros is the desire to be a being without any contingent occurrent desires. It is a second-order desire that all desires should be cancelled. This need that makes us pathetically vulnerable to chance is a need whose ideal outcome is the existence of a metal statue, an artifact." She sees the immutability of the pure form of beauty as a protection from this "vulnerability."

28. Nevertheless I shall argue (70–72) that later parts of Diotima's speech do warrant the stronger conclusion, though in a rather unexpected way.

29. *The Fragility of Goodness*, n., p. 178.

30. Such a relational theory of value would go a long way toward dealing with Nussbaum's complaint (ibid., p. 180), that differences in beauty or goodness are merely quantitative. Differences in intensity—or quantity—would be in the relation, not in the object. A given object would be beautiful (or good) for *this* subject at *this* time in *this particular* relationship. Since such relationships are not interchangeable, the objects likewise would not be interchangeable. Agathon as object in one particular relationship would

not be identical with Agathon as object in another particular relationship. (Cf. the treatment of personal identity on pp. 68–71, 72–75.) Some such view of value seems to have been proposed as early as Herakleitos. It is clearly implied by fr. 61, "Sea water is the purest and the most polluted. For fish it is drinkable and life-giving; for men, not drinkable and destructive" (trans. Kathleen Freeman, *Ancilla to the Presocratic Philosophers* [Cambridge, Mass.: Harvard University Press, 1970]). Fragments 4, 9, 13, and 37 also lend themselves to such an interpretation.

31. Cf. p. 48.

32. Cf. pp. 56–58.

33. Agathon's suggestion that Eros functions in nature procreatively is expanded by Sokrates (208c–209e) into the concept of Eros as the life-force (cf. pp. 77–81). That Sokrates prefaces this discussion by addressing Diotima as "wise" (σοφωτάτη) may be intended to reflect Agathon's claim that poetry is "wisdom" (σοφίασ, which Lamb translates as "skill;" cf. above, pp. 48–49). In any event, Sokrates is presenting her as wise, and that, in context with the passage that follows, implies that wisdom is a matter of the depth of one's participation in the life process.

34. *The Fragility of Goodness*, n., p. 178.

35. Cf. Rosen's very different treatment of the relation between beauty and the good, *Plato's Symposium*, p. 238ff.

36. Although the question of the relation between philosophy and the poet's capacity to create (using "poetry" in the broad sense implied here) has not been taken up explicitly, the resolution is clearly implied. The role of the philosopher is to determine what in any given instance the good is. (Cf. Sokrates' comment to Alkibiades at 219b–c, "we shall consider and do what appears to be best for the two of us in this and our other affairs." See also ch. 6, pp. 122–123). Without such knowledge to guide, the poet's productions are matters of chance, and may be instrumental for the attainment of good, of evil, or of nothing of value at all. Thus, the philosopher, not Eros, is the proper guide for the poets. Although for Agathon σοφία merely meant "skill," for Sokrates it means that wisdom the love of which so guides our skills as to make us human.

37. Pp. 68–69.

38. Pp. 65–66.

39. This explains the otherwise anomolous fact that Diotima here has adopted the role of *erastes* to Sokrates' *eromenos*.

40. *Symposium*, ed. Kenneth Dover (Cambridge: Cambridge University Press, 1980), p. 147.

41. Nussbaum (*The Fragility of Goodness*, p. 196ff.), I think rightly, sees Alkibiades as understanding love primarily in terms of power. "The attribution of value to an unstable external object brings internal instability of activity. There is a strong possibility that Alcibiades *wants* Socrates to be a statue—a thing that can be held, carried, or, when necessary, smashed. There is a possibility that this sort of intense love cannot tolerate, and wishes to end, autonomous movement." This in turn leads to the claim that failure to control the object turns the power the other way. "Practical reason shapes a world of value. But the lover, as a lover, ascribes enormous importance to another world outside of his own and autonomous from it. It is not clear that the integrity of his own world can survive this, that he can continue to feel that he is a maker of a world at all. To feel so great a commitment to and power from what is external to your practical reason can feel like slavery, or madness" (p. 197). In these terms, Alkibiades' fear results in just that failure of commitment that makes love impossible. That Alkibiades is portrayed as enmeshed in this problem seems beyond doubt. On the other hand, I disagree with Nussbaum's contention that this is Sokrates' or Plato's view of love (see ch. 6).

Chapter 5.

1. Since Euripides was a contemporary of those at the banquet, the fact that Alkestis was his creation would perhaps have been more obvious to them than the fact that Akhilles was Homer's creation.

2. Without giving too much weight to the details of this side of Samuel Butler's argument (*The Authoress of the Odyssey*, London, 1897) his work at least makes clear how little we know about "Homer." His work also points up the fact that even if "Homer" should not be Nausikaa, there is something to be said for the possibility that the *Odyssey* was written by a woman.

3. Artifactual evidence that seems clearly to associate an early goddess with metallurgy includes a Karanovo VI (4500–4300 B.C.E.) crucible with two pairs of breasts decorating its interior, and a Cucuteni vase (4700–4500 B.C.E.) decorated with breasts and chevrons, and containing over 400 copper pieces including two axes. (Marija Gimbutas, *The Language of the Goddess*, [New York: Harper & Row, 1989], pp. 69–70). Such evidence does not show conclusively that metallurgy was originated by women or by women priests, but it clearly opens up that possibility.

4. Cf. Dover, *Symposium*, p. 153.

5. Cf. the chance element in Aristophanes' speech (192b, 193c; above pp. 42–43), as well as Pausanias' description of the "baser love" (ch. 2, p. 27). Cp. also Ferrari's treatment in terms of *Phaidros* of the place of chance in a life of philosophic love as contrasted with a philosophic life. (*Listening to the Cicadas*, esp. p. 230ff).

6. The two Greek words, ἁπτόμενος (translated here as "contact") and ʽομιλῶν ("consort"), like their English translations, are ambiguous with respect to their sexual implications. Both can be used to refer to sexual activity, but neither requires it.

7. Note that Diotima's discussion of the various levels at which one pursues immortality roughly parallels the description of the ladder, but without the immutable form as a "top step." In the description of the ladder (cf. above, pp. 61–62.) Diotima makes clear that the highest level where philosophy has a place is that where the lovers have reached beauty as the class of all beautiful things, the penultimate step. There is no place for philosophy at the top step. This seems to support both the claim (211b) that if there is a pure form of beauty it is apart from the world, and the implication that such a form could have no function in the world.

8. The fact that Plato's own work has been reinterpreted over the ages and "immortally renewed" in this way is an interesting case in point.

9. Depending upon which was written first.

10. Note again the passive role of the perceiver.

11. The Greek word for "truth," ἀληθῆ, is the negation of λήθη, "forgetfulness," and in that literal sense means "the unforgotten." In context, however, Diotima is using the word to refer to the status of the pure form of beauty, which has been clearly and emphatically described as immutable. Her reference here to immortality seems to make sense only in terms of this.

12. For a very different handling of this theme, see Nussbaum, *The Fragility of Goodness*, p. 180ff. Her claim that one could "look at a body and see in it exactly the same shade and tone of goodness and beauty as in a mathematical proof" (p. 180) presupposes an objective theory of value, a theory clearly required by the description of the pure form of beauty, but incompatible with a relational theory of value (cf. above, pp. 65–67, and ch. 4, n. 30). On the other hand, the view of the world as process implies a relational theory of value, which in turn implies a polar relation between subject and object in terms of which each is creative of the other. The individual is incorporated into the process; the process creates the individual on all levels, and in turn on all levels interracts with and is modified by the individual. Plato may have had something of this view as early as the Trial Dialogues. Cf. my "Socrates' Concept of Piety" (*Journ. of Hist. of Phil.*, vol. 5, no. 1) where this view is worked out on the level of one's interactions with other persons and with the democratic state.

13. Ch. 4, pp. 56–58; and ch. 4, n. 14.

14. Cf. above, pp. 69–72.

15. I have borrowed this use of the concept of necrophilia from Mary Daly, *Gyn/ecology: The Metaethics of Radical Feminism* (Boston: Beacon Press, 1978).

16. See note 26 below.

17. All quotations from *Phaidros*, unless otherwise noted, are from the Loeb Library edition, trans. H.N. Fowler.

18. At least since Hackforth's landmark study of *Phaidros* (R. Hackforth, *Plato's Phaedrus* [New York: Bobbs-Merrill, 1952], pp. 162–64) the apparently self-defeating character of this passage has been the subject of much scholarly discussion. Nussbaum (*The Fragility of Goodness*, p. 126) claims that although Sokrates opposed writing, Plato did write because he "[felt] the need for written paradigms of good philosophical teaching. . . . But by placing Socratic criticisms of writing inside his own writing, Plato invites us to ask ourselves, as we read, to what extent his own literary innovations have managed to circumnavigate the criticisms." In the pages to follow I shall argue that he has circumnavigated them in a "playful," but very explicit way (perhaps too explicit). Ferrari (*Listening to the Cicadas*) devotes the final chapter of his book to this problem. There he steers a careful course through a field cornered by the "standard" interpretation as exemplified by Hackforth and de Vries (*A Commentary on the Phaedrus of Plato*, Amsterdam, 1969), the "ironic" interpretation (Ronna Burger, *Plato's Phaedrus: A Defense of a Philosophic Art of Writing* [University of Alabama Press, 1980], as well as the teachings of Leo Strauss), and a "third type" of interpretation anchored primarily in Derrida ("La Pharmacie de Platon," in *La Dissemination*, 71–197, Paris, 1972). Ferrari claims (pp. 220–21) that "through Socrates, Plato makes a serious but relatively straightforward, almost banal point about the written word (it would have seemed more novel, of course, in Plato's day). . . . [that] writing, with its capacity to capture words in a permanent form external to and potentially independent of their user, is especially prone to encourage that fetishising of words. . . which is the antithesis of genuine communicative art." In a footnote to this passage, he adds (n. 28, pp. 281–82) "that Plato thought his genuine opinions might be fetishised if committed to writing is reason for him. . . to be sure to alert the reader to his worry, but it is no reason at all to commit to writing the exact opposite of his genuine opinions, as 'ironic' interpreters would have it." In the end Ferrari sees interpretation as reflexive dialectic, i.e., as a dialectic one carries on with oneself in the presence of the dialogue: "the action invites us to ponder, as part of our interpretation of the work, our own performance as interpreters; and so the supposedly silent text. . . finds a voice with which to answer us after all. The live voice that we hear is our own—the voice of the interpretive performer—not Plato's. . . . Plato devised his text. . . such that for the event which we cannot experience—

his creative performance as author—we may substitute our own performance as interpreters'' (p. 211).

Although I am in general agreement with Ferrari's position, the present interpretation has the merit of following more closely what Plato has Sokrates (and through him, Thamos) say directly in criticism of the written word—and I end up with the claim that although much of what happens happens in the mind of the reader/interpreter, the dialectic is not reflexive. It is a dialectic between the reader/interpreter and Plato. Charles Griswold (*Self-Knowledge in Plato's* Phaedrus [New Haven: Yale University Press, 1986]) seems also to envisage something like a dialogue between the reader and the author. I find much in Griswold's position with which I agree; however, any attempt to explore in depth the various levels of reader participation he points toward in his epilogue is beyond the scope of the present essay. Griswold's major theses are that "if the *Phaedrus'* notion of dialogue is to hold, then a connection between conversation and self-knowledge must be established, as must a connection between conversation and anamnesis" (p. 237). As for the connection between dialectic and self-knowledge, cf. Appendix, esp. pp. 150–151. As should by this point be clear, I am sceptical of the usual interpretation of Plato's position regarding the pure forms entailed by the doctrine of recollection. (More on the latter below, nn. 20, 21. Also Appendix, esp. pp. 135–137 and 148–150.)

19. Cf. Appendix for an analysis of these "errors" and their implications for the interpretation of *Meno*.

20. Cf. Plato's treatment of this distinction between wisdom and the simulation of wisdom in *Meno*, Appendix, pp. 126–128. In the *Symposium* both Agathon's demand (175c–d) that Sokrates sit beside him so he could acquire wisdom by "contact," and Alkibiades' desire (217a) "to *hear* all that our Socrates knew" reflect the failure to understand this distinction. Griswold (*Self-Knowledge in Plato's* Phaedrus) sees the advantage of dialogue over writing differently. He believes Plato to hold both to the doctrine of recollection and to the doctrine of forms. As a result, the risk is not one of failing to learn, but of losing what one has: "The danger of *substituting* an opinion for knowledge is so ubiquitous and unavoidable...that a special form of discourse is required if the danger is to be checked. By questioning others and defending itself (as well as the reverse), the movement of thought does not settle *artificially* on a single system, concept, theory, method, proposition—on a single dogma, in short" (p. 215, emphasis mine). This relegates the dialectic to a purely negative role of defending recollections of forms from erroneous substitutes. Although in many dialogues the elenchus does function to free Sokrates' conversational partners of error, the effect seems usually (as in *Meno*, see below, pp. 128, 129–130 and 133–135) to bring them to "Sokratic ignorance," rather than to protect any knowledge of forms they might already have. Griswold avoids the implied

problem through his view of the role of self-knowledge in Plato's work: "Socrates practices his dialectic for his own benefit primarily. He teaches others insofar as he prepares the ground for them to recollect, and this consists in disabusing them of their firmly held opinions...and sparking their eros for wisdom" (215–216).

21. This must hold for any case, whether the knowledge in question is of Simmias or, as Griswold would have it, of an immutable form. As pointed out below (Appendix, pp. 131–132) this embodies one difficulty the doctrine of recollection must overcome: if all learning is recollection and knowledge must precede recollection, then the acquisition of knowledge remains unaccountable.

22. As Meno presented a paradox he did not understand (Appendix, pp. 125–126); and as Meno had "on countless occasions...made abundant speeches on [excellence]" (80b) without knowing what excellence is (Appendix, p. 128). Cf. also esp. Appendix, pp. 136–137.

23. Cf. Appendix, pp. 129–130, also p. 151.

24. I am in agreement with Griswold who says that "Plato's dialogues do ask and answer questions in that they pose riddles and aporiai...to the reader and then supply, in the form of deeper strata of significance, partial answers to the questions" (222). For a working out of this in terms of the *Symposium*, see ch. 5, sec. 4.

25. The contemptuous reference here to "those who engage in other amusements, refreshing themselves with banquets (συμποσίοις) and kindred entertainments" (276d) may be a subtle dig at Phaidros and the other speakers in the *Symposium*, in which case the further claim that "he who has knowledge of the just and the good and the beautiful...will pass the time in such pleasures as I have suggested" (276d) may be a comment on Sokrates' role in the *Symposium*.

26. Similar objections are raised against the written word in *Second* and *Seventh Letters*. The authenticity of each of the *Letters* has been challenged over the years. Bury, who translated them for the Loeb Classical Library edition (London, 1929) rejects I, IX, and XII as "certainly spurious" (p. 385) and goes on to say "that the only two which we can with any confidence regard as genuine are...the seventh and eighth" (391). Only a few scholars, he says, (himself not included) "less confidently" accept the *Second Letter* as authentic. Ludwig Edelstein (*Plato's Seventh Letter* [Leiden: E.J. Brill, 1966]) in turn rejects the *Seventh Letter*. More importantly, he points out (pp. 3–4) that any attempt to establish the authenticity of the *Seventh Letter* (and, presumably, any of the others) must come to rest on how our interpretation of the content of the letter squares with our interpretation of the rest of

Plato's work. Nicholas White (*Plato on Knowledge and Reality* [Indianapolis: Hackett, 1976]), who argues for the authenticity of the *Seventh Letter*, concurs, contending that "the better we can integrate...[the matters raised in the 'philosophical digression'] into Plato's thought, the greater the likelihood that the work is genuine" (pp. 201–02). He then adds in a footnote (n. 14, p. 211) that "much of the evidence for authenticity...being evidence that the ideas in the letter fit intelligibly with those of the dialogues, is equally compatible with the hypothesis that the letter was written by someone other than Plato but carrying on his line of thought." The circularity of then using the letters as a basis for interpreting Plato's other works is obvious. Moreover, if the *Letters* are not authentic, the relevant passages in the second and seventh are almost certainly a scan on *Phaidros*. For these reasons the present study cannot throw much light on that issue. Since the present interpretation of *Phaidros* is nonstandard, if these portions of the *Letters* should be subject to an interpretation similar to that given here of *Phaidros*, this might lend some credence either to the claim that they and *Phaidros* have the same author, or to the claim that whoever might have forged the *Letters* understood *Phaidros* in somewhat the same way I do. On the other hand, if they do not lend themselves to similar interpretations, then the reader has a "fielder's choice" between accepting my interpretation of *Phaidros* and rejecting either or both of the *Letters*, or of accepting the *Letters* and rejecting my interpretation of *Phaidros*.

27. Pp. 62–63

28. Ibid.

29. Pp. 63–64.

30. Cf. above, pp. 54–56.

31. Cf. above, pp. 71–72.

32. Another mention might be in order here of the assertion in the *Republic* (523b–c) that contradictions are the only "provocatives" to thought. The discovery of a contradiction parallels the elenchus. Until the contradiction is discovered I hold a belief about Plato's position (say, on the place of the pure form of beauty in his metaphysical scheme). Once the contradiction is discovered I "know what it is that I do not know," i.e., I have reached "Sokratic ignorance."

33. P. 92.

34. There is at least a possibility that Plato got this from Parmenides. Cf. my "The Paradox of Parmenides," *Southern Journal of Philosophy*, vol. 1, no. 3 (Fall 1963), pp. 20–29. If he did, this in turn might account for his choice of Parmenides as the character who gives us Plato's deepest and most complete criticisms of the doctrine of forms.

35. Cf. above pp. 84–86.

36. The more usual translation of ἀδελφός is "brother" or "sibling," i.e., "product of the same womb" (δελφύς).

Chapter 6.

1. Nussbaum and Rosen both take Alkibiades' speech seriously and treat of it at length. Nussbaum argues that Sokrates presents us with a disembodied pursuit of the good that pries us out of the world of particulars and of particular lovers. This is to be contrasted with Alkibiades' particularized love of Sokrates—"the deep importance unique passion has for ordinary human beings...its irreplaceable contribution to understanding" (p. 197). She sees Sokrates as stonelike and unapproachable, and suggests that Plato has written Alkibiades' speech into the dialogue as representing the place of individual "unique passion" in order to show that as human individuals we must choose between Sokrates' view of the philosophical life and the more human, but less philosophical life that includes such passions. Although such a perception of Sokrates seems to me to be inaccurate, it does seem to be precisely the perception Alkibiades has of him.

Rosen sees Alkibiades' speech as a portrayal of Sokrates as passive, hubristic, and coldly indifferent not only to Alkibiades' bodily charms, but to all earthly things—summer heat (312–13), winter cold (311–12), the gods ("Socrates' hybris is akin to atheism" [308]), the state ("Socrates is not a political man" [p. 319]—although this is perhaps to be contrasted with the claim that because of Alkibiades "we get an account of Socrates' political excellence" [284]), the people and the aristocracy ("the philosopher's dissimulation is designed to protect himself from the many, and the many from philosophy" [280], a dissimulation that is then practiced on the "gentlemen" as well [312]), danger (314–16, "Socratic coldness looks like courage" [316]), starvation, feasting, drinking, sexual activity of any kind ("Socrates excels in both excess and defect so far as eating and drinking are concerned, where he is abstinent or defective erotically" [311]), etiquette (304), or anything else that makes life human ("He does not care for human, but only for divine things" [318]). Rosen's view of Sokrates accords well with that of the Neoplatonists. In view of the fact that for an army on the march such things as heat, cold, danger and food supplies are beyond the control of the individual, and in view of the way the hoplite was constrained to act in a phalanx I might be inclined to substitute some such word as "discipline" where Rosen uses "indifference." Apart from that, however, the same comment seems in order here as above. Although I strongly disagree with this as Plato's perception of Sokrates, it may well be an accurate indication of Plato's portrayal of Alkibiades' perception of Sokrates.

2. Ch. 1, p. 13ff. Cf. also Rosen, *Plato's Symposium*, p. 287.

3. Pp. 7–8.

4. Dating at least as far back as Ficino. Cf. Rosen, *Plato's Symposium*, p. 233ff.

5. Which might better be translated here as "lusting for."

6. One need not accept the tradition that Sokrates' wife was a shrew in order to see that he spent much more time in the agora talking with people than he did making a living. Xanthippe's lament in *Phaido* (60a) is that he will no longer be able to spend his time with his friends talking about philosophy—and in the *Apology* (31b) Sokrates describes himself as having neglected his own affairs in order to concern himself with the interests of the Athenians.

7. Martha Nussbaum interprets Sokrates' "deceit" as a failure on Sokrates' part to fulfill the emotional side of human love. Cf. "The Speech of Alcibiades: A Reading of Plato's *Symposium*," *Philosophy and Literature*, vol. 3 (1979); also *The Fragility of Goodness*. Similarly, Rosen (*Plato's Symposium* p. 320 and p. 301) sees Alkibiades as warning "Agathon and the other beauties not to be deceived by Socrates' ostensibly erotic pursuit," adding that the warning is given not to protect the others, but to spite Sokrates.

8. Or the Roman, "in vino veritas." Even today many seem convinced that people who are drunk are less able to lie, more likely to speak the truth, than those who are sober, suggesting we are not yet entirely free of this superstition.

9. Francois Lissarrague (*The Aesthetics of the Greek Banquet: Images of Wine and Ritual*, trans. Andrew Szegedy-Maszak [Princeton: Princeton University Press, 1990] points out that symbols of Dionysos and of satyrs (as well as of Eros) were essential elements of the pattern woven through the fabric of a Greek symposium. In this case both Dionysos and satyrs have (at least formally) been forbidden to enter (cf. above, pp. 11–12). I have suggested that Dionysos has nevertheless been present throughout the evening. Now Dionysos, in the persona of Alkibiades, is pointing out that the dominant figure in the evening's entertainment has been a satyr in the persona of Sokrates.

10. That a case can be made in defense of Alkibiades' actions would not alter the fact that early readers of the dialogue would have perceived him as a defector. They probably would have felt that even if Alkibiades' flight from the Athenians could be justified, his joining with Sparta was unforgivable.

11. The charges of "irreligion" and of "corruption of the youth" are often seen as elliptical references to Alkibiades' sacrilege and his defection.

The reference in the *Apology* to Sokrates' "first accusers" (18a–e) is similarly seen as an attempt on Sokrates' part to reply to this unspoken allegation.

12. Cf. above, pp. 72–73, 78–80.

13. That Sokrates in this dialogue is also probably Plato's mask is perhaps worth noting.

14. It seems probable, too, that Plato intended the reader to take this as a rather broad hint that the speech Sokrates gives in the *Symposium* should be subjected to some careful scrutiny—a view that supports the interpretation arrived at by a different route above.

15. Cf. "Socrates' Concept of Piety," *Journ. of the Hist. of Philosophy,* vol. V, no. 1, where an argument is developed at some length not only that the dialectic controls its participants, but that in the three dialogues *Euthyphro,* the *Apology* and *Krito* the dialectic is portrayed as the hierarchically superior god.

16. Although, for different reasons, both Nussbaum and Rosen seem sceptical of the claim that in this part of the *Symposium* Plato is offering a defense of Sokrates against the accusation that he was somehow responsible for Alkibiades' defection, on its face that claim seems reasonable. Just the three obvious facts first, that such an accusation was in circulation, second that Sokrates is the central figure in all of the early and middle dialogues, and third, that Alkibiades figures so prominently in this dialogue, describing his perception of his relation to Sokrates, together add weight to such a claim. Further weight is added by the fact that two of the other guests, Phaidros and Eryximakhos, were accused along with Alkibiades in the desecration of the herms. By the time Plato wrote the *Symposium* he may have come to the point of disagreement with some of Sokrates' philosophical positions (as Nussbaum strongly suggests), but in this treatment of the Marsyas myth we are given a poignant portrayal and a lamentation for the teacher that the people could not allow to live.

17. If the vocabulary of the Eleusinian mysteries is indicative, she would have been in the priesthood of Demeter who, as one who by giving up her contact with the soil could cause all growth to stop, may, like Dionysos, have been a fertility god, and a symbol of the life force.

18. Cf. Appendix, pp. 129–130.

19. Ch. 1, pp. 11–12, ch. 3, 39–45.

20. Even this plays into the conflict between Dionysos and Apollo, since orgies were the province of Dionysos, but Apollo was traditionally regarded as the god who introduced male homosexuality to both the Greeks and their gods.

21. I fail to see that Eryximakhos' efforts to maintain the formal structure of the party has any significant effect. (Cf. Rosen, *Plato's Symposium*, pp. 287, 291.)

22. Even the reference here to the structure of his own conversation suggests a preoccupation with form.

23. Groden, Brentlinger and Baskin, *The Symposium of Plato* (Amherst, Mass.: University of Massachusetts Press, 1970), p. 2.

24. This, of course, does not in any way detract from Brentlinger's interpretation of Sokrates' behavior at this point as a symbol of rebirth—an interpretation which I find attractive.

25. Ch. 4, pp. 70–72, ch. 5, pp. 83–86.

26. Cf. above ch. 1, pp. 8–10.

27. As argued in "Socrates' Concept of Piety," *Journ. of the Hist. of Philosophy*, vol. V, no. 1 (Jan. 1967).

28. Cf. Appendix, pp. 150–151, for the development of this theme in terms of *Meno*.

29. Cf. Appendix, pp. 126–128, also 151 for an analysis of this concept of learning, and its effect on Meno.

30. Note, for example, the ending of *Meno* where Sokrates ironically suggests that Meno go and spend his time with Anytos; or Sokrates' sardonic plea at the end of *Euthyphro* that Euthyphro stay and instruct him. Sokrates also (as Professor Anthony Preus pointed out to me) frequently sends people to Prodikos.

31. 184a–c. See also the discussion above, ch. 2, pp. 26–28.

32. Certainly Alkibiades is portrayed in other dialogues—most notably, perhaps, in *Protagoras*—as a student with great talent and promise. Rosen, on the other hand, claims that "it is not sufficient to interpret Socrates' 'love' as a desire to make Alcibiades either a virtuous citizen or a philosopher. From the beginning of their relationship, Alcibiades is presented as obviously unfit for either role" (p. 281). He goes on to say that Sokrates' interest in Alkibiades is grounded in a wish to study "the young boy's hybris or pleonexia. . . . Extreme hybris, or the desire to be a god, is not simply a vice, but a quality deserving of study, and in a sense, of cultivation" (p. 282).

33. Guthrie (*Orpheus and Greek Religion*, p. 15, and n. 5, p. 24) points out that the latter part of this statement ("all else profane" etc.) parallels an Orphic hymn.

34. P. 46.

35. Alkibiades' gradual revelation of this most private and personally embarrassing incident to people at the party is perhaps not unlike the gradual exposure of Pentheos before the maenads in Euripides' *Bakkhai*.

36. Cf. above, pp. 72–75.

37. Lamb includes the word "so" at this point in his translation, which would suggest that Alkibiades is acting out on the couch he now shares with Agathon and Sokrates what he is describing to them. Although outrageous behavior of this sort would be entirely in character for Alkibiades, nothing in the Greek seems to support such a translation.

38. Cf. Dover, *Symposium*, p. 5.

39. Rosen, *Plato's Symposium*. The quote is from p. 311, but Rosen develops this thesis throughout his analysis of Alkibiades' place in the dialogue.

40. *The Fragility of Goodness*, p. 195ff.

Appendix.

1. This appendix parallels very roughly the argument of a paper I published many years ago entitled "The Theory of Recollection in Plato's *Meno*" (*Southern Journal of Philosophy*, vol. 9, no. 3 [Fall 1971]). The present article is much more fully developed and has been completely rewritten.

Much of the recent literature on *Meno* uses the dialogue as a stepping-off point for other studies (often of the development of Greek mathematics or logic). While such studies are of considerable interest in themselves, they tend to distort the view of the dialogue as a whole. They also are for the most part not pertinent to the concerns of this appendix. Other studies focus somewhat narrowly on the treatment of the doctrine of recollection in *Meno*. For a concise analysis of the more recent of these, see Michael Morgan, "How does Plato Solve the Paradox of Inquiry in the *Meno*?" in Anton and Preus (eds.), *Essays in Ancient Greek Philosophy III* (Albany: State University of New York Press, 1989), p. 169ff. Although I disagree with Morgan's solution of the paradox, if the doctrine of recollection is to be taken seriously, Morgan's claim that Plato's solution is metaphysical rather than epistemological would also have to be taken seriously: "The paradox of inquiry is solved by recognizing that the truths apprehended and affirmed at the culmination of the inquiry are always in the soul, always available as objects of our mental grasps" (p. 177). Since the forms are necessarily outside the soul, such an interpretation (as Morgan points out) is also incompatible with the doctrine of forms.

2. Here, as with the *Symposium*, all translations, unless otherwise noted, are from Lamb's translation in the Loeb Library edition.

3. Moravcsik ("Learning as Recollection," in Vlastos (ed.), *Plato I*, [Garden City, N.Y.: Doubleday, 1971] pp. 53–59) apparently misses this despite his insistence on "learning the forms of inquiry" (p. 54). He says: "though Meno...states the difficulty of directing an *inquiry* toward an unknown object, he adds the *question* of how one would know that what is found is the information sought initially" (emphasis mine).

4. The least that can be implied by this is that Sokrates (and, presumably, Plato) is not committing himself to the doctrine of recollection.

5. That Plato is making moves like this strongly suggests that here, as in the *Symposium* he is opening the door to a dialectic between himself and the reader. The reader, in recognizing the implications of such a move, would break through a "screen." Cf. ch. 5, sec. 4.

6. Jacob Klein, whose *Commentary on Plato's Meno* (Chapel Hill: University of North Carolina Press, 1965) has the merit of omitting nothing from scrutiny, also sees this as a dodge (p. 67), but he does not suggest that it might be the opening move in a coordinated plan to keep Sokrates off the subject.

7. Klein points out (p. 69) that the stress Sokrates here puts on habit is picked up in Sokrates' claim at 76d that his answer "was perhaps phrased according to what is habitual [συνήθειαν] with [Meno]" (Klein's translation), as well as in Meno's pathetic admission at 82a that in asking Sokrates to "teach" him the doctrine of recollection he "only spoke from habit."

8. As was the case with all of the characters in the *Symposium* except Aristophanes and Sokrates—but most notably, perhaps, with Alkibiades. (Cf. above, ch. 6, p. 116.) I am in agreement with Klein on this interpretation of Meno's view of knowledge.

9. Cf. pp. 130–132.

10. If this paradox did originate with Gorgias we have no independent evidence that it did. Nevertheless, it clearly is in keeping with Sextos' account of Gorgias (*Adv. Math.* VII, 65–87) as one who argued for the conclusions: first, that nothing exists; second, that even if something should exist it would be unknowable; and third, that even if something should exist and one should happen to have knowledge of it, that knowledge would be incommunicable.

11. In the sections to follow I shall argue that in fact these are two different gateways to the same questions: what is human excellence and how is it acquired?

12. Although the text seems to be corrupt here (Burnet, n. to 75d 7, Oxford ed.), allowing for the possibility that this passage refers not to "the

questioned person" but rather to the person *doing* the questioning, such an interpretation does not make sense in terms of the context. Klein (*A Commentary on Plato's Meno*, p. 63) paraphrases the passage, as giving answers "in terms which the interlocutor would *concede*. . .that he knows" (emphasis mine); however, he interprets this as entailing "agreement" on the part of Sokrates and his "interlocutor" regarding the content.

13. This concept of hubris is worked out above, ch. 1, pp. 8–10, and p. 155, n. 8. Also ch. 6, p. 115.

14. In this case it may be possible to pinpoint Sokrates' target. Guthrie (*Orpheus and Greek Religion* [London: Methuen, 1935, 1952], pp. 164–66) argues that this passage reflects Orphic doctrines. If so (and if such doctrines exist!) the implied criticism may be designed to show how and why that view fails to stand up to philosophical scrutiny.

15. Klein (*A Commentary on Plato's Meno*, p. 95f.) recognizes the problem, and resolves it by drawing a distinction between learning by recollection and learning by "seeing." There is some textual support for this ("has [seen ($\dot{\epsilon}\omega\rho\alpha\kappa\upsilon\hat{\iota}\alpha$)] all things" [81c]), but the argument nevertheless seems thin. If all learning is recollection (81d), then "seeing" could not in itself be viewed as a kind of learning; i.e., if "seeing" is another, different kind of learning, then it would not be the case that *all* learning is recollection. The most that could be said for what is "seen" (whether by means of the bodily senses or otherwise) is that it would function as a "reminder" facilitating recollection of what has previously been "learned." (Cf. the discussion of "learning by seeing" above, ch. 4, p. 59, and p. 165, n. 19.) Moreover, the possibility that the soul is created with such knowledge is precluded by Sokrates' insistence (98c–d) that "neither knowledge nor true opinion is a natural property of mankind" (i.e., innate), but both are "acquired" ($\dot{\epsilon}\pi\dot{\iota}\kappa\tau\eta\tau\alpha$). Although Guthrie, Vlastos and Moravcsik (cf. note 24 below) all come to the dialogue from a very different perspective, they seem to fall victim to essentially the same problem.

16. I am indebted to a student, Christine Stephenson, for this insight. In at least one instance (*Euthydemos*, 29e) Plato shows an awareness of this implication. After Euthydemos has claimed that Sokrates knows everything, Sokrates takes him to task by demanding, "how am I to say that I know certain things, Euthydemus; for instance, that good men are unjust?" (Loeb ed., trans. Lamb). Another student, Alberto Mendez, pointed out to me that if one has learned *all* falsehoods, then "that *x* is true" might turn out to be another falsehood. Thus, recollection could never justify belief.

17. For a different interpretation of the significance of Sokrates' restatement of the paradox, cf. Morgan, ("How Does Plato Solve the Paradox of Inquiry in the *Meno*?"). Moravcsik ("Learning as Recollection," p. 57)

notes the dropping of τὸ παράπαν, explaining "that the intended solution covers only those cases in which we in a sense know what we are searching for," pointing out that one cannot "recall" that of which nothing is known. He does not examine the implications of Meno's failure to notice.

18. Although Klein's translation of this passage (*A Commentary on Plato's Meno*, p. 91) reflects the difference between the two statements of the paradox, he treats them as the same—and then criticizes the argument (p. 92) as ignoring "the way the 'unknown' generally presents itself *as* an 'unknown,' circumscribed by questions that arise 'naturally' whenever we become aware of some inconsistency or a lack of connection between the 'known' pieces of our experience."

19. Klein points out (*A Commentary on Plato's Meno*, p. 98) that "Socrates makes sure that he and the boy speak the same language," but then (in a footnote) connects this to a passage in *Kharmides* (159a) that he interprets as indicating that if Kharmides speaks his native language he must have some sense of the meaning of the words in it. In point of fact, *Kharmides* 159a does not refer to language. Sokrates says, "if you have [*sophrosyne*] with you, you can hold an opinion about it. For being in you, I presume it must, in that case afford some perception from which you can form some opinion of what [*sophrosyne*] is, and what kind of thing it is" (Loeb ed., trans. Lamb). That is, if Kharmides has the *quality* (not the word or the concept), he must have an inkling of what that quality is. The fact that neither Kharmides nor Kritias can come up with an adequate characterization of it implies that neither of them "has" it (not too surprising in light of what we know of them at the time of the Thirty). If this reasoning should be applied to *Meno* it would imply that Meno did not "have" human excellence. Although Plato would probably agree with that conclusion (cf. the discussion, pp. 136–140), he does not argue the case that way.

20. The slave gives this particular reply only twice, the other at 84d where he is asked if he understands (μανθάνεις) what Sokrates has told him. Usually the slave limits his replies to more noncommittal expressions of agreement such as πάνυ γε and ναί.

21. In this instance we may see the dialogue being manipulated not by Sokrates, the character, but by Plato, the author.

22. This runs counter to Moravcsik's claim that "in the case of inquiries terminating with the knowledge of a priori truths, knowing and not knowing cannot be strictly separated as understanding and verification" (p. 58). Counting the squares does not seem different in kind from finding or not finding Larisa (97a–e) at the end of the road.

23. For a suggestion as to how Sokrates may have manipulated Meno in a similar way, cf. Klein (*A Commentary on Plato's Meno*) pp. 52–56.

24. The doctrine of recollection is not easily reconciled with ordinary experience. Guthrie points to the difference between mathematical and other sorts of knowledge, arguing ("Translator's Preface," in *Plato's Meno*, ed. Malcolm Brown [New York: Bobbs-Merrill, 1971, p. 12) that "what the [slave dialogue] teaches could be expressed as the difference between empirical and a priori knowledge...it suggests that whereas we have to learn facts of the former kind either from our own experience of the outside world or on the authority of another, the latter type of truth does seem in some way to come from inside us." This is an interesting suggestion, but there seems to be no support for such a distinction in the text. Since "seeking and learning are in fact nothing but recollection" (81d, trans. Guthrie), our (empirical) experience could result in learning if and only if it functioned as a "reminder" of something that had been learned at some earlier time. Moreover, there is throughout the dialogue a subtle, but sustained attack on "learning by hearing" that would preclude the acceptance of anything on grounds of "authority."

Moravcsik ("Learning as Recollection") and Vlastos ("*Anamnesis* in the *Meno*," *Dialogue*, vol. 4 [1965], 143–67) both argue for a similar view, limiting recollection to a priori knowledge. Morgan points out ("How Does Plato Solve the Paradox of Inquiry in the *Meno*?" p. 174), "Not only is it doubtful that Plato would have treated geometrical inquiries as *a priori*, the formulation of the doctrine of recollection (81c) and the later discussion about true beliefs and knowledge of the road to Larissa show that Plato did not in the *Meno* yet have in mind what would later come to be treated as a distinction between empirical and *a priori* truths." Moravcsik ("Learning as Recollection," p. 59) contends that "the theory...can be understood as the claim that the mind is furnished innately with a set of concepts which it contains in a way analogous to the way in which what is remembered is stored in the mind." This runs counter to Sokrates' statement at 98c–d that knowledge is not "natural" ($\phi\acute{v}\sigma\epsilon\iota$), but "acquired" ($\dot{\epsilon}\pi\acute{\iota}\chi\tau\eta\tau\alpha$).

Klein (*A Commentary on Plato's Meno*, p. 105) maintains that recollection is to be interpreted in terms of the acceptance rather than of the content of a belief. Comparing it to the simple "repeating" of what one has been told, he maintains that "we may assent to, or reject, [a] 'proposition' by drawing the assent or denial from ourselves. Such assent to, or rejection of, a proposition...constitutes an opinion of a different kind. It cannot be 'induced' or 'manipulated' because its source is not 'outside' the person who holds it. It is the completion of our own thinking." This seems somewhat facile. On the one hand, Meno is not "induced" to give up either what he holds to be the proper method of learning ("being told") or the content (e.g., Sokrates' definition of "figure"—even after Sokrates "told" him it was unacceptable). On the other, even Sokrates claims to be willing to be persuaded to give up his beliefs if he is "manipulated" in the right way (i.e., by giving him more or better reasons). The fact that Klein supports his interpretation by sixty-five pages (a fourth of his book) of analysis of other dialogues, and of Aristotle—a passage which he himself calls a "digression"—suggests that his position might be difficult to support in terms of *Meno* alone.

Let me emphasize again that I do not intend that this analysis of *Meno* be taken as applying to any other Platonic dialogue—least of all to *Phaido*.

25. Although Klein notes the comparison between Meno and his slave (*A Commentary on Plato's Meno*, p. 173f.) he argues (p. 89f.) that Sokrates draws no image of any kind because he will strip Meno bare without an image. "And there is no telling what a faithful image of Meno the 'beautiful,' might look like." Again (p. 190): "That is *not* what Socrates has done. He has made *us* see Meno as Meno is" (emphases his).

26. Note that Sokrates refers to what the slave is doing as "learning" even here where he is apparently trying to convince Meno that learning is not what is taking place.

27. The *Symposium* may in part be an attempt to solve this more basic, tougher problem. If so, the attempt is not completely successful. Cf. the treatment of "similarity" and "difference" in ch. 5, sec. 5. If the *Symposium* does attempt to solve a problem raised but not dealt with in *Meno*, this would imply that the *Symposium* was written later—but not much later—than *Meno*.

28. As Klein points out (*A Commentary on Plato's Meno*, p. 36f.), whether Plato's readers had actually read Xenophon or Ktesias is unimportant. "There can hardly be any doubt that Meno's image as that of an archvillain was fixed in the minds of Plato's contemporaries" (p. 37).

29. Although Lamb's translation allows for a distinction between "what *can* be taught" ("is teachable") and "what *is* taught," that distinction seems not to be reflected in the Greek. With the exception of the dialogue with Anytos (where they are describing the education various citizens gave to their children), Plato limits himself almost completely to the single form, διδακτόν, for which I have offered the neutral "to be taught."

30. H.-P. Stahl ("Beginnings of Propositional Logic in Plato," in *Plato's Meno*, ed. Brown, pp. 180–97) interprets this passage (p. 187) as indicating that Plato did not distinguish between implication and equivalence. I suspect that the distinction Plato failed to draw is that between what today would be called a class logic and a propositional logic. In the discussion of the distinction between "figure" and "a figure," and between "color" and "a color" (74b–d), Sokrates is clearly dealing with a universal affirmative proposition in class logic. Implication is one propositional form that can be easily rephrased as such a proposition; e.g., "If it rains the streets will be wet" can (awkwardly but accurately) be restated, "All cases of rain are

cases of wet streets." Equivalence, however, must be stated as two universal affirmative propositions: "All cases of x are cases of y, and also all cases of y are cases of x." This fact is perhaps what made it easier for Plato to *avoid* confusing implication with equivalence.

31. I am indebted to one of my anonymous readers for pointing out that "the second proposition can just as easily be taken as an additional premise rather than an inference, since it is introduced by δέ γ̇ ('and indeed') rather than ἄρα ('then')." If it is an additional premise, this would free Sokrates of the apparent fallacy. The rest of the argument that follows would remain unaffected.

32. Note that this roughly parallels Diotima's claim that these and similar things are loved for the sake of the good (204e–205a and 205e; see also above, pp. 70–71.

33. Plato seems to be using ἐπιστήμη, "knowledge," and φρόνησις, "prudence," pretty much interchangeably. His use of φρόνησις ("prudence" or "practical wisdom") serves to point up the fact that the various qualities he is discussing become "excellences" if and only if they are properly applied. (Lamb sometimes translates φρόνησις as "prudence," sometimes as "wisdom.")

34. Most translators render εὐμαθίαν as "intelligence;" however, "quickness to learn" seems to better preserve the ambiguity of the Greek, which might refer to intelligence, but could also be interpreted as skill in committing to memory. By this point in the dialogue Sokrates has drawn a distinction between these two even though Meno fails to understand it.

35. The two propositions are not equivalent, but the inference, if it is one, is valid.

36. Klein (*A Commentary on Plato's Meno*, p. 224) points out that Sokrates' introduction of Anytos includes the claim that Anytos' father "gave his son, Anytus, a good upbringing and education." Since Anytos led the prosecution of Sokrates (to say nothing of his arrogant behavior in the present context), he becomes a prime example of the failure of the father to teach human excellence to the son (as Klein notes on p. 233).

37. I am indebted to Professor Eric Snider for calling my attention to this aspect of Anytos' speech. (Eric Snider, "The Structure and a Point of the *Meno*," read before the Ohio Philosophical Association on 3 April 1987, and published in the *Proceedings*, pp. 2–14.

38. P. 131.

39. This difficulty is the same as that implied by the claim that if knowledge is to be defined as being able to give reasons in support of a

belief—a definition that *Meno* shares with *Symposium*—we should distinguish "good" reasons from "bad" ones (cf. above ch. 4, pp. 54–57; p. 164, n. 10). Although in the *Symposium* this points toward the dialectical character of knowledge, here it serves merely to point up the shallowness of Anytos' view of learning.

40. Pp. 136–140.

41. Ch. 4, pp. 54–57, also p. 164, n. 7.

42. This would explain why Sokrates, in restating Meno's paradox, did not include Meno's "question of how one would know that what is found is the information initially sought" (Moravcsik, "Learning as Recollection," p. 57). If this definition of knowledge is taken seriously, one could *never* with finality know that the answer had been found—rather than Moravcsik's explanation that "if one understands what one investigates, then one will know when an answer is given to the original question." Whether an answer is relevant is resolved by Sokratic ignorance, but whether an answer is correct is never fully resolved.

43. This process could be used to describe the actual development of geometry through the ages. On the one hand, there is the application of conic sections to astronomy by Kepler a millennium and a half after they were introduced by Archimedes. On the other hand, the questioning of the "self-evidence" of the postulate of parallel lines—perhaps as early as Euclid (who gave it last place in his list of postulates)—was in the nineteenth century to free mathematics of its ties to the empirical world, leading first, to the development of non-euclidean geometries, and through them to projective geometry and, in more recent times, topology.

44. Protagoras, for example, seems to have felt compelled to extend his relativism to the ontological level in order for it to work epistemologically: "Of all things the measure is Man, *of the things that are, that they are, and of the things that are not, that they are not*" (Freeman, fr. 1, emphasis mine). This, of course, justified his teaching of the arts of persuasion.

45. Since such a commitment would imply that Sokrates knows everything in the universe in all its interrelations. Not only would such a claim be hubristic in the extreme, it would also run counter to what has been said of Sokratic ignorance. This may be why he claims only to "speak as one who does not know, but only conjectures."

46. Note that these are not "parts" of excellence in the sense that "justice" might be considered a "part" of excellence at 73d (cf. the discussion in Vlastos, "Socrates on 'the Parts of Virtue'," *Platonic Studies*, second ed. [Princeton: Princeton University Press, 1981], p. 418ff.). In the

present case each is a component, a "part" in the sense of being a necessary, but not a sufficient condition of excellence—but together they constitute a sufficient condition (i.e., there seem to be no other necessary conditions).

47. Cf. above, pp. 142–143.

Bibliography

Anderson, D. E. "The Theory of Recollection in Plato's *Meno*," *The Southern Journal of Philosophy*, vol. 9, no. 3 (Fall 1971).

_____. "The Paradox of Parmenides," *The Southern Journal of Philosophy*, vol. 1, no. 3 (Fall 1963).

_____. "Socrates' Concept of Piety," *Journal of the History of Philosophy*, vol. V, no. 1 (1967).

Aristotle. *The Works of Aristotle*, ed. Jonathan Barnes (Princeton: Princeton University Press, 1984).

Bell, Malcolm. "Stylobate and Roof in the Olympieion at Akragas," *American Journal of Archeology*, vol. 84, no. 3 (July 1980).

Brentlinger, John A. Introduction to *The Symposium of Plato*, Suzy Q Groden, John A. Brentlinger and Leonard Baskin (Amherst: University of Massachusetts Press, 1970).

Burger, Ronna. *Plato's Phaedrus: A Defense of a Philosophic Art of Writing* (University of Alabama Press, 1980).

Butler, Samuel. *The Authoress of the Odyssey* (London, 1897; reprinted, Chicago: University of Chicago Press, 1967).

Clay, Diskin. "The Tragic and Comic Poet of the *Symposium*" in *Essays in Ancient Greek Philosophy*, vol. II, ed. John Anton and Anthony Preus (Albany: State University of New York Press, 1983).

Daly, Mary. *Gyn/Ecology: The Metaethics of Radical Feminism* (Boston: Beacon Press, 1978, 1990).

Derrida, Jacques. "La Pharmacie de Platon," in *La Dissemination* (Paris: Editions de Seuil, 1972).

DeVries, G. J. *A Commentary on the Phaedrus of Plato* (Amsterdam: Adolf Hakkert Publications, 1969).

Diogenes Laertius. *Lives of the Philosophers*, trans. Robert Caponigri (Chicago: Henry Regnery Co., 1969).

Dover, K. J. *Greek Homosexuality* (Cambridge, Mass.: Harvard University Press, 1978).

_____. *Greek Popular Morality in the Time of Plato and Aristotle* (Oxford: Blackwell, 1974).

_____. *Symposium* (Cambridge: Cambridge University Press, 1980).

Edelstein, Ludwig. *Plato's Seventh Letter* (Leiden: E. J. Brill, 1966).

Ferrari, G. R. F. *Listening to the Cicadas: A Study of Plato's Phaedrus* (Cambridge: Cambridge University Press, 1987).

Freeman, Kathleen. *Ancilla to the PreSocratic Philosophers* (Cambridge, Mass.: Harvard University Press, 1970; orig. publ. 1948).

_____. *The PreSocratic Philosophers: A Companion to Diels*, Fragmente der Vorsokratiker (Oxford: Basil Blackwell and Mott, Ltd., 1946).

Gimbutas, Marija. *The Language of the Goddess* (New York: Harper & Row, 1989).

Griswold, Charles L. Jr. *Self-Knowledge in Plato's Phaedrus* (New Haven: Yale University Press, 1986).

Groden, Suzy Q, John A. Brentlinger and Leonard Baskin. *The Symposium of Plato* (Amherst: University of Massachusetts Press, 1970).

Guthrie, W. K. C. *Orpheus and Greek Religion* (London: Methuen, 1935, 1952).

_____. Translator's Preface to *Plato's Meno*, ed. Malcolm Brown (New York: Bobbs-Merrill Co., 1971).

Hackforth, R. *Plato's Phaedrus* (New York: Bobbs-Merrill Co., 1952).

Heath, Sir Thomas. *Aristarchus of Samos: The Ancient Copernicus* (Oxford: Oxford University Press, 1913, 1959, 1966).

Henderson, Jeffrey. *The Maculate Muse* (New Haven: Yale University Press, 1975).

Kern, O. ed. *Orphicorum Fragmenta* (Berlin, 1922, 1963).

Klein, Jacob. *A Commentary on Plato's Meno* (Chapel Hill, University of North Carolina Press, 1965).

Lissarrague, Francois. *The Aesthetics of the Greek Banquet: Images of Wine and Ritual*, trans. Andrew Szedy-Maszak (Princeton: Princeton University Press, 1990).

Long, A. A. "Empedocles' Cosmic Cycle in the 'Sixties," in *The Pre-Socratics*, ed. P. D. Mourelatos (Garden City, N.Y.: Doubleday and Co., 1974).

Moravcsik, Julius. "Learning as Recollection," in *Plato I: Metaphysics and Epistemology*, ed. Gregory Vlastos (Garden City, N.Y.: Doubleday and Co., 1971).

Morgan, Michael L. "How Does Plato Solve the Paradox of Inquiry in the *Meno*?", in *Essays in Greek Philosophy*, vol. III, ed. John Anton and Anthony Preus (Albany: State University of New York Press, 1989).

Nehamas, Alexander. "Episteme, Logos and Essence in Plato's Later Thought," paper given before the Society for Ancient Greek Philosophy, December, 1982.

Nussbaum, Martha. *The Fragility of Goodness* (Cambridge: Cambridge University Press, 1986).

_____. "The Speech of Alcibiades: A Reading of Plato's Symposium," in *Philosophy and Literature*, vol. 3 (1979).

Nye, Andrea. "The Hidden Host: Irigaray and Diotima at Plato's Symposium," in *Hypatia*, vol. 3, no. 3 (Winter 1989).

O'Brien, David. *Empedocles' Cosmic Cycle* (Cambridge: Cambridge University Press, 1969).

Plato. Loeb Classical Library editions of *Charmides, Euthydemus, Meno* (translated by Lamb), the *Republic* (Shorey), the *Symposium* (Lamb), *Phaedo, Phaedrus* (Fowler) and *Letters* (Bury).

Robbins, Emmet. "Famous Orpheus," in *Orpheus, The Metamorphosis of a Myth*, ed. John Warden (Toronto: University of Toronto Press, 1982).

Rosen, Stanley. *Plato's Symposium* (New Haven: Yale University Press, 1968; second ed. with notes, 1987).

Snider, Eric. "The Structure and a Point of the *Meno*," in *Proceedings* of the Ohio Philosophical Association, 1987.

Stahl, H.-P. "Beginnings of Propositional Logic in Plato," in *Plato's Meno*, ed. Malcom Brown (New York: Bobbs-Merrill Co., 1971).

Vlastos, Gregory. "Anamnesis in the Meno," in *Dialogue* vol. 4 (1965).

White, Nicholas. *Plato on Knowledge and Reality* (Indianapolis: Hackett, 1976).

Wright, W. R. *Empedocles: The Extant Fragments* (New Haven: Yale University Press, 1981).

Index

a priori, 172n.24; 181n.22; 182n.24

Abstraction, 60, 61, 62, 93, 99, 169n.7; and beauty, 60, 61, 93, 99; class of all beautiful things, 61, 169n.7; definition of, 60; differences, 99; Diotima on, 60; and generalization, 60, 61; the ladder of, 60, 61; and philosophy, 61, 62; and reasons, 61, 62; and revelation, 62

Admetos, 24, 52

Adultery, 43; and homosexuality, 43

Aesthetics of the Greek Banquet; Images of Wine and Ritual, Francois Lissarrague, see: Lissarrague, Francois

Agathon, 7, 10, 11, 13, 15–16, 18, 29, 40, 46–50, 51, 64–67, 70, 74, 77 103, 110, 111, 115, 116, 117, 119, 121, 156n.21, 22; 157n.28; 158n.11; 161n.29, 31, 33, 34; 162n.33–38; 167n.30, 33; 171n.20; and Alkibiades, 110, 115, 116, 117, 119, 156n.21; and Aristophanes, 15, 45; as beloved, 74; on creativity and Eros, 48, 49; and Dionysos, 10, 15, 47, 49; and dominance, 49; on Eros, 46–49, 67, 70, 77, 162n.36; 167n.33; eloquence of, 49; "host of fools", 46, 47;

insults, 46, 47; and language, 49, 67; not listening, 46, 49; and love object, 64, 66; on lovers as poets, 48; mask of, 49–50, 74; mistake of, 67, 74; and music, 51; and Pausanias 10, 15–16, 21, 29, 47, 49, 65, 67, 158n.11: and Phaidros, 162n.35; and poetry, 48, 51, 70; and procreation, 70, 77; as self-centered, 67; and Sokrates, 10, 14, 15, 18, 46–49, 51, 64–67, 116, 162n.33, 34, 41; 171n.20; Sokratic ignorance of, 67; style (manner) of, 49, 161n27; as transvestite, 49, 162n.38; and wisdom and poetry, 48, 167n.33; see also: Lovers, Pausanias and Agathon

Aiskylus, 26

Akhilles, 24, 26, 52, 78, 79, 168n.1; and love relation-ship, 24; as lover, 26; mask of, 79; as ideal warrior, 79

Akron, 31

Alkestis, 24, 25, 52, 78, 79, 168n.1; as beloved, 25

Alkibiades, IX, 11, 13–14, 16, 17, 19, 101–07, 109, 112, 113–114, 115–24, 156n.13, 21, 22; 158n.10; 161n.31; 163–64n.5; 168n.41; 171n.20; 174n.1; 175n.7, 9, 10, 11; 176n.16;

Lykeion, 104, 111–112; and
    Sokrates, 111, 112
Lykon, 108

Maculate Muse, Jeffrey
    Henderson. See: Henderson,
    Jeffrey
Marsyas, 14, 71, 104, 106–08, 110,
    112; and Apollo, 107; and
    Dionysos, 71; and the contest,
    107; and the flute, 107, 112;
    as musician, 107; myth of,
    106–07; and Olympos, 112
Masks, 8–10, 14, 22, 23, 25, 27,
    28, 29, 31, 38, 39, 40, 50, 51,
    53, 67, 74, 104, 106, 112, 176n.13;
    and Agathon, 49–50, 74; and
    Akhilles, 79; and Alkibiades,
    121; and Aristodemos, 10;
    and Aristophanes, 40; and
    conventional virtues, 23; and
    Dionysos as god of, 8, 14, 106,
    112; and Diotima, 51, 53; and
    elenchus, 9; and Empedokles,
    31, 40; and Eros, 106; and
    Eryximakhos, 31, 38, 39, 40,
    74; and immutable forms,
    112; and lovers, 22–23, 24,
    25, 28, 29, 67, 74; and
    Pausanias, 27, 74; and Phaidros,
    22, 23, 24, 74; and Plato's,
    176n.13; and removing of, 8;
    and role-playing, 74; and
    satire, 40; and self, 74; and
    Sokrates, 51
Medicine, 7, 11, 34–38, 39, 42;
    and Apollo, god of, 7, 36, 37,
    42; and attunement, 36, 37,
    42; and conception, 154–55n.5;
    and love, 35–37; mask of, 39;

and physicians, 35–38. See
    also: Apollo; Empedokles;
    Eros; Eryximakhos; Love,
    noble; Strife.
Medicine, theory of, 35–38, 42.
    See also: Medicine
Meletos, 107, 108, 145; in the
    Apology, 107; flattery of, 107;
    and Sokrates, 145
Memoranda, see: Memory;
    Word, written
Memory, 58, 67, 87, 88, 89, 90,
    91, 92, 98, 116, 142–43, 150–51,
    164n.14; and birth, 58; and
    change, 69, 98, 148; and the
    dialectic, 58, 89, 90, 91; and
    forgetfulness, 58, 89, 90, 92;
    as harmful, 143; and hearing
    and remembering, 116; and
    knowledge, 57, 58, 88–91,
    142; and memoranda, 88–92;
    and Meno, 142–43; and Plato,
    89–91, 92; and replacement,
    67, 98; and Sokrates, 98, 142;
    and Theuth (Thoth) to Thamos
    (Ammon) on, 87, 88; and
    wisdom, 88, 91; and the
    written word, 88–91
Mendez, Alberto, X, 180n.16
Menexenos, 163n.2
Meno, 108, 125–32, 135–150,
    151, 177n.29; 179n.3, 7, 8;
    181n.17; 182n.24; 183n.25, 28;
    185n.42; and avarice, 142;
    and the dialectic, 128–29, 137,
    140, 151; and the eristic,
    130–31; and excellence,
    128–29, 130, 139, 140–46, 150;
    and dramatic style, 127; and
    inquiry, 125, 139, 179n.3; and
    insults, 128, 137, 138; and

Meno (*continued*)
learning, 136–38, 140, 141–44,
147, 150, 151, 177n.29; 179n.7,
8; and memory, 142, 143, 151;
and noticing, 181n.17; paradox
of, 125, 128, 131–33, 139, 145,
172n.21; 178n.1; 185n.42; and
simulation of knowledge,
128; and the slave, 139, 140;
the slave dialogue in, 133–34;
and Sokrates, 108, 125–35,
137, 138, 139, 140–45, 147–50,
179n.7; 181n.23; and Sokrates
as "stingray", 128, 137; and
teaching, 125–29, 144, 145,
150, 151, 179n.7; and treachery
of, 140, 183n.28; values of, 142;
Xenophon's account of, 140
Meno, IX, 3, 4, 9, 22, 54, 55, 57,
87, 108, 125–27, 128, 130–32,
135, 136–37, 148, 155n.7;
164n.9; 171n.19, 20; 177n.28;
178n.1; 182–83n.24; 183n.27;
184n.37, 39; characterization
of knowledge in, 54, 155n.7;
and doctrine of recollection,
57–58, 125–27, 130–32, 135,
178n.1; Epimenides in, 87;
the geometry lesson in,
132–35, 138, 148–49; knowledge
and opinion in, 55, 148; and
simulation of knowledge,
128; and the *Symposium*, 125,
148. See also Knowledge;
Meno; Recollection, doctrine
of; Slave dialogue
Metallurgy, 80, 168n.3
Metaphysical themes, IX, 41
Metaphysics, IX, 44, 63, 64, 82,
96, 150, 178n.1

Metaphysics, Plato's, IX, 63, 82;
and change, 82; and pure
forms, 82
Method, (the author's), 1–6
Moravesik, Julius, 179n.3;
180n.15, 17; 181n.22; 182n.24;
185n.42
Morgan, Michael L., 178n.1;
180n.17; 182n.24; and Meno's
paradox, 178n.1; 180n.17
Mortal nature, 68–69, 71, 74,
77, 78, 81–83, 84, 85, 94, 95,
98; mortals as processive, 95
Mortality, 37, 78, 85, 86, 94;
and knowledge, 94. See also:
Immortality, Immutability,
Mortals
Mortals, 32, 37, 56, 57, Chap. 4,
sec. 6, 67–72; 74, 77, 81–86; and
attunement, 37; and death,
37, 78, 85, 86; Diotima on,
68, 69, 71, 82, 84, 85; and
immortality, 68, 69, 71, 72,
77, 81–83, and mortal existence,
56–57, 67–72, 82, 83; mortal
nature. See: Mortal nature;
as processive, 56, 77, 84, 85;
self-preservation defeated, 78.
See also: Change, Eros,
Growth, Immortals, Immor-
tality, Life force, Life as
process, Love, Love and
immortality, Self
Mourelatos, P. D., 160n.11
Muses, 107
Music, 35, 36, 51, 70, 106–07,
112; Agathon on, 51; and
Apollo, 107, 112; Eryximakhos
on 35, 36; and the flute,
106–07, 112; and Olympos,
112; and poetry, 51, 70

Women, 25, 30, 34, 41, 42, 43,
53, 81, 103, 155n.5; 158n.12;
162–63n.1; 163n.2; 168n.2; as
author of *Odyssey*, 168n.2;
Empedokles on, 42;
Eryximakhos on, 34; females
as offspring of earth, 41;
homosexuality, 43; lesbianism,
43; Pausanias on, 30; Phaidros'
attitude toward, 25; and procreation, 155n.5; 158n.12; as
teacher of Sokrates, 53, 81, 103,
162–63n.1; 163n.2; woman's
argument, 162–63n.1. See also:
Birth; Diotima; Procreation
Word, 86–92; dialectic method
of education, 89; as part of
dialectic process, 89, 91; as
seeds, 91; Sokrates' objections to, 89, 90, 91; written
in the soul, 86. See also:
Word, written
Word, written, 5, 86–92, 111,
170–71n.18; and Apollodoros,
111; and change, 89; and
processive character of
knowledge, 91; and the
dialectic, 89, 90, 91; as
immutable, 92; and the

learning process, 86, 88, 90;
and memoranda for old age,
89, 90; and memory, 88–91;
and Phaidros, 86–92; and
Plato, 5, 89–91, 92,
170–71n.18; and Plato's
reasons for, 5, 92; and
questioning, 86, 89, 91; and
screening the audience, 88,
90, 91, 92; and Sokrates'
objections to, 89, 90, 91; and
Theuth (Thoth) to Thamos
(Ammon) on, 88. See also:
Knowledge, Memory
"World line" (physics), 70, 71
Wright, M. R., 159n.10;
160n.12; 161n.23

Xanthippe, 175n.6
Xenophon, 183n.28

Zeus, 8, 42, 47, 48, 49, 154n.2,
5; Agathon on, 47, 48, 49;
and creativity, 48; and Eros,
47, 48, 49; and origin of
humans, 42; and Phanes,
154n.2; and strife, 42